POLITICS AND CHANGE
IN A TRADITIONAL SOCIETY
LEBANON, 1711-1845

POLITICS AND CHANGE
IN A TRADITIONAL SOCIETY
LEBANON, 1711-1845

ILIYA F. HARIK

PRINCETON, NEW JERSEY
PRINCETON UNIVERSITY PRESS
1968

Publication of this book has been aided by
the Whitney Darrow Publication Reserve Fund
of Princeton University Press

Printed in the United States of America
by Princeton University Press, Princeton, New Jersey

Acknowledgments

THE writer is indebted to many people who helped in making this study possible and gratefully acknowledges their support. In particular I wish to thank Mr. Albert Hourani, Mr. Leonard Binder, and Mr. Marshall Hodgson for the interest they have taken in this work and for their advice and criticisms. While I am very indebted to them, I alone take responsibility for shortcomings in this work.

I would also like to acknowledge with gratitude the Committee for the Comparative Study of New Nations, in the University of Chicago, for the financial support and intellectual stimulation when I was a Carnegie Fellow with the Committee from 1962 to 1964, during which period this book was prepared. I am also grateful to Indiana University for Faculty Research grants which have enabled me to prepare this manuscript for publication.

My wife has shared with me the burden of putting this manuscript into shape. She has my gratitude for the work and moral encouragement which she has offered generously.

Contents

APPENDICES

List of Illustrations

Glossary

Amir—highest noble title in Mount Lebanon, equivalent to prince.

'Ammiyyah—commoners; also the name given to the peasant uprisings of 1820, 1821.

'Aqil—a Druze initiated in the tenets of his religion.

'Awayid—benefits received by original owners of a monastery.

A'yan—nobles.

Al Dawlah—refers to the Ottoman state or government.

Dhimmah (Ahl al)—in Muslim law are the people of the revealed religions like Christians and Jews, who are also under Muslim protection.

Divan (also Diwan)—administrative council.

Gharad—faction.

Hakim—literally ruler; in Mount Lebanon it was the name by which a Shihabi overlord was known.

Huwalah—retainers of the Hakim who were similar in certain respects to gendarmes.

'Idiyyah—presents and gifts received by a muqati'ji from his subjects on feast days and special occasions.

Iltizam—tax farming system associated with Ottoman provincial administration particularly in Syria and Egypt.

Imarah—principality.

Iqta'—feudal, feudalism.

Ismiyyah—loyalty of the subject to his lord and lord's house. Literally, it means taking another person's name for one's own.

Jabal—mountain

Kabir ismiyyah⎫
⎬—paramount head of a clan.
Kabir 'uhdah⎭

Kakhya—same as mudabbir.

Khul'ah—usually a fur coat sent as a symbol of investiture by

Ottoman authorities to lords under Ottoman suzerainty like the one sent customarily by the Vali of Sayda to the Hakim of Mount Lebanon.

Manasib—the muqati'jis in their general capacity as political leaders in the Imarah. Used when the emphasis is on political role rather than the day-to-day administration of 'uhdahs.

Maydan—a court where sports and military practices were exercised.

Miri—the annual tax on land and produce.

Mudabbir—adviser and administrator in the Hakim's service.

Muqaddam—a noble title next in rank to amir.

Muqata'ah—fief in the name of a clan.

Muqati'ji—a hereditary chief who is also a fief holder.

Naf'—a discount from the miri collected by a muqati'ji left to him by the Hakim for his personal use.

Pasha—noble and military rank in the Ottoman Empire. Valis held this title.

Qadi—judge.

Ra'aya—subjects.

Ra's—head, chief.

Sharakah—tenant farming.

Sharik—a tenant farmer.

Shaykh—noble title next to muqaddam in Lebanese usage.

Shurtah—same as huwalah.

Tawa'if—powerful commoner clans known in Mount Lebanon during the iqta' period. Not to be confused with the current meaning of the term as religious sect.

'Uhdah—the fief of a particular muqati'ji.

'Uqqal—plural of 'aqil.

'Uzwah—belonging to the clan, faction, usually in reference to the following of a muqati'ji.

Vali—Ottoman governor of a province, vilayet.

Vilayet—largest Ottoman administrative unit headed by a governor or vali.

Wakil—literally delegate, representative. A commoner chosen by village people as their political leader and representative. See Chapters VIII and IX.

Waqfs—mortmain.

POLITICS AND CHANGE
IN A TRADITIONAL SOCIETY
LEBANON, 1711-1845

ABBREVIATIONS

AL	*Awraq Lubnaniyyah*
KTS	Munayyar's *Kitab al Durr al Marsuf fi Tarikh al Shuf*
MAA	Mudiriyyat al Athar al 'Ammah (Lebanon: National Department of Antiquities)
MAE	Ministère des Affaires Étrangères (France: Correspondance Consulaire)
MB	*Al Majma' al Baladi* (ed. Bulus Mas'ad)
MQ	*Al Mashriq*
MTL	'Aynturini's *Mukhtasar Tarikh Jabal Lubnan*
PAB	Patriarchal Archives of Bkirki
TA	Duwayhi's *Tarikh al Azminah*
TML	*Tarikh al Majma' al Lubnani*, published in *al Usul al Tarikhiyyah*
TRLM	Bulaybil's *Tarikh al Rahbaniyyah al Lubnaniyyah al Maruniyyah*
TTM	Duwayhi's *Tarikh al Ta'ifah al Maruniyyah* (ed. Rashid al Khury al Shartuni)
TZ	Ma'luf's *Tarikh Zahlah*
UATS	Rustum's *Al Usul al 'Arabiyyah li Tarikh Suriyyah fi 'Ahd Muhammad 'Ali Basha*
UT	*Al Usul al Tarikhiyyah* (eds. Bulus Mas'ad and Nasib al Khazin)
Dimashqi, *Tarikh*	*Tarikh Hawadith al Sham wa Lubnan*
Haydar, *al Ghurar*	*Kitab al Ghurar al Hisan fi Tawarikh Hawadith al Zaman* by Haydar Shihab
Haydar, *Lubnan*	*Lubnan fi 'Ahd al Umara' al Shihabiyyin* (eds. Bustani and Rustum)
Haydar, "Nuzhat"	"Nuzhat al Zaman fi Hawadith 'Arabistan" (MS)
Ma'luf, *Dawani*	*Dawani al Qutuf fi Tarikh bani al Ma'luf*
Mashaqah, *al Jawab*	*Muntakhabat min al Jawab 'ala Iqtirah al Ahbab*
Propaganda	Archivio Sacra Congregazione de Propaganda Fide (Rome)
Shidiaq, *Akhbar*	*Akhbar al A'yan fi Jabal Lubnan*
Yaziji, *Risalah*	*Risalah Tarikhiyyah fi Ahwal Lubnan fi 'Ahdihi al Iqta'i* (ed. Qustantin al Basha)

CHAPTER I

Introduction: Problem and Method

LEBANON today stands out among her Arab neighbors in one important respect: she enjoys a distinct system of government which is basically democratic. For about a quarter-century of independent political life, she has succeeded in maintaining her democratic form of government, which is essentially the same as that introduced by the French mandatory authorities in 1925 and which has remained unchanged amidst a political environment plagued with successive military coups and revolutions. Since her independence in 1943, Lebanon has felt the shocks of both regional and world crises, some of which have shaken her to the very foundations. Her democratic institutions, nevertheless, have endured.

Lebanon's unique position at present is not of recent origin. Her political organization was fundamentally different from the rest of the Arab lands throughout the Ottoman period.[1] I do not wish here to give the impression that the following work is a study in historical continuity. I am concerned, rather, primarily with change in a traditional political organization, the *iqta'* (feudal) order under the Shihabi Imarah, and the period with which we shall be dealing extends only to the middle of the nineteenth century.

At the same time, the historical limitations ought not to obscure the fact that this study should be quite relevant for understanding the political life of present-day Lebanon, especially with respect to explaining its distinctive characteristics in the Middle East region. As has already been mentioned, the iqta' system in Mount Lebanon was itself markedly different from the prevailing political order in the rest of the Arab parts of the Ottoman Empire. Further, the revolutionary changes which the country went through during the nine-

[1] See my article, "The Iqta' System in Lebanon: A Comparative Political View," *The Middle East Journal*, XIX (Autumn 1965), 405-421.

teenth century prepared the way for the transition to modern democratic life. The considerable reduction in the power of the feudal aristocracy, the direct participation of the common people, and the introduction of legal political institutions to take the place of the fallen iqtaʻ system were among the striking results of these changes leading to the present political conditions in Lebanon. It should also be pointed out in this context that the iqtaʻ institutions themselves were basically conducive to the development of a tradition of sound and relatively free and responsible political life in Lebanon. The propinquity between rulers and their peasants and the balance of pluralistic political forces were main factors in the social, economic, and political freedom and security of the Lebanese under the Imarah.

The purpose of this study is thus twofold: it is theoretical, thus concerned with the comparable; and also particular and rooted in the historical. It is my intention to illuminate the processes of change in the traditional political institutions in Lebanon—their causes, principles, and direction. The following study should also help underline the point, at this time when the social sciences are evidencing keen interest in the problems of change and development, that fundamental and revolutionary change in the social, political, and economic life of the new nations is neither very new nor so predominantly the result of external modernizing influences. Traditional societies have the ability and initiative to introduce change and adapt to it in a manner and logic of their own. Thus this study of Lebanon promises to be comparative in purpose and should shed some light on the uniformities in political behavior and change which prove relevant for comparison in other traditional societies.

For me, however, this work is of somewhat more than a scientific interest—it has a practical meaning, too. It is my hope that this book will present a picture of Lebanese history in one of its most vital periods with sufficient coherence to give the Lebanese people additional understanding and insight into the political life of their country.

In my approach to this study, I am treating Lebanon during the Shihabi Imarah period (1697-1841) as a political system. We may regard the term "system" as a field of action made up of constituent parts, each of which is interrelated with the others. A "field of action" may be defined as consisting of actors who, in making decisions, are guided and constrained by values and established norms of conduct. In its more common usage in political science, the system concept is applied to a whole country or society; in the present study we are simply using it as an analytic tool which should apply to any interrelated facts constituting a field of action and isolated solely for the purpose of study.

Thus in viewing the Imarah as a separate political unit and treating it as a system, we have simply assumed that there is sufficient evidence at the initial stage of observation to permit us to consider the people and their relations under the Imarah together as an interrelated field of action. In other words, if parts of a field of action are observed to be of consequence for one another, then one is justified in treating them as a system.

The constituent parts of a system which are taken here as a conceptual framework for analysis are (1) the principle of legitimacy, (2) the institutions, and (3) the social composition of the actors. "Legitimacy" refers to the principles in terms of which people justify political action. It is an expression of a group's value orientations and the norms accepted in their culture.

By a political institution I do not mean whole structures or organizations, but normative regularities which govern political behavior and define the ways people may or may not act.[2] Institutions thus refer to imperative rules of conduct

[2] In using the term "institution" in this sense we are following Talcott Parsons, *Structure and Process in Modern Societies* (Glencoe: The Free Press,

honored by the members of society, which may be embedded in their culture or belief-system. These rules express the world-view with which they are consistent and define the class of men they affect. They may take either a positive or a negative form: one ought to do this but not do that. For example, in Mount Lebanon the Shihabi overlord had no right to inflict personal injury in punishing a feudal lord, but the rules specified other means of punishment such as exile or destruction of property. Thus the rules governing punishment of lords can be considered normative regularities which had the effect of command, even though they were not written in the form of law. In the traditional political system of Mount Lebanon, the rules governing political relations were not written but were handed down in the form of oral tradition from one generation to the next.

The third and last category of which a system is constituted is the actors—those holders of legitimate authority whose commands are generally obeyed. In this study we shall focus primarily on the social composition of the actors and the attributes that distinguished them from the rest of society.

The conceptual framework just outlined regards the field of action under study as a self-contained unit. However, in examining the interrelations of the constituent parts of the system rather than its relations with the external world, we do not mean to ignore forces which come from outside. External forces will be taken into account in this study, but only when they directly bear upon the system and the particular problems with which we are dealing. What we shall not do here, however, is to trace the origins of such external factors or to analyze the systems of which they form a part. For example, in discussing the impact of the Roman Catholic Church upon the Maronite people, we shall be concerned with

1963), p. 177; also Lloyd Fallers, *Bantu Bureaucracy: A Study of Integration and Conflict in the Political Institutions of an East African People* (Cambridge: W. Heffer and Sons, n.d.), pp. 5, 9.

the ways in which these influences affected the people of Lebanon and their political institutions, without going into detail about the Church of Rome itself or the forces which determined its relations with Lebanon. This will also hold regarding Ottoman and European relations with Lebanon during the period under study.

Studies of nineteenth-century Lebanon, and also of other Middle Eastern countries, seek explanation for change primarily by tracing internal developments to external forces. Thus one finds that the theme of the impact of the West is one of the most common subjects in studies of the Middle East. However, the following study suggests that the problem of change could be made considerably clearer if it could be defined in terms of its constituent parts. Such an approach requires the student to look at the principles governing political relations within the system itself and to locate the inherent sources of change there. Moreover, if these principles and problems are clearly defined, then we may be better able to understand the system's response to external forces of change. The assumption here is that the iqta' political system of Lebanon, which had its culture and institutions, also contained its own principle of motion. We hope to show that this is true descriptively and that the approach is fruitful analytically.

With the main concepts delineated, we can now discuss the plan of the study and define the central problem of this inquiry. The first part of this work will be devoted to describing the iqta' political system with reference to its principle of legitimacy, its institutions, and the composition of its actors. Reconstructing the system as it existed in the eighteenth century before it was disrupted by profound change meant using such historical material as chronicles, official documents and records, diplomatic correspondences, narratives of events, some memoirs, reports, and other sources of secondary nature. Obviously, sources of this kind have their limitations, particularly when one is seeking information relevant for particular patterns of relations. What therefore happens in a study based on such material is that some generalizations are less certain and less well verified than others because of the gaps in historical data. Hopefully, with further historical research on the period, some of these problems will be better resolved in the future. In the meantime I feel it is better to go out on a limb than not to go anywhere at all. In the study of political change, historical depth is necessary and data is always less ample than we would like it to be; but this is no reason to sidestep the question.

Since we are primarily concerned with conflict and change in this study, it seems pertinent to start with the meanings of these two terms. By "change" I mean a variation in observable regularities, not in discrete events. A "regularity" is a persistent relationship between two or more facts, and only a disturbance of this uniform relationship is here considered to constitute a change. Since an institution, as it is understood here, is one kind of regularity, we want to find out if any of these institutions underwent some change, partial or complete, during the period under examination. We also want to look for changes in the patterns of relationships obtaining between the three system variables, i.e., to see if the whole system is transformed, for what reasons, and in what direction.

The second term is "conflict," by which I mean the negative effect one pattern of action has upon another. For instance, political institutions may be considered to be in conflict when the command of one rule requires a person to act in such a way that his actions have an adverse effect on, or contradict, the commands from another rule of conduct. An "adverse effect" means that chances of conformity with the injunctions of one rule are diminished as a result of conformity to another. Incompatibility between authority and kinship relations and between delegated and constituted authority are two examples of conflict in the iqta' system. There is a corollary to this definition of conflict, related to institutional ambiguity. When we speak of "ambiguity" in institutions, we mean the failure of normative rules to provide clear guidelines for action in recurrent situations, thereby leading to friction among the actors. A clear example of ambiguity in the iqta' institutions of the Shihabi Imarah was the principle of succession, as we shall later see.

Since we are interested here in political change, we should naturally look for trends in peoples' behavior which have the effect of disturbing established relations and institutions. Thus in the chapters following the reconstruction of the iqta' system, we shall be concerned with forces which were leading to the modification of the existing order. The kind of problem with which we shall be dealing is one in which members of society, whether deliberately or because of compelling forces, try to break the established rules and impose new patterns and a new order.

Institutional analysis thus reveals how a political society is organized and what are the norms which guide the behavior of its members. Important realities, however, would be missed if we were to limit ourselves to institutional analysis in the study of politics in general and political change in particular. It is not feasible for any society, no matter how comprehensive its political institutions and conformist its members, to lay down all the rules for all situations. Men often find themselves in situations in which the existing rules either do not apply or are not clear enough to make a decision easy, and they have to innovate. Institutional analysis is not sufficient, in the second place, because of the fact that men have a choice, no matter how restrictive the rules under which they labor. Individuals have some capacity to break or undermine the rules, and if this kind of behavior becomes persistent it leads to change in the institutions of society. Third, institutions understood as general rules for action are defined in terms of classes of activities, rather than individual instances. For this reason they leave a margin of choice to the actor when he applies them to particular cases.

In this study I am asking the question: Why did the iqta' political system break down and its character become transformed? First, I examined the patterns of relations obtaining in the system, and where I observed forces acting to modify them, or certain inherent conflicts, I isolated those factors for further study. This enabled me to suggest some hypotheses regarding political change in the iqta' system. Then I proceeded to find out if these could be upheld.

The main hypothesis of this study is that in a relatively integrated political system, its constituent parts—the principle of legitimacy, the institutions, and the actors—stand in consistent relationship. If one of these constituent parts of the system fails to enforce and instead contradicts another, the system will be in a state of conflict. That is, if one of the constituent parts of the system changes, causing conflict with the other variables, the ensuing conflict will generate a similar reaction in the other parts. A return to the *status quo ante* is possible, however, if the source of disturbance in the relationship of the constituent parts is removed. In the first case we then speak of "system transformation," which means a change in the definition and relations of the system variables. When, for instance, the principle of legitimacy in a political system is based on ethnic values, a rule demanding that a person be loyal and obedient to someone of another ethnic group will clearly result in conflict, which will lead to a change in the incompatible institutions. A person who is subject to such contradictory demands finally has to make a choice between them, often with revolutionary effects.

The second main hypothesis is that conflict between political institutions creates strain in the system and contributes to change. Imperative rules of conduct governing political relations in a system are numerous, and harmony among the specific rules is of great consequence in the study of integration and change. Thus while describing the iqta' institutions, we shall also pay attention to the analysis of institutional conflict and its implications for the other constituent parts of the system.

I have found this approach useful in studying political change and conflict in a traditional small community, nineteenth-century Lebanon. Its comparative merit can be determined only after it has been tried in other cases. It would be, of course, more profitable and meaningful for this conceptual framework to be tested in comparable small communities rather than in large societies.

CHAPTER II

The Country and the People

THE STORY of Lebanon in modern times is the story of strangers who settled together in one rugged and inhospitable terrain, because of a common plight. The strangers were the Maronites and Druze; the terrain, the coastal mountain range on the eastern shore of the Mediterranean, stretching from Tripoli in the north to Sidon in the south. The hardship from which they had earlier suffered, as described by a modern Lebanese historian, was that each was the representative of a lost cause.[1] The Maronites were remnants of a once flourishing Christian population in the eastern Mediterranean area, while the Druze were a heterodox offshoot from the dominant political and cultural body of Islam.

Could these strangers achieve a successful life together on the rocky mountains of Lebanon? The difficult mountain terrain provided for the immediate need for protection, but that could not alone ensure complete security for an unmolested existence—at different periods throughout history foreign soldiers have managed to tramp over most of Mount Lebanon. Thus it was chance that made Maronites and Druze neighbors; but for an enduring social community to evolve which could face challenges from outside and from within, accident had to be followed by intelligent purpose and action.

The differences which separated these two communities, in their religious beliefs, historical background, and areas of habitation, were gradually overcome by a process of integration starting around the beginning of the seventeenth century. The integrating force was the political institutions of the Imarah, first under the Ma'ni dynasty (1516-1697) and then under their successors, the Shihabis (1697-1841). It is these

[1] Philip Hitti, *Lebanon in History: From the Earliest Times to the Present* (London: Macmillan & Co., Ltd., 1957), p. 246.

political institutions and their eventual transformation during the nineteenth century with which this study is concerned. In this chapter, however, we shall first look at the societal differences of the two main groups which formed the Imarah society. Our survey will start with the geographical terrain in which the Imarah of Mount Lebanon developed.

MOUNT LEBANON

Mount Lebanon as a political community of pluralist character goes back no further than the seventeenth century. The peoples of Mount Lebanon lived for centuries in separate geographic regions without relations with each other, except perhaps for occasional hostilities. The country did not even have a single name until late in the eighteenth century. The Maronites called their part of the country Mount Lebanon, and the Druze called their region Jabal (Mount) al Shuf, or Jabal al Druze. A look at the map (Fig. 1) will help with this question of nomenclature. To the extreme north, around the famous Cedars, lies the original home of the Maronites, which was known as Mount Lebanon.[2] It does not seem, however, that the geographic meaning of the term was always limited to that area. For instance, patriarch and chronicler Istfan al Duwayhi (d. 1704) showed that he had an idea of a geographic Lebanon extending beyond the region of Jibbat Bsharri, bounded in the south by the country of the Druze and in the north by Bilad 'Akkar.[3] Thus before the end of

---

[2] This is clear from accounts given by various chroniclers and writers from the days of Jibra'il al Qila'i (d. 1516); see Kamal S. Salibi, *Maronite Historians of Mediaeval Lebanon*, "American University of Beirut, Faculty of Arts and Sciences Publications: Oriental Series No. 34" (Beirut: Catholic Press, 1959), pp. 23-87. Also Istfan al Duwayhi, *Tarikh al Tai'fah al Maruniyyah*, ed. Rashid al Khury al Shartuni (Beirut: n.p., 1890), pp. 78ff. (hereafter cited as *TTM*); also Duwayhi, *Tarikh al Azminah: 1095-1699*, ed. Ferdinan Tawtal, in *MQ*, XLIV (Beirut: al Matba'ah al Kathulikiyyah, 1951), 103, 214, 276 (hereafter cited as *TA*). Similarly, Jerom Dandini, *Voyage to Mount Libanus*, published in John Pinkerton, ed. *General Collection of Voyages and Travels* (London: Longman, Hurst, Rees, and Orme, 1811), x, 285-295.

[3] Duwayhi, *TTM*, p. 98; also *TA*, p. 201.

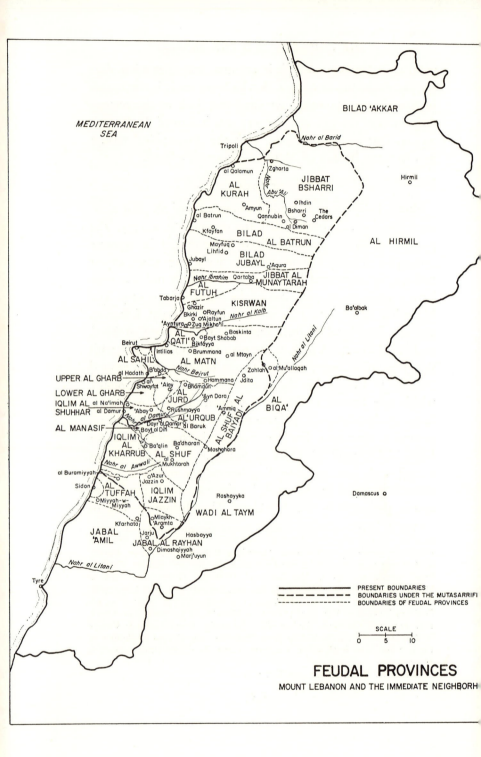

MEDITERRANEAN
SEA

BILAD 'AKKAR

Tripoli

Nahr al Barid

al Qalamun   Zgharta

JIBBAT
BSHARRI

Hirmil

AL
KURAH

Amyun   Ihdin
Qannubin   Bsharri   The
Cedars

al Batrun

Kfayfan

al Diman

BILAD
AL BATRUN

AL HIRMIL

Mayfuq
Lihfid
Jubayl

BILAD
JUBAYL

Aqura

JIBBAT AL
MUNAYTARAH

Nahr Ibrahim   Qartaba

AL
FUTUH

Tabarja

KISRWAN

Ba'albak

Ghazir
Bkirki   Rayfun
'Ajaltun
'Ayntura Zuq Mikha'il

Nahr al Kalb

AL
QATI'

Baskinta
Bayt Shabab
Biktayya
Brummana

al Mtayn

Beirut

Intilias

AL SAHIL

AL MATN

Nahr al Litani

B'abda

al Hadath

Zahlah   al Mu'allaqah

UPPER AL GHARB

'al
Shwayfat 'Alay

Hammana   Jdita

Nahr Beirut

Bhamdun

LOWER AL GHARB

AL
JURD

'Ayn Dara

IQLIM AL   al Na'imah
SHUHHAR   al Damur

'Abay

Rushmayya

'Ammiq

AL
BIQA'

al Damur

AL MANASIF

Dayr al Qamar al Baruk
Bayt al Din

AL'URQUB

IQLIM
AL
KHARRUB

Ba'qlin

Ba'dharan

Mashghara

AL SHUF

al
Mukhtarah

al Buramiyyah

Nahr al Awwali

'Azur

Sidon

AL
TUFFAH

Jazzin

IQLIM
JAZZIN

Rashayyka

Damascus

Miyyah-w-
Miyyah

Kfarhata

Mlaykh-
'Aramta

WADI AL TAYM

JABAL
'AMIL

Jarju

JABAL AL RAYHAN

Hasbayya

Dimashqiyyah
Marj'uyun

Nahr al Litani

Tyre

PRESENT BOUNDARIES
BOUNDARIES UNDER THE MUTASARRIFI
BOUNDARIES OF FEUDAL PROVINCES

SCALE
0   5   10

FEUDAL PROVINCES
MOUNT LEBANON AND THE IMMEDIATE NEIGHBORH

the eighteenth century geographic Lebanon could be defined by a line starting at the mouth of the Dog River in the south-west, following the river east to its source and turning north-east all the way to Afqa, the Hirmil, and 'Aqqar regions. On the west it was bounded by the Mediterranean Sea, excluding the seaport and town of Tripoli. European travelers in the late eighteenth century used the name in this sense.[4]

To the south of the Maronite lands was the Jabal al Shuf, also known as Jabal al Druze.[5] In this case the country took its name from the inhabitants, the Druze who made their home in southern Lebanon as early as the eleventh century, not long after their religion was founded. Under the Ma'nis and before the advent of Fakhr al Din II (1585-1635), the Druze mountain was limited to al Shuf, al Gharb (the upper and the lower), al Jurd, and al 'Urqub, not including the Matn, the Biqa', the districts (*iqlims*) of Jazzin, al Tuffah, al Kharrub, and Jabal al Rayhan. The *iqlims* were directly under the Pasha of Sayda, and the Biqa' and Matn under the Vali of Damascus.[6] During the rise of Fakhr al Din these regions were integrated under his suzerainty and remained so for most of the Ma'ni and Shihabi periods. This area became known as the Mountain of the Druze, officially as well as among the common people. Ottoman letters of investiture sent to the Shihabis were addressed to Jabal Shuf or Jabal al Druze.[7] This remained the official practice up to the time of the last Shihabi ruler; thus in 1840 an Ottoman firman went

---

[4] See C.-F. Volney, *Travels Through Syria and Egypt in the Years 1783, 1784, and 1785*, II (London: G.G.J. and J. Robinson, 1788), 168. Also John L. Burckhardt, *Travels in Syria and the Holy Land* (London: J. Murray, 1882), p. 25.

[5] Not to be confused with present-day Jabal al Druze in the southwestern part of Syria.

[6] Hananiyya al Munayyar, *Kitab al Durr al Marsuf fi Tarikh al Shuf*, ed. Ighnatius Sarkis, *MQ*, XLVIII-LI (1954-1957), XLIX, 270 (hereafter cited as *KTS*).

[7] Haydar Shihab, *Lubnan fi 'Ahd al Umara' al Shihabiyyin*, eds. Asad Rustum and Fu'ad Afram al Bustani (Beirut: Lebanese Government Publication, 1933), passim 597-681 (hereafter cited as Haydar, *Lubnan*).

to Bashir Shihab III investing him as Amir of "Jabal al Druze."[8] However, the official Ottoman terminology was outdated by that period, as is clear from a letter written by the same Amir in which he refers to his domain as "Mount Lebanon."[9]

During the Imarah period the Ottoman government did not use the term Mount Lebanon in official papers. Northern Lebanon was referred to as "Jubayl" and "al Batrun." Perhaps the Ottomans did not use "Mount Lebanon" because the name was not current except among the Maronites, who had no political status at the time of the Ottoman conquest.

By the beginning of the nineteenth century, "Mount Lebanon" was being commonly used in reference to the whole country under Shihabi rule from 'Akkar to near Sayda, the country of the Druze as well as that of the Maronites. Other names like Jabal al Druze were not completely dropped but continued to appear occasionally.[10] The first written document in which Maronites, Druze, Shi'is, and Sunnis all refer to a common territory as their country goes back to 1840. The statement, a joint declaration of revolution against the Egyptians, reads, "We the undersigned Druze, Christians, Matawilah, and Muslims, who are known as inhabitants of Mount Lebanon . . . ," followed by signatures, "We the Druze people of Mount Lebanon, the Christians, Matawilah, and Muslims in general."[11]

---

[8] Asad Rustum, ed., *Al Usul al 'Arabiyyah li Tarikh Suriyyah fi 'Ahd Muhammad 'Ali Basha*, 5 vols. (Beirut: American University of Beirut, American Press, 1930-1934), v, 172-174 (hereafter cited as *UATS*).

[9] *Ibid.*, v, 234.

[10] This is clear from the writings of such chroniclers as Antonius al 'Aynturini (d. 1821) and Amir Haydar Shihab (1761-1835). See Antonius Abi Khattar al 'Aynturini, *Kitab Mukhtasar Tarikh Jabal Lubnan*, ed. Ighnatius al Khury, in *MQ*, XLVI-XLVII (1952-1953), XLVI, 332-333 (hereafter cited as 'Aynturini, *MTL*); Haydar, *Lubnan*, passim.

[11] Bulus Mas'ad and Nasib Whaybah al Khazin (eds.), *Al Usul al Tarikhiyyah: Majmu'at Watha'iq*, 3 vols. (Beirut: Matabi' Samya, 1956-1958), I, 146-147 (hereafter cited as *UT*).

The literary revival in Lebanon at the beginning of the nineteenth century brought a new impetus and significance to the name. The poets gathered around Amir Bashir II gave it an emotional and patriotic content, reflecting the early stirrings of national consciousness among the Lebanese. In a long panegyric, Nasif al Yaziji calls Bashir "the great pillar of Lebanon," and on another occasion the poet applauds the Amir for the prestige he brought to Lebanon during his rule:

> Lebanon you have clad with the light
> of the angel Gabriel over the mountain.[12]

Another of the Amir's poets, Niqula al Turk, makes common use of the term "pillar of Lebanon," referring to the Amir. On an occasion in which the Amir emerged victorious in a military campaign in 1810, al Turk wrote, "He is the foundation on which the edifice of Lebanon rises," and further:

> The homeland he honored, its life he made pleasing;
> Remembered for ages the prestige he has brought it.[13]

The application of the term "Mount Lebanon" to the whole mountain range coincides with the period in which Amir Bashir Shihab II governed the Mountain. There is no evidence at all that he had anything to do with its widespread acceptance, nor that it was the result of a special design or conscious effort on the part of the people. Two factors, however, can be considered of particular importance in this change in terminology: the spread of the Maronite population throughout all the Mountain, mixing with the Druze and other peoples, and the unification of Maronite and Druze Lebanon under the Shihabis during the second half of the eighteenth century.

[12] Antonius Shibli (ed.), "Al Athar al Matwiyyah," *MQ*, XLVIII-LVI (1954-1962), XLVIII, 162, 400. Also in the same sense see Haydar, *Lubnan*, p. 715.
[13] *Ibid.*, pp. 561, 563.

THE MARONITES

The Maronites are a Christian people of the Catholic faith. For several centuries past they have lived almost exclusively in Mount Lebanon,[14] and their Church may be described as a national Church of Lebanon. The name Maronite is derived from the name of the sect's patron saint, the monk Maron, who probably lived in the latter part of the fourth century.[15] The Maronites' spoken and written language is now Arabic, but for more than three centuries after the Arab conquest of Syria they continued to use their national language, Aramaic. In the fifteenth century their language was already Arabized, although they continued to use Aramaic script for Arabic words (Karshuni) until late in the eighteenth century. The clergy still use Syriac liturgies in the mass.

The connections which developed between the Maronites and the Papacy in Rome had great effect upon the community and its Church. This will be discussed in detail later, but here we shall take note of the origin of these relations. The Maronites' contacts with the Church of Rome cannot be dated with conclusive historical evidence to a period earlier than that of the Crusades in the twelfth century.[16] Previously, it seems, they had been a monotheletic sect. Intermittent contacts with the popes occurred from that period on, until a

[14] Some Maronites lived in Cyprus, Aleppo, Damascus, and Bilad 'Akkar, but generally in negligible numbers. They also seem to have started to take up residence among the Druze in the sixteenth century, as witnessed by the Papal delegate to the Maronites at that time. See Lewis Shaykho, "Al Ta'ifah al Maruniyyah wa al Rahbaniyyah al Yasu'iyyah fi al Qarnayn al Sadis 'Ashar wa al Sabi' 'Ashar," *MQ*, xvii-xxi (1914-1923), xvii, 761-762.

[15] 'Abdallah Ghibra'il, *Tarikh al Kanisah al Intakiyyah al Siriyaniyyah al Maruniyyah*, 2 vols. (B'abda, Lebanon: al Matba'ah al Lubnaniyyah, 1900-1904), i, 84; also Philip Hitti, *Lebanon in History*, p. 247.

[16] See, for these intermittent contacts, Salibi, *Maronite Historians*, pp. 138-143; also Kamal Salibi, "The Maronite Church in the Middle Ages and Its Union with Rome," *Oriens Christianus*, xlii (1958), 92-105; also Shaykho, "Al Ta'ifah al Maruniyyah," *MQ*, xvii, 321-324.

measure of continuous relationship was established in the year 1578.

As for their government, the Maronites were subject to the governors of Tripoli, in Mamluk times, who appointed chiefs from among them to collect tribute and maintain public order. When Sultan Salim conquered Syria in 1516, the Maronites did not appear to be a political community like the Druze, whose chiefs figured as important political leaders in western Syria. There is no record that Sultan Salim took any notice of them. The regions of northern Lebanon where the Maronites lived were given over by Sultan Salim I to the Turkoman house of 'Assaf.

The Maronite patriarchs, unlike other Christian sects in the Ottoman Empire, did not seek investiture from the Sultan, but rather from the pope. This was doubtless due to the Ottomans' lack of interest in such a politically insignificant small group, rather than a legal concession. The practice continued up till World War I, when the Turkish military governor of Syria and Lebanon forced the patriarch to seek investiture from the Sultan.[17]

Of Maronite social organization we know very little before the seventeenth century. For some time Bsharri seems to have been the major town and the seat of their most important chief, known as the *muqaddam*, who was subject to the governor of Tripoli from Mamluk days. Other villages in northern Lebanon also had muqaddams of their own during different periods in history.

Certainly the Maronites did not always have the privileged social and political status they enjoyed in the eighteenth and nineteenth centuries. Like the rest of the Christian peoples living in a traditional Muslim society, they were a *dhimmah*

---

[17] According to Bishop 'Abdallah Khury, patriarchal secretary to Patriarch Huwayik. 'Abdallah Khury, "Al Batriyark al Maruni wa Jamal Basha Ibban al Harb," *MQ*, xxii (1924), 161-167.

people. The dhimmah were the Christians and the Jews living under Muslim dominion. They were guaranteed certain rights of free religious practice and security in life and property. In return they paid the state a poll tax and a land tax and suffered certain social and political disabilities as a caste inferior to their Muslim fellow subjects.[18] For instance, as dhimmah people the Maronites were forbidden to carry arms, ride horses, wear Muslim garb, or ring bells in their churches. Not until their country was taken over by the ruling Amir of Jabal al Druze, Fakhr al Din II, were the Maronites to enjoy free status.

> During the rule of Fakhr al Din the Christians raised their heads, they built churches, rode on saddled horses, and wore white turbans, . . . and drooping belts[19] and carried the bow and inlaid rifles, and in his days French missionaries came to live in Mount Lebanon; for most of his armies were Christians and his advisors and servants were Maronites.[20]

This did not last for long, however. With the decline of Ma'ni power in the middle of the seventeenth century, the Maronites' status reverted to the previous unhappy conditions, except for Kisrwan which became incorporated in the Imarah.

The Hirmil, a region in the northernmost part of Mount Lebanon, was controlled by the Himadah house who were Shi'ites (known in Lebanon as Matawilah). During the second part of the seventeenth century the Himadahs were able to expand their domain to include the Maronite lands of northern Lebanon, except for Kisrwan which remained in the hands of the Khazins. Himadah rule over the Maronite

---

[18] Hamilton Gibb and Harold Bowen, *Islamic Society and the West: A Study of the Impact of Western Civilization on Moslem Cultures in the Near East* (London: Royal Institute of International Affairs, Oxford University Press, 1957), I, Part 2, 208.

[19] Dhimmah people were not allowed to wear the customary wide belts which drooped low to the feet; they had to wear a string instead.

[20] Duwayhi, *TA*, p. 329.

country continued, with occasional interruption, until the middle of the eighteenth century. In 1759 the Maronites rose up in arms and expelled their Himadah lords and invited a Shihabi governor to rule over them. The condition of the Maronites improved considerably under the Shihabis. This fact is borne out by the eighteenth-century French traveler Volney, who visited the Maronites after their political union with the Druze under the Shihabi Imarah. Volney writes, "The Maronites are, to this day, equally strangers to the oppressions of despotism, and the disorders of anarchy."[21] As for property, it was not owned by the Sultan but by the people themselves. "Property," he writes, "is as sacred among them as in Europe."[22] Nor did the Maronites and the Druze pay inheritance tax, for "by a particular privilege, the Druze and Maronites pay no fine for their succession; nor does the Emir, like the Sultan, arrogate to himself original and universal property. . . ."[23]

In a rural community like Mount Lebanon of the eighteenth century, social stratification was very simple. Society was divided into two groups—shaykhs and peasants. The shaykhs were local village headmen, not marked out by great distinctions or wealth but, rather, derived from the peasant class itself. They were large property owners and cultivated their lands with the aid of tenants. Only in Kisrwan were there wealthy and powerful shaykhs, like the Khazins. The shaykhs, as Volney observed them, were distinguished from the rest by "a bad Pelisse, a horse, and a few slight advantages in food and lodging."[24] The peasants were either small landowners or tenants who cultivated the lands of shaykhs and shared the produce with them in equal portions. They grew olives, grapes, tobacco, cotton, some grain, and mulberry for silk manufacturing.[25] Silk culture was the one industry of the country and formed the basis of the economy.

[21] Volney, *Travels Through Syria and Egypt*, ii, 17.
[22] *Ibid.*, p. 18.   [23] *Ibid.*, pp. 79-80.   [24] *Ibid.*, pp. 17-18.
[25] John Bowring, *Report on the Commercial Statistics of Syria*, Great

The Maronite population was not very large. In 1578 the Maronites were estimated to be about 40,000[26] living in some 200 villages.[27] The large majority of these were in Jibbat Bsharri. The Maronites started to emigrate to Jabal al Druze after the Ottoman conquest in 1516.[28] In the last decades of the sixteenth century, five or six villages in Jabal al Druze had some Maronite people living in them.[29] During the Ma'ni period (1516-1697), especially the time of Fakhr al Din II, Kisrwan started to attract the Maronites; and by the beginning of the eighteenth century it became predominantly Maronite in population. Most of the people who went to live in Kisrwan were originally from the north in the regions of Jibbat Bsharri and Jubayl, which eventually, for a time, became almost deserted.[30] The population of these two regions did not start to grow again until the second part of the eighteenth century when the country became a domain of the Shihabi Imarah. Under Shihabi rule there was a marked increase in the Maronite population in the north, as well as in the rest of the Mountain. By the end of the eighteenth century the population figure for the Maronites was fairly large compared to the earlier periods and to the other communities living in the Mountain. The number usually given is close to Volney's estimate, which must be a reasonable figure. The estimate Volney made is 115,000[31] excluding the southern re-

---

Britain, Presented to both Houses of Parliament by Command of Her Majesty (London: H.M. Stationery Office, printed by William Clowes and Sons, 1840), p. 102.

[26] Estimate by Eliano Battista who visited the Maronites during the years 1578-1580. See Shaykho, "Al Ta'ifah al Maruniyyah," MQ, xvii, 758.

[27] Patriarch Mikha'il al Rizzi (1567-1581) in a letter to the pope. See Shaykho, "Al Ta'ifah al Maruniyyah," MQ, xvii, 758, n. 1.

[28] Duwayhi, *TA*, p. 236; also Shaykho, "Al Ta'ifah al Maruniyyah," MQ, xvii, 761; see also letter to Rome by Patriarch Istfan al Duwayhi, Mas'ad and al Khazin, *UT*, iii, 39.

[29] Shaykho, "Al Ta'ifah al Maruniyyah," MQ, xvii, 761.

[30] Duwayhi, *TA*, pp. 295-296.

[31] Volney, *Travels Through Syria and Egypt*, ii, 365.

gions of the Imarah, which were inhabited by Maronites and Druze mainly. With the figures of these included, the Maronite population at that time should have been something like 150,000.[32]

The first victims of this migration were the Matawilah, who had had a long history of political rivalry with the Imarah of Jabal al Druze. With the passing of northern Lebanon into Shihabi hands, the Matawilah there were crushed and the industrious and law-abiding Maronites were encouraged to replace them in Kisrwan, Bilad Jubayl, and al Batrun, and even in the south of Jabal al Druze. As a result, the Matawilah were persistently pushed out until they ended up living outside Mount Lebanon, around which they formed a belt. Thereafter, the population of Jibbat Bsharri and Bilad Jubayl showed a remarkable rate of growth. Figures given by chroniclers and travelers indicate that the Maronites there in the middle of the nineteenth century numbered more than twice the population of Kisrwan;[33] a century earlier, Kisrwan had had almost three times the population of those regions.

The Druze

The Druze are a religious sect which originally stemmed from Shi'i Islam, but developed as a completely separate

---

[32] Volney is often quoted wrongly in Arabic and French sources as giving the figure 115,000 for the entire Maronite population of Mount Lebanon. This is wrong because he mentions explicitly that the figure is for Kisrwan, by which he means the whole of northern Lebanon including Jibbat Bsharri. The figure of 150,000 was reached by adding the population figure of the Maronites in the south to that given by Volney. The figure for the south was determined through a conservative estimate based on the figures given in the following sources: Tannus bin Yusuf al Shidiaq, *Akhbar al A'yan fi Jabal Lubnan*, ed. Munir Whaybah al Khazin (Beirut: Matabi' Samya, 1954), I, 32 (hereafter cited as *Akhbar*); Camille de Rochemonteix, *Le Liban et l'Expédition Française en Syrie (1860-1861)*, (Paris: Librairie August Picard, 1921), p. 347; Achille Laurent, *Relation Historique des Affaires de Syrie depuis 1840 Jusqu'en 1842: Statistique Générale du Mont Liban*, 2 vols. (Paris: Gaume Frères, 1846), I, 433-468. The last is the most detailed account.

[33] Shidiaq, *Akhbar*, I, 32, see table of census; also Rochementeix, *Le Liban*, Appendix, opposite p. 346.

community with their own religious organization and practice. Not long after the sect was founded, its religious leaders ceased to accept new converts or to allow anyone to give up his Druze faith.[34] Thus by their own choice the Druze have remained few in number to this day.

The sect originated in Egypt in the beginning of the eleventh century during the reign of the Fatimid Caliph, al Hakim (996-1021). As the new faith met with little success there, its proponents concentrated their efforts on the Isma'ily sects in Syria and particularly in Wadi al Taym in southern Lebanon.[35] Their early history is just as obscure as that of most other groups in Lebanon; but by the sixteenth century the Druze population was concentrated in the regions of Wadi al Taym, the Jabal al Shuf, and al Gharb, with a few in the Vilayet of Aleppo.

A strong tendency to stress social unity and solidarity as a community is manifested in the ethical teachings of the Druze religion. Brotherhood in the faith, one of the seven ethical injunctions, urges the believers to observe the religious ranks in the ladder of initiation, to love their co-religionists, to show deference to the high among them, and to be accessible and helpful to those of inferior position in life.[36] In their social attitudes the Druze have shown a definite inclination to conform to these moral and social imperatives. A Maronite historian who has lived among them and studied their history and culture describes their national character as one of "intense community loyalty, high sense of

---

[34] In later years, however, it seems that Muslim people of noble families like the Tannukhs, the Arslans, and the Jumblats who ruled in Druze-populated regions did accept the Druze faith; see Hitti, *Lebanon in History*, p. 262.

[35] For the beginning of the sect see Marshall G. S. Hodgson, "Al-Darazi and Hamza in the Origin of the Druze Religion," *Journal of the American Oriental Society*, LXXXII, No. 1 (January-March 1962), 5-20.

[36] Hananiyya al Munayyar, *Théogonie des Druses; ou Abrégé de leur Système Religieux*, ed. and trans. Henri Guys (Paris: Imprimerie Impériale, 1863), pp. 78-79. For a detailed account see Silvestre de Sacy, *Exposé de la Religion des Druzes*, 2 vols. (Paris: Imprimerie Royale, 1838).

solidarity, vigorous spirit of independence, endurance in the face of adversity."[37]

Religious life and practice during the period we are studying was not well organized nor of central importance in the Druze community, as was the case in the Maronite community. It seems that strong political organization and traditional ties of social cohesion among the Druze made up for indifference toward religious life. Travelers who visited Lebanon before the beginning of the nineteenth century do not seem to have been struck by an awareness of religiosity among the Druze, as they were with the Maronites and Sunni Muslims. Volney, for example, was greatly impressed by Druze spirit of social solidarity, but speaks of their "indifference for religion, which forms a striking contrast with the zeal of the Mahometans and Christians."[38]

In their religious organization the Druze have no clear distinction between clergy and the laity. The entire Druze population is divided into two categories, those initiated into the secrets of the faith (*'uqqal*) and those not initiated (*juhhal*). The latter, observers have reported, know hardly anything about the articles of faith in their religion, but they belong to the Druze religious community all the same and identify as Druze.[39]

The 'uqqal, all those men and women who have received some information regarding the tenets of their religion and who are allowed to sit within the halls for worship, are also divided into two categories—the general and the special classes. The former are those who have passed the simple test of trust and can be permitted to know some elementary facts of re-

[37] Hitti, *Lebanon in History*, p. 262.

[38] Volney, *Travels Through Syria and Egypt*, II, 81; also Butrus Ghalib, "Taqrir al Sayyid Ghranji 'an Biladina fi al Qarn al Thamin 'Ashar," *MQ*, XXVIII (1930), 583.

[39] Nasif al Yaziji, *Risalah Tarikhiyyah fi Ahwal Lubnan fi 'Ahdihi al Iqta'i*, ed. Qustantin al Basha (Harisa, Lebanon: Matba'at al Qiddis Bulus, [1936]), p. 24 (hereafter cited as *Risalah*).

ligion. The special class may be described as those well founded in the knowledge of the mysteries of their religion. Except for some ostentatious signs of piety and asceticism, the 'uqqal had no social or political qualities which separated them from the rest of the population. They themselves did not think of themselves as clerics; they did not charge fees for the performance of religious ceremonies, they lived like other men, and like the rest, they went to war and enjoyed the reputation of being good fighters.[40]

Druze religious leaders were not able to keep independent from the political heads of the community. Political chiefs succeeded in drawing the 'uqqal into their competing factions very easily.[41] The Shaykh al 'Aql, though the community's religious head, was in political matters entirely subject to the leaders of the two Druze factions. In fact, from the latter part of the eighteenth century each faction elected a Shaykh al 'Aql of its own, and thus instead of having one religious head the Druze community had two, one for each of the two iqta' parties. There was a Jumblati Shaykh al 'Aql and a Yazbaki Shaykh al 'Aql, a division which persists to this day.[42]

Education among the Druze, religious men as well as lay population, was almost nonexistent. The only learning they had in the eighteenth and early nineteenth century, reported a nineteenth-century writer who lived among them, was that of the stars and talisman. In case one aspired to become a judge, he added, one studied the *shari'ah*.[43] But how many among them could become judges? During the Shihabi rule the Druze government had only one judge at a time, who handled cases of a civil nature. In matters of personal status, the Shaykh al 'Aql was in charge. Volney, who became well acquainted with their way of life, wrote that Druze children

[40] Shayban al Khazin, *Tarikh Shayban*, in *UT*, III (1958), 519.
[41] Cf. Haydar, *Lubnan*, pp. 766-767.
[42] Yusuf Khattar Abu Shaqra, *Al Harakat fi Lubnan ila 'Ahd al Muta-sarifiyyah*, ed. 'Arif Abu Shaqra (Beirut: Matba'at al Ittihad, n.d.), pp. 191-192.
[43] Yaziji, *Risalah*, p. 27.

"are neither taught to read the Psalms, as among the Maronites, nor the Koran, like the Mahometans; hardly do the Shaiks know how to write a letter."[44] We know of no schools of any sort for children in the Druze community except for a short-lived school established in 1849 at al Mukhtarah.[45]

Social stratification among the Druze, unlike their religious organization, was sharply defined. As with the Maronites, society was divided economically into three classes: tenants, property owners, and *muqati'jis* (hereditary chiefs). We do not have a very clear record of the proportion of tenants to landowners in Mount Lebanon, and only rough estimates or guesses are possible in this respect. Volney indicated a high percentage of property owners, but unfortunately he did not find it necessary to distinguish between tenants and propertied peasants; he believed there was not much difference between the two groups since tenants rented the land and it became their responsibility. Shaykh Shayban al Khazin, at approximately the same time as Volney, seems to confirm the latter's account, at least insofar as Maronite Kisrwan was concerned. According to this account, apparently the larger part of the land belonged to small peasants.[46] One also gets the impression from chronicles and other records that property ownership was widespread among the Maronites from Kisrwan to Jibbat Bsharri, as well as among the Druze population.

As for the muqati'ji class, both Druze and Maronite, only a few remained the owners of great estates by the first part of the nineteenth century, among whom the Jumblats were the largest landowners. The muqati'jis gradually alienated a large proportion of their land through sales and donations as *waqfs* (mortmain). Their property itself was parceled into small plots as a result of increase in their numbers in the late

---

[44] Volney, *Travels Through Syria and Egypt*, ii, 82.

[45] See Shakir al Khury, *Majma' al Masarrat* (Beirut: Matba'at al Ijtihad, 1908), pp. 20-21.

[46] Shayban, *Tarikh*, pp. 445-447. A similar observation is made by Bowring, *Report*, pp. 8, 102.

eighteenth and early nineteenth centuries, especially in the case of the Maronite muqati'jis.

There is no available figure which can be considered reliable for the Druze population before the nineteenth century.[47] However, they seem never to have been large in numbers.[48] The earliest figures we have go back to the third decade of the nineteenth century. One estimate gives a total population of no more than 60,000 people;[49] and another makes the number of men 10,000, which should actually give about the same total population as the first.[50]

POLITICAL HISTORY

In 1516 the Ottomans under Sultan Salim I occupied Syria and defeated its Mamluk masters. The Ottoman conqueror confirmed the existing feudal system in southern Lebanon and rewarded some of the Lebanese chiefs for supporting him. One of these was Amir Fakhr al Din al Ma'ni I, who thereafter started to acquire power and prominence. The Imarah of Jabal al Druze was founded by the Ma'ni dynasty when they gained precedence over other feudal houses and became overlords of south Lebanon.

The Ma'nis extended their domain, which was originally confined to al Shuf, both in south Lebanon and toward the north. As a result of Ma'ni expansion in the north, a bitter conflict developed between the Turkoman chiefs of that region and Fakhr al Din II (1585-1635). Fakhr al Din's first success was in Kisrwan, which he annexed and bestowed upon

---

[47] Volney gives the figure of 120,000 people for Jabal al Druze, which must have included the Maronites and others living with the Druze. See Volney, *Travels Through Syria and Egypt*, II, 365. Also Laurent, *Relation Historique*, I, 433-468.

[48] Shayban comments that they were a very small group; *Tarikh*, p. 519.

[49] Jean Joseph Poujoulat and Joseph Michaud, *Correspondance d'Orient: 1830-1831*, VII (Paris: Ducollet, 1835), 342. They exaggerate the number of the Druze and the effects of the Egyptian occupation on the size of their population.

[50] Yaziji, *Risalah*, p. 28.

his Maronite advisor, Abu Nadir al Khazin, in 1616.[51] Thus the Khazins became the first Maronite house to achieve muqati'ji status. Kisrwan, which up till then had been inhabited by Muslims, mainly Matawilah, was gradually settled by the Maronites with the encouragement of Fakhr al Din. The Maronites, attracted by the security, freedom, and employment in government under the Ma'nis, emigrated in large numbers to Kisrwan and other regions of Jabal al Shuf.[52] In the south, Fakhr al Din's early campaigns took the lands of the Sanjak of Sidon[53] which are known as the *iqlims* (districts) of al Kharrub, Tuffah, Jazzin, and the Jabal al Rayhan. After a long struggle these *iqlims* were finally incorporated permanently into Mount Lebanon under the Shihabis.

The continued expansion of Fakhr al Din in Syria finally led the Ottoman government to send a major military expedition against him. He was captured and executed. Shortly after Fakhr al Din's downfall, the affairs of the Imarah fell to his brother, who was able to restore Ma'ni rule in southern Lebanon. In 1697 the last Ma'ni died without an heir and with him the dynasty came to an end. Thereupon, a Shihabi descended from the Ma'nis on the maternal side started the Shihabi dynasty, which was politically a continuation of the Ma'ni one.

The legacy which the Ma'nis left to the Shihabis was of a modest nature compared with the glory of Fakhr al Din's reign. The territory consisted only of al Shuf, al Gharb, al Jurd, al Matn, and Kisrwan.[54] Kisrwan was the one Maronite land left to the rulers of Jabal al Druze after Fakhr al Din. The rest of the Maronite lands and other parts of northern Lebanon

[51] Haydar Shihab, *Kitab al Ghurar al Hisan fi Tawarikh Hawadith al Zaman*, ed. Na'um Mughabghab (Egypt: Matba'at at Salam, 1900), pp. 649-650 (hereafter cited as Haydar, *al Ghurar*). Cf. Mas'ad and al Khazin, *UT*, III, 311.

[52] Shaykho, *MQ*, XVII, 761; also Duwayhi, *TA*, p. 236; 'Aynturini, *MTL*, XLVI, 436.

[53] Hitti, *Lebanon in History*, p. 374; also Munayyar, *KTS*, XLIX, 270.

[54] Shayban, *Tarikh*, p. 403.

remained in the hands of the Pasha of Tripoli, who appointed different chiefs, mainly Matawilah, to farm out the country.

After the downfall of Fakhr al Din II, the Ottoman government reorganized the administration of Syria to keep closer vigilance over the Druze. To make this easier for the Vali, the city of Sayda was made the seat of the Vilayet of Sayda in 1660. Bilad Jubayl, Batrun, and Jibbat Bsharri became attached to the Vilayet of Damascus in 1638.[55] The Shihabis therefore had to deal with two Valis at the same time—they were tributaries to the Vali of Sayda for the Mount of the Druze and Kisrwan, and to the Vali of Damascus for the northern territories of Lebanon. Thus the rulers of Mount Lebanon were affected by what went on around them and became quite involved in the politics of the Syrian vilayets.

From the beginning of their rule in 1697, the Shihabis had to fight Ottoman encroachments upon their mountain on two fronts. They had to curb the ambitions of the Valis and Pashas on the one hand, and on the other they had to crack down on a rival dynasty in the Mountain itself, the 'Alam al Din house, who were the chiefs of the Yamani faction. The background of this rivalry, briefly, is as follows: from the days of the Ma'nis, the Yaman and Qaysi political factions, widely spread over different parts of the Arab Middle East, in Lebanon had taken the character of rivalry between two dynasties, the Ma'nis and the 'Alam al Dins, for the government of the Mountain. The 'Alam al Dins showed more loyalty to the Ottomans and were supported by the Valis. The Ma'nis, who were the chiefs of the Qaysi faction, stood for greater autonomy in the affairs of the Imarah and generally distrusted the Ottoman government and its Valis. Although the Ma'nis were Sunni Muslim, most of the Druze supported them rather than the Druze house of 'Alam al Din.[56]

[55] Haydar, *al Ghurar*, p. 724.

[56] Although there is no clear evidence that the Ma'nis changed their

After a period of setback, the Qaysis reemerged under the leadership of Amir Haydar Shihab (1703-1732). They finally gave the Yamani faction in Jabal al Druze the coup de grace in 1711 in a decisive battle fought in 'Ayn Dara, a village in Jabal al Druze. After this the Shihabis reasserted their power and, to the end of their rule, were free to attend to their affairs without any serious threat to their dynasty.

As for their relations with the Valis in Sayda and Damascus, the Shihabis were by no means subservient. Especially after the 'Ayn Dara battle, and for most of the rest of their rule, the Shihabis could deal with the Valis practically on equal terms. On several occasions Valis sought Shihabi assistance to help establish their own authority. Early in the eighteenth century the Shihabis reasserted their rule over the regions known as the *iqlims* and over the city of Beirut. This city remained under Shihabi rule only from 1748 till 1776, when Ahmad Pasha al Jazzar of Acre annexed it to his little empire.

The Shihabis continued to enlarge their domains during the eighteenth century, and their expansion culminated in the incorporation of northern Lebanon under their rule. This was the first lasting unification of Mount Lebanon. Because of the significance of the event and the fact that little is known about it, we shall give it special attention here.

The Maronite country of northern Lebanon was under the Matawilah lords of the Himadah house during the first half of the eighteenth century. The Himadahs also controlled the Sunni Muslim regions of northern Lebanon such as al Dinniyah and 'Akkar. However, in 1759 the Maronites of Jibbat

---

Sunni Muslim religion, some historians believe they were converted to the Druze religion. The Druze historian Yusuf Muzhir takes their conversion for granted; see Yusuf Muzhir, *Tarikh Lubnan al 'Am*, 2 vols. ([Beirut]: n.p., n.d.), I, 370, and Hitti, *Lebanon in History*, p. 262; also Gibb and Bowen, *Islamic Society and the West*, I, Part 1, 222. Cf. for the opposite view, the account of Fakhr al Din's contemporary and judge, al Shaykh Ahmad ibn Muhammad al Khalidy, *'Ahd al Amir Fakhr al Din al Ma'ni*, eds. Fu'ad Afram al Bustani and Asad Rustum (Beirut: Lebanese Government Publication, al Matba'ah al Kathulikiyyah, 1936), pp. 2, 4.

Bsharri, Bilad al Batrun, and Bilad Jubayl revolted against their Himadah rulers and expelled them from Jibbat Bsharri, following the expulsion of the Himadahs from the Sunni *muqata'ahs* of al Dinniyah and 'Akkar. Thereafter, each of the Maronite village shaykhs rented the iqta' of his village directly from the Pasha of Tripoli, who had encouraged the Maronites in their uprising against the notorious Matawilah lords.

As hostilities continued between the Maronites and the Himadahs, however, the former sought the help of the Shihabis and asked them to come and rule their country.[57] The shaykhs of Jibbat Bsharri asked the Maronite muqati'jis of Kisrwan, the Khazins, to plead their cause with Amir Mansur Shihab, who was then ruling Jabal al Druze. The Khazins, though, failed to help the Maronites of the north,[58] thus losing a very important opportunity to regain some of their waning political power. At that point the struggle in northern Lebanon entered the arena of partisan political contest in Jabal al Druze. The Himadahs, who had also sought to draw Amir Mansur to their side, appealed to the Yazbaki faction leaders to keep the Shihabi Amir from helping the Maronites.[59] As a result, Amir Mansur only took a stand of compromise; he accepted the Maronites' request that they should receive the iqta' of their country through him but did not back them with the military force necessary to hold off the Himadahs.[60]

By this time the Jumblati faction was starting to assume a role of opposition to Amir Mansur. They thereupon entered into negotiations with Sa'd al Khury,[61] the Maronite advisor of the young Amir Yusuf Shihab, son of the former governor Amir Mulhim Shihab. The Jumblati faction promised Sa'd support for his master in seeking investiture from the Ottoman governor of Damascus for the Maronite country of

[57] 'Aynturini, *MTL*, XLVII, 45-46.
[58] *Ibid*.   [59] *Ibid*.   [60] *Ibid*.
[61] Shayban, *Tarikh*, pp. 512-513; also Haydar, *Lubnan*, pp. 60-62.

Jibbat Bsharri, Bilad al Batrun, and Bilad Jubayl. At this, Sa'd al Khury and Amir Yusuf immediately went to Damascus,[62] with enough cash collected from the Maronites of northern Lebanon[63] to win the Pasha to their side. As Amir Yusuf and his advisor were able to present the Pasha readily with the yearly tribute of the muqata'ahs in question, he agreed to grant the investiture.

Amir Yusuf and Sa'd al Khury then promptly put an end to the Himadahs' rule in Bilad Jubayl and took disciplinary measures against them wherever they still showed resistance.[64] In 1773 the Himadahs suffered a complete defeat by Sa'd al Khury, after which they never rose again in northern Lebanon. Amir Yusuf encouraged the Maronites to resettle in the regions the Himadahs had earlier forced them to leave. The state of insecurity in those regions under the Himadahs had left the country desolate and poor, so impoverished, in fact, that Amir Yusuf found the revenues from all his domains still too little to meet the expenses of government.[65] He therefore embarked on a policy of imposing peace and encouraging peasants to settle and cultivate the land. As for the Maronite chiefs who had supported him in his efforts to be invested governor, he appointed them muqati'jis over Jibbat Bsharri, Bilad al Batrun, and Bilad Jubayl.[66]

After 1764 the Shihabis controlled Mount Lebanon from the Cedars to Jabal 'Amil. At first there were two governing amirs, one in the north and one in the south, independent from each other until 1770 when Amir Yusuf succeeded in becoming the ruling amir of both regions. After him, his sons and Amir Bashir Shihab struggled for power and again divided Lebanon between them into a northern and a south-

---

[62] *Ibid.* Also 'Aynturini, *MTL*, xlvii, 45-46.

[63] *Ibid.* Also Mansur al Hattuni, *Nabdhah Tarikhiyyah fi al Muqata'ah al Kisrwaniyyah* (Beirut: n.p., 1884), pp. 178-179.

[64] Haydar, *Lubnan*, p. 62; 'Aynturini, *MTL*, xlvii, 46.

[65] Haydar, *Lubnan*, p. 64.

[66] 'Aynturini, *MTL*, xlvii, 46; also Hattuni, *Nabdhah*, pp. 178-179.

ern region. In 1807, Bashir asserted himself over the two sections, which were not separated again until the downfall of the Shihabi dynasty in 1841. As mentioned earlier, Maronites had been living among Druze in the south since the days of the Ma'nis, and under the Shihabis the most populated Maronite muqata'ah was Kisrwan. Nonetheless, the incorporation of the Maronite country into the Mountain of the Druze had serious effects on the political institutions of Lebanon, as we shall see later.

In 1776, Ahmad Pasha al Jazzar was appointed Vali of Sayda and made his seat at Acre. His ambition led him on a course of constant intrigue aimed at subjugating Mount Lebanon, especially as his power increased with his appointment in 1785 as Vali of Damascus as well as of Sayda. Al Jazzar's attempts to deprive the Mountain of its freedom and autonomy failed, although he brought the Shihabis to their knees by playing them one against the other. The Vali's policy weakened Shihabi rule and kept political conditions unstable in Lebanon until shortly before his death in 1804.

After al Jazzar's death, Bashir Shihab successfully asserted his authority over Lebanon until 1832, when the Egyptian occupation of Syria forced him to ally his fortunes with the military prowess of Muhammad Ali and his son Ibrahim. Although at first this alliance with the victorious Egyptians gave him prestige, its long-run effects seriously imperiled Shihabi rule in Lebanon. It widened the gap between Bashir and the Druze chiefs which had already developed by the time of the Egyptian conquest. At the same time, the presence of the Egyptian military might in Syria made interference in the internal affairs of the Shihabis inevitable. The Lebanese lost some of the freedom they had enjoyed in preceding eras and were forced to serve as conscripts in the Egyptian expedition. Finally, the Egyptians' heavy pressures led the Mountain people to revolt in 1840. Maronites and Druze fought the Egyptians with the assistance of an international expedition, composed mainly of the British and the Ottomans. Bashir II fell with his ally Ibrahim Pasha, and the Ottoman government named in his place Amir Bashir Mulhim Shihab, known in Lebanese history as Bashir III. This Amir failed to unite the Druze and Maronites under his authority, and in 1841 a civil war broke out between the two communities which brought the Shihabi dynasty to an end.

The Egyptian affair not only jeopardized the Shihabi dynasty but also caused the internationalizing of the Lebanese question for the first time in history. Henceforth, Lebanon became an object of concern for the European powers which were squabbling for the spoils of the Sick Man of Europe. The Ottomans themselves became very much antagonized by the Shihabis, who had proved a potential enemy to the Sultanate. When the Shihabis failed to solve the predicament of political struggle for domination between the Druze and the Maronites, the Ottoman government had no problem in removing them from their position in Lebanon.

Following the demise of the ruling Shihabi house, a political reorganization took place in Lebanon carried out by the Ottoman government and the European powers. The country was divided into two administrative units, one under a Druze governor and the other under a Maronite. Each division was called *Qa'immaqamiyyah*. The Maronite *Qa'immaqamiyyah* constituted all the country from al Matn to Jibbat Bsharri, and that of the Druze, south of al Matn to Jabal 'Amil. The problem in this partition arrangement was that the Lebanese were not really willing to divide their country. Resistance became particularly acrimonious because of the presence of a good number of Maronite people under the Druze government, since the old Jabal al Druze had acquired a mixed population of both Druze and Christians. A few Druze were also to be found in the Christian section.

In 1860 civil war broke out again between Druze and Christians. Lebanon was then again reorganized by the Ottoman government and the European powers under a new constitution. An Ottoman Christian, non-Lebanese, was to govern the whole of the Mountain for a term of five years subject to renewal. This governor, called *Mutasarrif*, was to be appointed by the Sultan with the approval of the European Powers which were signatories to the Lebanese Organic Law. A central council of twelve members elected by the people would aid the Mutasarrif and advise him on matters of policy. The council represented the religious communities living in the Mountain, each having two members. In 1864 the apportionment of seats was revised in favor of the two main communities: the Maronites were given four members and the Druze three. Lebanon was divided administratively into six departments with a prefect for each; the prefect was appointed by the Mutasarrif from the religious community of the majority of people in his department. The iqta' system of the Imarah was formally abolished.

As we conclude this brief historical survey, one feature of the political experience of Mount Lebanon requires special attention. This was the successful integration of heterogeneous religious and ethnic groups under one political system over a long period of time. No political inequality was caused by the fact of religious difference. Tolerance and liberty proved to be a legacy which is valued today in Lebanon and which forms the main requisite of its political success.

CHAPTER III

The Political System of the
Shihabi Imarah

THE CONCEPT of iqta' in Middle Eastern history has generally
been used interchangeably with that of *iltizam*, more or less
in the sense of the tax-farming system prevalent in the Ottoman Empire. In contrast, I am using the term iqta' in a
more specialized and distinct sense, as a political concept
relating to the political system of Mount Lebanon. Thus the
term iqta' is defined here as a political system in which authority is distributed among a number of hereditary aristocratic chiefs subordinate in certain respects to a common overlord.

The iqta' political order of the Shihabi Imarah had a number of characteristics which allow us to view it as a single
system. There was a certain degree of political unity in that
authority at the center constituted a point of reference for
both muqati'jis and subjects. Also, the same political institutions prevailed in the various parts of the country under
Imarah jurisdiction. Finally, there was a geographic base
where the same historic groups lived and interacted for a
long period of time. From the sixteenth to the nineteenth
century there was one change in dynasty and several changes
in geographic boundaries, but political unity and the type
of political institutions persisted. This discussion does not
take into account the whole period since the sixteenth century, but is limited to the Shihabi era from the beginning of
the eighteenth to the middle of the nineteenth century.

In this chapter we shall describe the iqta' political system
of the Shihabi Imarah with respect to its three main constituent parts: the principle of legitimacy, the institutions, and the
actors. Our main effort will be to determine the extent to
which the system was integrated, i.e., the degree of consistency

in the relationships of its constituent parts; and second, to examine the sources of conflict within it.

LEGITIMACY AND POLITICAL ALLEGIANCE IN THE SHIHABI IMARAH

Here some explanation of the technical language of the iqta' system in Mount Lebanon will make our task easier later on. In the language of the time, no general term seems to have been used by the participants in the system or the official documents to designate the whole order. The Shihabi ruling Amir was referred to variously as *al Amir al Hakim* or *al Hakim*. The phrases *Hukm Jabal al Shuf wa Kisrwan* and *Hukm Jabal Lubnan*, that is, the government of Mount Lebanon, were often used by Haydar and other chroniclers.[1] A general term, *'uhdah* (plural, *'uhad*), was commonly used to designate government by a muqati'ji. A muqati'ji was a hereditary noble chief who enjoyed political authority over a 'uhdah, the region over which his governmental rights extended. The muqati'jis were also known as *manasib* (in the plural) when they were described in their capacity as political leaders collectively in contrast to their roles as particular rulers of specific 'uhdahs.

The principle of legitimacy in the iqta' system was derived from more than one source. In general perspective, the arrangement of authority fitted within the framework of Ottoman dominion. The Sultan was theoretically the highest authority over the feudal rulers of Mount Lebanon and their subjects, and the Hakim of Lebanon sent tribute (the *miri*) in the Sultan's name to the Valis of Sayda and Tripoli. Similarly, investiture of the Amir al Hakim was also done in the name of the Sultan. For al Shuf and Kisrwan, investiture came by way of the Vali of Sayda, and for Jubayl and its dependencies, from the Vali of Tripoli. The period for which the investiture was granted was one year; this can be con-

---

[1] Haydar, *Lubnan*, pp. 649, 690.

firmed for the period after 1775, although there is no available evidence that it was true of earlier periods.[2] There were exceptions to this practice even after 1775, when Amir Bashir II received investiture for life in 1810 from Sulayman Pasha and again in 1820 from 'Abdallah Pasha.[3] However, the fact that the Hakim was invested with his office on a yearly basis did not mean that the regulation of succession was in the hands of the Ottoman Valis, as we shall soon see.

Every year upon receiving the tribute, the Vali sent the Hakim a *khul'ah*, a sable coat[4] which was the token of investiture and symbol of authority, and the Amir put it on with some show of public ceremony as soon as he received it. The Amir's reception of the khul'ah had a special significance in the political institutions of the Imarah. As seen by Amir Bashir's poet, Niqula al Turk, the khul'ah "confirms the ties of loyalty"[5] between the Hakim and the Ottoman State. On the whole it gave the Lebanese a general feeling of satisfaction that the Ottoman State, which represented for them a higher civil order, had legitimized the government of their chiefs. It also gave them the expectation of peace, that is, the feeling that no disorder or hostility with the State was forthcoming. For a small community like Mount Lebanon the sanction of the Ottoman State also meant recognition by the outside and neighboring world. Imperial power over the whole area surrounding Lebanon gave the Lebanese the opportunity for useful intercourse with their neighbors.

However, in practice the Lebanese viewed their relations with the Ottoman government with some caution and did not show much trust in its dealings. When, for example, Amir Mulhim Shihab (1729-1754) had to yield his brother 'Ali as

[2] Ottoman Valis were invested on a one-year basis in the eighteenth century; see Hamilton Gibb and Harold Bowen, *Islamic Society and the West*, I, Part I, 201.

[3] Haydar, *Lubnan*, pp. 552-554, 680.

[4] See Marsums in Haydar, *Lubnan*, pp. 553, 649.

[5] Niqula al Turk, *Diwan al Mu'alim Niqula al Turk*, ed Fu'ad Afram al Bustani (Beirut, Lebanese Government Publication, Nusus wa Watha'iq, 1949), p. 230.

a hostage to the Vali of Sayda, he made his brother stay in the French khan there because "there was no trust in al Dawlah."[6] The Shihabi Hakims were always careful not to give the Ottoman government or its viceroys a pretext or opportunity for encroaching on their traditional autonomy. The Valis as a rule did not interfere with the internal affairs of the Imarah, and, excepting Ahmad Pasha al Jazzar, the independent power of the Lebanese Hakims was greater than that of the Valis of Sayda and Tripoli. In short, so far as Lebanon was concerned, the Ottoman sovereignty was virtually a fiction—the Sultan was recognized as the supreme lord, yet he was so far removed in distance and power that the Amir al Hakim was the actual ruler in his land.

The second and major legitimizing principle, or source of authority, lay in the social norms as expressed in the practices and traditions of the Lebanese people. These traditions were handed down from one generation to the next and were held in great respect. Traditional social values included veneration for the ways of the elders, respect for each person's place and station in the social order, and adherence to the rules affecting each class and title. To the people of Mount Lebanon, the division of society into a hierarchy of classes was the normal order, which could be traced back to antiquity. Men were not equal, for each had a place determined by his birth. Men were born as commoners (*'ammiyyah*), shaykhs, muqaddams, or amirs; each class had its special place and rights in society.

A title of nobility applied to all the members of a patrilineal kinship group, not to one or a few members only. Marriages and social protocol were defined by the noble rank which a person held. It was in the light of these facts that the muqati'jis acted, for instance, when they chose a Shihabi amir to rule over them after the death of the last Ma'ni Hakim. The Shihabis intermarried with the Ma'nis, like them were of amir rank, and were also political allies of the Ma'nis. To

---

[6] Haydar, *Lubnan*, p. 41.

elect a Shihabi was therefore the natural course of action, according to the world-view of the Lebanese of the seventeenth century.

There was, then, an inborn sense of social order and custom, which was not easily broken by the passing of time. The continuity of tradition can be illustrated by the statement the first Shihabi Amir made to the Maronite prelates soon after he assumed power in 1697. He wrote: "We shall look after your interests and protect you; we shall also treat you according to your customs, letting nothing change for you."[7]

Like most other traditional cultures, Lebanese society under the Shihabi Imarah esteemed the inherited practices and the elders' ways of doing things. But respect for age and heritage alone would not have sufficed had there not also been a feeling that the accepted customs manifested justice. Thus it was not only acceptance of tradition that legitimized the institutions of the Imarah, but also a sense of utility and benefit. One can detect in accounts of the period the feeling that the order under which the people lived gave them security in their lives and property as well as relative independence and liberty.

The importance of the historically derived principle of legitimacy as a restraining force in the system should not be underestimated, especially when it is remembered that the rulers of the Imarah had neither army nor police. As in medieval Europe, the lords considered it an affront to their honor and independence to have hired men fight their battles for them. The Amir himself could not rely much on force to produce conformity and obedience to his policies and orders. He had but a small number of retainers, who served essentially for administrative purposes. These were known as *al shurtah* or *huwalah*, and their position was not held in much esteem. On some occasions the Amir resorted to Albanian and North African mercenaries to help repel outside danger; and in the

---

[7] See letter in Butrus Ghalib, "Nawabigh al Madrasah al Maruniyyah al Ula," *MQ*, XXII (1924), 110.

civil wars instigated by al Jazzar, mercenaries were employed.

If the people in the iqta' system were not governed by force, neither were they held together by religious bonds. The population was of mixed religious affiliation, which did not coincide with social stratification. Both general classes, muqati'jis and subjects, contained a mixture of Druze and Maronites.[8] The ruling family of Shihab was Sunni Muslim; and although some of the family became converted to the Maronite faith starting in the mid-eighteenth century, the early converts were not in line for succession.[9] The general population was also quite mixed. The great majority were Maronites and Druze, and then came Christians of various other sects, Shi'is, and Sunnis.

Political allegiance was not based on religious or ethnic considerations, and political loyalty cut across sectarian lines. A man's allegiance was first to his muqati'ji and then to the ruling Amir, whether they were of his religious group or not. As a subject under the jurisdiction of a muqati'ji, a man was considered to be of the 'uhdah of the muqati'ji; and as it was usually the case that a subject's political affiliations were with those of his master, he was said to be of the *'uzwah* of his lord.[10] In the one case the person was a subject; in the second, a follower. Another term hardly distinguishable from 'uzwah is *ismiyyah*, which refers to the iqta' bond holding a number of subjects in loyalty to the muqati'ji's house. It meant, literally, taking another man's name; but in the iqta' sense it meant taking the name of the muqati'ji's house as a definition of one's place in society. Socially and politically the individual was identified as an adherent of the muqati'ji. In

---

[8] There was one Christian Orthodox muqati'ji family, the 'Azars of al Kurah, and one Shi'i family, the Himadahs.

[9] Sayyid-Ahmad Mulhim was the first Maronite Shihabi amir to become Hakim, but for hardly a year, in 1778; Bashir II was the next among the Christian amirs to ascend to the highest office. However, owing to the secrecy in which they kept the fact of their conversion, it is not possible to hold for sure that these were the first two Maronite amirs to rule.

[10] This term is still used, but not widely.

referring to his subjects, in fact, the muqati'ji used the term *nasna*, our men.[11] This customary relationship of allegiance was often buttressed by written contracts between the muqati'ji and some of his stronger subjects or leading clans, a fact which should remind us that custom alone was not always wholly dependable.

For a man to be of the 'uhdah of a muqati'ji involved moral obligations not only on his part but also on that of the lord, who would come to the aid of the subject and protect him. In the language of the period the muqati'ji's responsibility for the subject's welfare was described as "tending and protecting."[12] To maintain his integrity and position in the political life of the Imarah, a muqati'ji was well aware that he had to have a strong following and a loyal one. Sometimes, in protecting their followers, muqati'jis went so far as to place political considerations above accepted rules of good conduct on the part of the subject. Some examples of the mutual feeling of interdependence between muqati'jis and subjects will illustrate this point.

In the last decade of the eighteenth century, Amir Faris Abillama' became annoyed by the unruly behavior of members of the Qintar and Hatum clans, subjects in his 'uhdah. The Hakim was equally angered and wanted the muqati'ji to do something to save the common people from the culprits' aggressions, but Amir Faris refused to be pressured by the Hakim. His reason for not taking action was that if he inflicted harsh punishment on the Qintars and Hatums he would weaken his own following in relation to those of other rival muqati'jis. Amir Faris, it is also worth noting, was a Maronite, while the Qintars and Hatums were Druze.

In another case a Christian from Dayr al Qamar, who was of the 'uhdah of Shaykh Kulayb Abu Nakad, became notori-

---

[11] See iqta' documents published in Lewis Bulaybil, *Tarikh al Rahbaniyyah al Lubnaniyyah al Maruniyyah*, in *MQ*, LI, 506, n. 3 (hereafter cited as *TRLM*).

[12] The Arabic terms are "haqq al ri'ayah wa al himayah."

ously aggressive and troublesome, regardless of the shaykh's warnings to him. Shaykh Kulayb, however, steadfastly resisted the Hakim's requests that he punish his subject. When the Amir finally lost patience and ordered the shaykh to kill the man, the shaykh pleaded with his overlord in these words:

> Sire, I am your obedient servant and raise my men and children to serve you; I have warned the fellow several times, but to kill my men with my own hands, that is impossible for me.[13]

This principle of responsibility for subjects was demonstrated even by a Hakim who was famous for his ruthlessness, Amir Bashir II. In the war between the Amir and Shaykh Bashir Jumblat in 1825, the Amir had some mercenary soldiers sent to his aid by the Pasha of Sayda. While the battle was on, the lieutenant with these soldiers advised the Hakim to use the cannons and finish off his opponents, but the Amir replied:

> Were I able to repulse them without wounding a single man, I would not hesitate to do so; for they are poor subjects forced to be here by their shaykhs. It is enough what they have to suffer in being taken away from their work and thrown in the face of danger on the battlefield. Should I, who am enjoined by God and the State [al Dawlah] to look after them and protect their lives, kill them with my own hands?[14]

The importance of the principle of responsibility with respect to the welfare of the subjects is worthy of a separate study aimed at assessing the salutary effects of the iqta' institutions upon the people of Lebanon. Here we shall have to be content with a relevant comment by the French traveler Volney, who was in Lebanon a few years before the French

---

[13] Mikha'il Mashaqah, *Muntakhabat min al Jawab 'ala Iqtirah al Ahbab*, eds. Subhi Abu Shaqra and Asad Rustum (Beirut: Lebanese Government Publication, Nusus wa Watha'iq, 1955), p. 56 (hereafter cited as Mashaqah, *al Jawab*).

[14] *Ibid.*, p. 101.

Revolution broke out. Speculating about the density of population in the rugged mountain country of Lebanon, Volney wrote:

> I can discover no other cause than that ray of liberty which glimmers in this country. Unlike Turks every man lives in a perfect security of his life and property. The peasant is not richer than in other countries; but he is free, "he fears not," as I have often heard them say, "that the Aga, the Kaimmakam, or the Pacha, should send their Djendis, to pillage his house, carry off his family, or give him the bastinado." Such oppressions are unknown among the mountains. Security, therefore, has been the original cause of population. . . .[15]

He also observed:

> As they are not exposed to the violence and insults of despotism, they consider themselves as more perfect than their neighbours, because they have the good fortune not to be equally debased. Hence they acquire a character more elevated, energetic, and active; in short, a genuine republican spirit.[16]

Similar comments were later made by other travelers and observers.

The subject's political loyalties were not limited to the muqati'ji or his house, but went beyond to the faction (*gharad*) to which the feudal house belonged. These factions were alliances of long standing among the manasib, each including several muqati'ji houses. The factions among which the manasib were divided under the Shihabi Imarah had no connection with the Qaysi and Yamani partisanship of old, which in Mount Lebanon ended in 1711 with the complete destruction of the Yamani faction. The new groupings originated sometime during the reign of Amir Mulhim Shihab (1729-

[15] Volney, *Travels Through Syria and Egypt*, ii, 73.
[16] *Ibid.*, p. 74.

1754)[17] as a result of a struggle among the chief manasib: the Jumblats, the 'Imads, and the Abu Nakads. Those who customarily allied themselves with the Jumblats were known as Jumblatis and those who followed the 'Imads, the Yazbakis.

This factionalism meant the primacy of certain muqati'ji houses—namely the Jumblats, 'Imads, and Nakads—over others. But this was only a general and informal recognition of their leadership and was not institutionalized formally except in political protocol. The manasib were opposed to a fixed relationship of control by one house over others. They protested vehemently, for instance, when 'Abdallah Pasha of Sayda issued a decree in 1820 declaring Shaykh 'Ali 'Imad chief of the shaykhs of al Shuf.[18] Although the 'Imads were considered the heads of the Yazbaki gharad, the Yazbaki shaykhs joined in the protest. As the French consul in Sayda reported to his government on the occasion:

> Une grande discussion vient d'avoir lieu entre les quatre familles des principaux cheks de la montagne qui ne veulent pas reconnaître pour leur chef, chek Ali Amad, chaque famille voulant être indépendante. . . . Les divers cheks ont écrit a ce sujet au Pasha dont ils attendent la décision.[19]

The party groupings, again, cut across religious lines. Christians, Druze, and even Muslims could belong to any of these factions regardless of their religion,[20] and the common people followed their muqati'jis' affiliations. The Maronite muqati'jis, though, were not greatly affected by the party divisions. For

[17] See Haydar, *Lubnan*, p. 49.
[18] France, Ministère des Affaires Etrangères, Correspondance Consulaire, Seyde [Sayda, Lebanon], Tome xxvii, December 16 and 24, 1820.
[19] *Ibid.*
[20] Nasib Nakad, "Tarikh al Nakadiyyin," MS (Jafeth Library, American University of Beirut), pp. 2-9. Also Arsanius al Fakhury, "Tarikh ma Tawaqqa'ah fi Jabal Lubnan min Shahr Ayyar Sanat 1840 wa Sa'idan," MS (Jafeth Library, American University of Beirut), p. 33. See also Mashaqah, *al Jawab*, p. 11, and Yaziji, *Risalah*, p. 17.

instance, the Khazins were only loosely associated with the Jumblati faction,[21] and the house of Hubaysh still more loosely with the Yazbakis. The Abillama' amirs did not align themselves permanently with either side; rather, they took sides according to the dictates of the moment. The Shihabs were theoretically nonpartisan, that is, above party.[22] As for the small Maronite shaykhs of Jubayl and its dependencies, they were hardly involved at all. Among the Christians it was mainly those of southern Lebanon who were caught up in the party spirit.

The weak attachment to party among the Christian manasib might be explained by the fact that these factions were alliances formed for the purpose of controlling the political life in the Imarah. During the eighteenth century the Christian muqati'jis did not play an important role in the political activity which determined the top leadership or in the election of Hakims. The Khazins were resigned to an ineffectual status, and the Abillama' amirs, while somewhat more active than the Khazins, were still to a certain extent isolated and weak. On the other hand, the Druze manasib showed a keen interest in the political life of the country and were most active.

Nevertheless, it is clear that religious affiliation was not a factor in shaping the politics of the Imarah before the end of the eighteenth century. While secularism was not consciously held as a normative principle, in practice iqta' institutions were based on a secular spirit. The following poem, written around 1842 by a Muslim living in the Christian town of Zahlah,[23] suggests the earlier state of harmony among the different religious groups and bemoans the decline of this spirit in his own time.

[21] Hattuni, *Nabdhah*, pp. 226-227.

[22] Yaziji, *Risalah*, p. 19.

[23] Identified by Ma'luf as Husayn Abu al Hassan. 'Isa Iskandar al Ma'luf, *Tarikh Madinat Zahlah* (Zahlah, Lebanon: Matba'at Zahlah al Fatat, 1911), p. 203, n. 1 (hereafter cited as *TZ*). We have no material evidence upon which we can question the authorship of the poem. Collective village feeling was not unknown during that period.

The old days have passed,
And new ones come on us like racing clouds.
Since Fakhr al Din's time have the Druze and we
Existed together without ill will.
But now when mistrust and unseemly things
Have fallen among us, the passion grows;
And intrigue and bitterness flourish well.[24]

Political Institutions and Actors

The cultural values we have just discussed define the principle of legitimate authority in the iqta' system of Mount Lebanon. Now we may proceed to examine the other constituent parts of the system, namely the actors in whom authority was invested, and the institutions, or rules and practices in terms of which the system functioned. In this traditional system which we are examining, political institutions defined the category of men in whom authority was invested and the character of the actors could not therefore be viewed separately. The individual actor conformed to the institutions which defined his place and role, and he had no visible or legitimate role in which he as an individual could change or reshape political rules governing authority relationships. The following is a description and analysis of these institutions.

The Pyramidal Structure of Authority

The first noticeable feature of the system was the relative gradation of authority. The muqati'ji was subordinate to the Hakim, the Hakim to the Vali, and the Vali to the Sultan. However, since the higher Ottoman authorities were at a distance and relations with them were limited to the Hakim's payment of *miri* (the annual tax on land and produce) and the Vali's sanction of the Amir's authority, we shall concern ourselves here with the more basic relationship between muqati'jis and Hakim. These two levels of authority were the primary political offices in the iqta' system.

[24] *Ibid.*

The general office of muqati'ji was not differentiated; everyone, no matter what his noble title, officially had the same privileges and duties. However, the political actors were differentiated in title and, to a relative extent, in the actual power which each held. With respect to noble title, there was a hierarchy, at the top of which came the title of amir, followed by that of muqaddam, then by the title of shaykh. Three houses held the title of amir, one of muqaddam, and several were entitled shaykhs. The hierarchy of ranks could be further differentiated; within each stratum were houses of the same noble rank, but with different degrees of prestige according to the esteem which each enjoyed in the eyes of the Shihabi Hakims.

This arrangement was all formalized by fixed rules of protocol respected in the court of the Hakim and outside it. For example, in writing to someone in these houses, the Hakim would use customary complimentary terms which differed from one house to another. Similarly, with the courtesies demanded when receiving members of the *a'yan* (nobles), if a Shihabi amir, for instance, entered the Amir al Hakim's presence, the Hakim immediately stood up for him before the visitor spoke the usual greetings. If the guest was one of the Abillama' or Arslan amirs, the Hakim stood only after the greetings. One of the peculiarities of this protocol was that the Hakim had to stand up for a Shihabi guest every time that person entered to see him, no matter how many times it happened during the day.[25]

The Shihabi-ruling amirs did not create all the titles of nobility, nor, for that matter, did the Ma'nis. The titles of the Arslans and 'Alam al Din amirs went as far back as those of the Ma'nis and Shihabis themselves. The shaykhs of the houses of 'Imad, al Qadi, al Khazin, and others were entitled before the Shihabis succeeded the Ma'nis in 1697. However, many of the houses who held titles in the Shihabi Imarah re-

[25] For the rules of protocol, see Yaziji, *Risalah*, pp. 6-8.

49

ceived them from the Shihabi amirs after the battle of 'Ayn
Dara in 1711, for instance the Talhuqs, the 'Abd al Maliks,
the 'Ids, and in 1712 the Jumblats.[26]

The hierarchy of rank may be summarized as follows. At
the top was the house of Shihab, followed respectively by the
Abillama' and the Arslan amirs.[27] Then came the Shi'i shaykhs
of the Himadah house[28] and the muqaddams of the Muzhir
house.[29] Below them were the following shaykhs in the higher
order of their class: the Jumblats, the 'Imads, and the Abu
Nakads.[30] Then came the Talhuqs, the 'Abd al Maliks, the
Khazins, the 'Ids, and the Hubayshes, who were more or
less of the same rank.[31] These were followed[32] by the Khuris,
the Dahdahs, the Abi Sa'bs, the Karams, and the 'Azars.[33]

[26] Haydar, *Lubnan*, p. 14.

[27] Yaziji, *Risalah*, pp. 6-7; also 'Isa Iskandar al Ma'luf, *Dawani al Qutuf fi Tarikh Bani al Ma'luf* (B'abda, Lebanon: al Matba'ah al 'Uthmaniyyah, 1907-1908), p. 249 (hereafter cited as Ma'luf, *Dawani*).

[28] Nasif al Yaziji, "Fi Taqsim Jabal Lubnan" (Jafeth Library, American University of Beirut, n.d.), p. 10; also *Risalah*, p. 15.

[29] In protocol they were treated like shaykhs (see Yaziji), except for minor distinctions in public ceremony; see Nawfal ibn Ni'matallah Nawfal, "Kitab Kashf al Litham 'an Muhayya al Hukumah wa al Ahkam fi Iqlimay Misr wa Barr al Sham," MS (Jafeth Library, American University of Beirut), p. 39. It is maintained by 'Isa al Ma'luf and Istfan al Bash'alani that the muqaddams of Abillama' were amirs before 1711 and that the title of muqaddam was not one of social rank but of the kind of responsibility; for instance, in the case of the Abillama', they maintain, it stood for their position as holders of iqta'. These two writers support their argument by documents going back to before 1711. See al Bash'alani, "Al Amir Haydar al Lama'i wa 'Asruhu," *al Manarah*, I, 221, 452, 453; and 'Isa Iskandar al Ma'luf, *Tarikh al Amir Fakhr al Din al Ma'ni al Thani min Sanat 1590-1635* (Juniyah: Matba'at al Risalah al Lubnaniyyah, 1934), p. 410; and *TZ*, p. 93, n. 2. This confusion of title was not unknown in the feudal history of Western Europe; see, for instance, Rushton Coulborn, *Feudalism in History* (Princeton: Princeton University Press, 1956), p. 18.

[30] Nakad, "Tarikh al Nakadiyyin," p. 28, and Yaziji, *Risalah*, pp. 6-7; also Abu Shaqra, *Al Harakat fi Lubnan*, p. 6.

[31] Yaziji, "Fi Taqsim Jabal Lubnan," p. 10. They also appear in this order in a Marsum from the Pasha of Sayda; see Haydar, *Lubnan*, p. 681.

[32] Yaziji, "Fi Taqsim Jabal Lubnan," p. 10, and Nakad, "Tarikh al Nakadiyyin," pp. 2-9, 28-29.

[33] Yaziji, "Fi Taqsim Jabal Lubnan," p. 10. The small Maronite shaykhs of Jibbat Bsharri and Bilad Jubayl ranked low in the hierarchy as did the Orthodox 'Azars.

In addition, the title of shaykh was enjoyed by some other persons who served the Hakim in the capacity of chancellor (*mudabbir*) and judge (*qadi*). It is of interest to note that the judge in the Hakim's court ranked very high in the social hierarchy, for in the official protocol he was treated as a person of the amir rank, even if he was previously a commoner. In contrast, the head of the shurtah (retainers) was treated officially like a commoner, even though he might have been of a noble birth.[34]

Basically, the distribution of prestige among different houses was not arbitrary or transitory, but stable and continuous. To tamper with the order of rank would have meant to invite the displeasure of the manasib, who jealously guarded the balance of power and prestige. Conformity to the code of behavior governing relations among these classes was strict, especially in questions of marriage and public ceremony.[35] "There is strong respect for ranks according to protocol [*bi i'tibar al usul*] in this country," the great nineteenth-century poet Nasif al Yaziji, who was also a scribe in the service of Amir Bashir, wrote in 1833. He further observed, "Honor [*al karamah*] does not vanish because of poverty, nor will it be upgraded because of wealth."[36]

The aristocracy of rank did not, however, correspond to a hierarchy of authority or power. A shaykh might be more powerful than an amir, and while an amir enjoyed a higher title, this did not necessarily imply the right of jurisdiction over a shaykh. In the governing of his muqata'ah, each muqati'ji was independent from the others, regardless of title. There were two ranks of authority only, the office of Hakim and that of muqati'ji.

Shihabi Sovereignty

As we have seen clearly by now, the house of Shihab was the royal family of Mount Lebanon. Only a Shihabi descended

---

[34] Yaziji, *Risalah*, p. 8. [35] Nakad, "Tarikh al Nakadiyyin," p. 28.
[36] Yaziji, *Risalah*, pp. 16-17.

from the line of Amir Haydar Musa (1685-1731), son of the daughter of Amir Ahmad al Ma'ni, was eligible for the highest political office in the Mountain. Before 1711 this right of sovereignty was challenged by the Yamanite faction and its supporters, including the Vali of Sayda, Bashir Pasha,[37] but with the victory at 'Ayn Dara in 1711, the right of the Shihabis was established beyond question.

Three factors determined the Shihabis' assumption of sovereignty in Mount Lebanon. First, they were legal heirs by marriage to the extinct Ma'ni house which had previously ruled the country, and also political allies, since they were of the same Qaysi faction. In the second place, they were chosen by the manasib. The manasib of the seven muqata'ahs[38] met at al Simqaniyyah village in al Shuf and elected a Shihabi amir, descended from the Ma'nis on the maternal side, to succeed as Hakim.

A third principle upon which Shihabi supremacy rested was military leadership. It should be remembered that their dynastic rule was not finally established until they defeated their rivals at 'Ayn Dara in 1711. What the Shihabis were defending at 'Ayn Dara was not a piece of land, but the right to rule over the manasib of Jabal al Druze. The important place of the warrior in the Imarah should not be overlooked in this context. All of the Shihabi-ruling amirs were warriors who had seen action in the field. The manasib were also warriors who had to rally to the service of the Amir in time of war. The *maydan*, the large court where horsemen practiced skills in arms and sports, was a prominent feature in the palaces of the Amir and the manasib.

The principle of Shihabi sovereignty was embodied first in protocol and second in political practice. In protocol, the Shihabi amirs came first in the hierarchy of prestige, as we have seen. They received special honors from the ruling Amir of their house and were given highest respects by the public.

[37] See Haydar, *Lubnan*, pp. 10-15.
[38] Munayyar, *KTS*, xlviii, 672.

No person would ever precede a Shihabi on any official occasion or in any public ceremony. Furthermore, they were above parties, Yazbaki or Jumblati, for as Yaziji observed, "People are identified with them [the Shihabis], but they are not identified with anyone else."[39]

In practice Shihabi sovereignty was demonstrated by the tradition which forbade any of the manasib, and the people in general, to fight or rebel against a Shihab—except in the name of another Shihab. Nasif al Yaziji wrote on this point:

> No one rises against them [in his own name]; but if the manasib of the country wished to rise against the ruling Shihabi Amir, they had to have another Shihabi amir in their ranks, in whose name resistance to the ruling Hakim could be made. . . .[40]

The political history of the Shihabi Imarah shows that adherence to this rule was strict.

Another indication of supremacy was that the Amir al Hakim was the only person who could raise commoners to the rank of nobility, and only he could enfeoff any person, whether a commoner or a man of title. His exercise of this right, however, was not frequent, and the actors remained a closed group perpetuating themselves in power. Available sources do not mention any ceremony similar to the European feudal custom of dubbing on the occasion of granting a title or enfeoffment. On such an occasion, the Hakim simply wrote to the person receiving the honor the customary greeting for the nobility: "dear brother."[41]

While the Hakim had the right to enfeoff a person, he had no legal right to deprive a muqati'ji of his title or his 'uhdah. Once a muqati'ji, a person remained a muqati'ji for life, passing the same position to his children after him. The fact that on a few occasions a Shihabi Amir actually did deprive cer-

---

[39] Yaziji, *Risalah*, p. 19.
[40] Yaziji, *Risalah*, p. 20; see also Munayyar, *KTS*, LI, 464.
[41] Yaziji, *Risalah*, passim.

tain muqati'jis of some of their holdings was due to the fact
that those muqati'jis were weak, like the Khazins, or disgraced, as in the case of the Arslans in 1711.

The Problem of Succession

To become Hakim of Mount Lebanon a contender had to
meet two conditions: first, he had to be a Shihabi descended
from the line of Haydar Musa Shihab, and second, he had to
be accepted by the manasib. As can easily be seen, the first
condition left the candidacy open to a large number of
potential heirs to the office. Unlike the principle of fixed succession in medieval Europe, there were no formal or definitive
rules which determined the new Hakim in advance. Another
difference between the two systems was that in feudal Europe
the practice of fixed succession made it possible that the people
might acquire a new ruler who was a complete stranger to
them, whereas in the Shihabi Imarah this could not happen.
That is, since the rule of primogeniture did not apply in the
Imarah and women were not eligible to succession, a daughter could not be married to someone from another country
who would then assume the rule, as in Europe.

The institution of open candidacy meant that a change in
the office of Hakim was always a possibility and an occasion
for politicking among the manasib. In this contest which characterized the history of the Imarah, we see the inherent conflict between the principle of succession and that of election.

The history of the struggle for the office of Hakim demon-
strates two things: first, that, over time, the role of the manasib
in electing the Hakim was growing in importance; and second, that, taking the whole period, there was a noticeable
tendency for the manasib to favor the eldest son of the former
Hakim. A look at the table of succession (Fig. 2) clearly
shows that the line of succession was not regular; but a more
careful examination proves that neither was it completely
without pattern. The office frequently went to the eldest son
of the Hakim.

A brief survey of succession among the Shihabi Hakims helps to clarify this point (see Table 1). After Haydar, his eldest son Mulhim ruled; but when Mulhim's illness weakened his hold on the government, he was made to abdicate, and his brothers Ahmad and Mansur, who were next to him in age, were elected in 1754. Mulhim's sons were still very young in 1754—Muhammad, the elder, was deaf and half blind and therefore excluded from succession,[42] and Yusuf was then only about six. But in 1763, nine years after his father had stepped down, Yusuf was able to take over the government of northern Lebanon and in 1770 to rule all of Mount Lebanon, north and south. After Amir Yusuf there followed the great struggle between his sons and a candidate far removed from the line of succession, Amir Bashir Qasim 'Umar Haydar, known in Lebanese history as Bashir II. Only in 1807 was Bashir finally able to remove the sons of Amir Yusuf from the government for good.

Thus on the whole, those of the Hakims who fell in the line of succession by the elder ruled for a longer total period than those from outside the direct line. The latter, excluding Bashir II, ruled a total of nineteen years from the days of Haydar to 1841, and even counting the very long term of Bashir II, their combined rule fell short of that of the legitimate heirs. Seven of those not in the direct line of succession together ruled for no more than five and a half years, and none of them held the office alone but always jointly with another Shihabi amir.

In examining the line of succession among Shihabi Hakims we clearly see that the Hakims had less power in designating their successors during the second half of the eighteenth century than during the first part, an evidence of the growing influence of the manasib. Amir Haydar, because of his growing physical weakness, abdicated in the interest of his eldest

[42] Haydar Ahmad Shihab, *Tarikh Ahmad Basha al Jazzar*, eds. Antonius Shibli and Ighnatius Khalifah (Beirut: Maktabat Antwan, 1955), p. 221; also Shayban, *Tarikh*, p. 509.

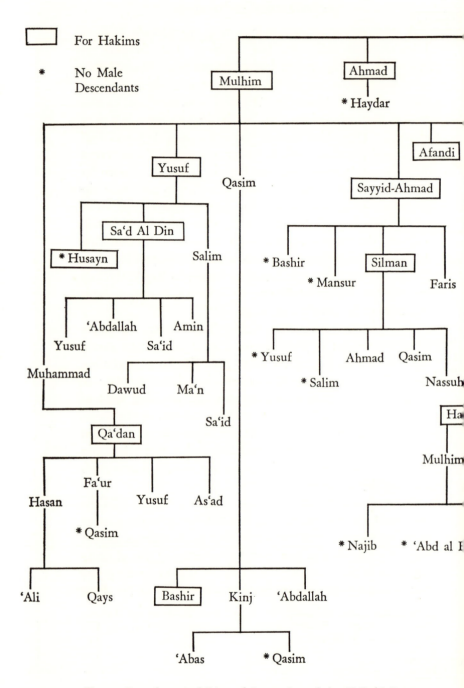

Fig. 2. Genealogy and Line of Succession of the Shihabi Dynasty

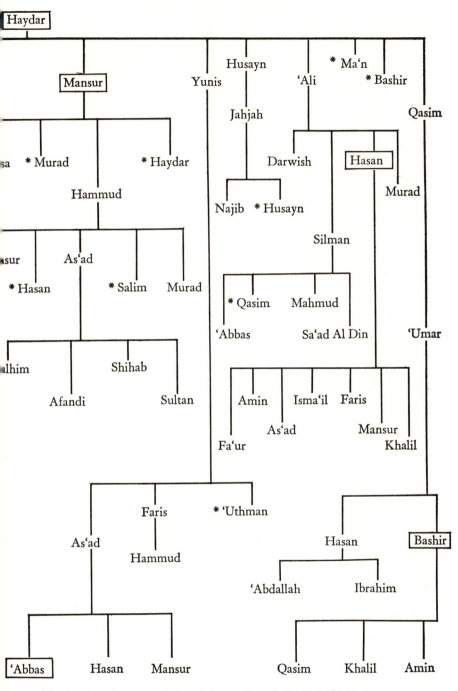

Fig. 2. Genealogy and Line of Succession of the Shihabi Dynasty

TABLE 1

CHRONOLOGY OF SHIHABI HAKIMS

| Name | Birth date | Accession | | Deposition or abdication | Deat |
		Shuf	Jubayl		
Haydar	1685	1706	—	1729	173
Mulhim	1701	1729	—	1754	176
Ahmad	1703	1754	—	1762	177
Mansur	1714	1754	—	1770	177
Yusuf	1748	—	1763	—	—
Yusuf	—	1770	1770	1788	179
Sayid-Ahmad Mulhim	1743	1778	—	1778	180
Afandi Mulhim	—	1778	—	1778	—
Yusuf	—	1778	—	1788	—
Bashir II	1767	1788	—	1790	—
Haydar Mulhim	1756	1790	1790	1792	180
Qa'dan Muhammad	—	1790	1790	1792	181
Husayn Yusuf	1783	1792	1792	1793	—
Sa'd al Din Yusuf	1785	1792	1792	1793	—
Bashir II	—	1793	1793	1794	—
Husayn Yusuf	—	1794	1794	1795	—
Sa'd al Din Yusuf	—	1794	1794	1795	—
Bashir II	—	1795	1795	1799	—
Husayn Yusuf	—	1799	1800	1800	—
Sa'd al Din Yusuf	—	1799	1800	1800	—
Bashir II	—	1800	—	—	—
Husayn Yusuf	—	—	1800	1807	182
Sa'd al Din Yusuf	—	—	1800	1807	184
Bashir II	—	1800	1807	1820 (10 March)	—
Hasan 'Ali	—	1820 (15 March)	1820 (15 March)	1820 (12 July)	182
Silman Sayid-Ahmad	1779	1820 (15 March)	1820 (15 March)	1820 (12 July)	185
Bashir II	—	1820 (12 July)	1820 (12 July)	1821 (July)	—
'Abbas As'ad Yunis	1773	1821 (22 July)	1821 (22 July)	1822 (May)	184
Bashir II	—	1822 (May)	1822 (May)	1840 (Sept.)	185
Bashir III	—	1840 (3 Sept.)	1840 (3 Sept.)	1842 (13 Jan.)	—

son Mulhim. We know of no challenge to this designation on the part of the manasib nor any sign of discontent. After Mulhim, however, it was election, not designation, which determined the succession. In 1754, Mulhim became ill, as we have just seen. His confinement to his home weakened his grasp on the reigns of government, so his brothers Ahmad and Mansur and a number of the manasib conspired against him.[43] At that point he abdicated in the interest of his two brothers. Although the chroniclers state that the Jumblati and Yazbaki parties originated during his reign and at his instigation,[44] they do not report any conflict between the two parties upon his abdication. During the rule of Ahmad and Mansur, however, the factionalism between the Yazbakis and Jumblatis apparently was instrumental in electing the Amir al Hakim. When Amir Ahmad and Amir Mansur fell out, the former was supported by the Yazbakis and the latter by the Jumblatis. In 1762 the two came into conflict, and Ahmad and the Yazbakis were defeated in a show of strength. Thus Ahmad was deposed and Mansur ruled alone.

Henceforth most, if not all, of the accessions and depositions were either determined by Yazbaki-Jumblati differences or were influenced by these considerations. The general procedure was that a party dissatisfied with the ruling amir would start to establish relations with the Shihabi aspirant, or if there were no available candidate at the time, would try to create one.[45] On the other hand, an ambitious Shihabi aspirant might himself start the movement among the manasib.[46]

The behavior of the ruling Amir under these circumstances was limited by fixed traditions. He could not, for instance, dispose of his rivals of the Shihabi house, nor could he exile any one of them unless the rival had actually fought him. The political traditions of the land were very much opposed

[43] Haydar, *Lubnan*, p. 43; Shidiaq, *Akhbar*, II, 30.
[44] Haydar, *Lubnan*, p. 49.
[45] *Ibid.*, pp. 63-64.
[46] See Shidiaq, *Akhbar*, II, 239; and Haydar, *Lubnan*, p. 104.

to political execution, particularly since it was considered improper for a Shihabi Hakim to maltreat a member of his own house. When Amir Yusuf in a moment of anger killed his half brother Afandi, who was caught conspiring against him, he had to apologize promptly to all the members of the Shihabi family.[47] Haydar reports of this incident:

> The next morning Amir Yusuf called the Shihabi amirs who were then living in Dayr al Qamar, and apologized for killing his brother, saying that they [i.e., Afandi and Sayyid-Ahmad] were planning to kill him. Then he wrote to all the rest of the amirs who were not in Dayr al Qamar. For he knew that people were offended by what he had done.[48]

Not all the manasib were equally influential or took part in the election of the Amir. There were no rules as to who among the manasib qualified as an elector, but the most influential leaders among the manasib usually determined the outcome. Although most of the muqati'jis enjoyed more or less similar positions, some of them were richer and more powerful than others. The richest of all were the Jumblats, and consequently they were also more influential most of the time. The persuasiveness of wealth could not be better demonstrated than by the cases of the Jumblats paying the poorer 'Imad shaykhs to have their support against the ruling Amir.[49] The 'Imads and Nakads were next in order of power and fully engaged in the interplay of influence, especially in the problems of elections.

It should be noted that it was the Druze manasib who had the most influence and formed the body which determined the fate of the highest office in the Imarah. They had great interest in politics; as Shayban al Khazin observed, "They are the keenest tribes on earth."[50] The Christian manasib did not show as much interest in the struggle over the suc-

[47] Munayyar, *KTS*, L, 205. [48] Haydar, *Lubnan*, p. 128.
[49] *Ibid.*, p. 129. [50] Shayban, *Tarikh*, p. 402.

cession of Hakims. As for the members of the Shihabi house themselves, they took active part in elections and general jousting for power, and often rivals instigated the manasib to rally behind them against the ruling Amir.

Government by Muqati'jis

The most salient feature of the iqta' system was the political supremacy of each muqati'ji in his particular domain. Every muqati'ji was a hereditary chief who had autonomous legitimate authority rooted in the people and the region over which he ruled. The Hakim in this arrangement did not govern, but represented the principle of imperative coordination and order among what otherwise might have been the disparate and conflicting interests of the different muqati'jis. Thus the Amir al Hakim stood for the principle of unity in a politically pluralistic society.

One of his major responsibilities as overlord of the muqati'jis was to defend his realm from neighboring chiefs as well as from Valis who tried to move in on his domain. He could decide whether or not to go to war, and had the right to demand military service from the muqati'jis. In battle he personally led the muqati'jis and their men. The military role among the muqati'jis in Mount Lebanon should not be underestimated, for it was through this military prerogative that they extended the boundaries of their country. Unlike the practice in Western feudalism, the period for which the muqati'jis provided military service for their overlord was not fixed. Much depended on the actual relations between the particular Hakim and the muqati'jis. If the muqati'ji was personally committed to the cause for which the Amir was fighting, he would stay with him indefinitely. However, if he happened to be half-hearted about it, he might withhold his support; this happened usually when the Hakim was personally weak and the muqati'jis felt sure that no serious consequence would follow. The muqati'ji who failed to support the Amir was taking risks, nonetheless, for he might find himself out of favor or even suffer retribution by the Hakim.

The role of the muqati'ji in the system was to rule directly and to administer his 'uhdah. Muqati'jis were not town dwellers; they lived in the villages over which they ruled, and attended to the business of government in person. The muqati'ji was the ruler, the leader, and the protector of his people. He judged his subjects, called them to arms, demanded their loyalty, and protected their rights.

The 'uhdah was the exclusive domain of the muqati'ji, over which he alone exercised authority. The Hakim had no rights of authority over the subjects of a muqati'ji; if he had any business with a subject he had to settle it through the muqati'ji.[51] The latter did not necessarily have to carry out the Hakim's wishes regarding his own subjects. The Hakim's jurisdiction even in his own seat of Dayr al Qamar was very tightly circumscribed. A person who committed some misdemeanor in front of the Hakim's palace had only to run a few feet toward the Shaluf water fountain to be beyond the Hakim's grasp, for then he entered the domain of his lords, the Nakad muqati'jis.[52]

The muqati'ji also performed a judicial function.[53] He heard cases and imposed punishment of various kinds, such as imprisonment, beating, forced labor, or financial exactions. However, the muqati'ji's judicial function was limited to those cases which did not involve personal matters such as marriages and inheritance, which fell under the clergy's jurisdiction. Another limitation on the muqati'jis judicial function was the Hakim's court which heard most cases concerning property and other civil matters. Also, the muqati'ji could not try criminal cases or inflict capital punishment, for such

---

[51] Shayban, *Tarikh*, p. 471.

[52] See Mashaqah, *al Jawab*, p. 34.

[53] Mudiriyyat al Athar al 'Ammah (National Department of Antiquities), Ministry of Education, Republic of Lebanon, MS, no. 7450 (hereafter cited as MAA); also Yaziji, *Risalah*, pp. 8-9; also Abu Shaqra, *al Harakat fi Lubnan*, pp. 175-177.

cases were referred to the Hakim who alone could try them.[54]

Just as the manasib had no authority to take the limbs or lives of their subjects, no higher authority had that power over them. The Hakim could not kill, amputate, beat, or even imprison a member of the a'yan.[55] The manasib were very strict about this matter. In 1711 after the battle of 'Ayn Dara, for instance, they refused to allow Amir Haydar to kill their bitterest enemy, the defeated Shaykh Mahmud al Harmush, even though he was a captive of war. They did not want to establish a precedent for the Hakim and therefore argued that tradition did not give a Hakim the right to kill a member of the manasib. The fact that the Hakim could not inflict such a severe punishment as death upon the manasib, however, did not mean that he lacked effective disciplinary power over them. On the contrary, he could inflict harsh measures affecting their property, but not their persons. If the Amir wished to punish one of the manasib he would exile him, confiscate his property temporarily, cut down his trees, or in some similar way damage his property.[56] The person of the muqati'ji was inviolate, and the Amir could not insult him or show him disrespect at any time. No matter how angry he happened to be with a muqati'ji, if the gentleman appeared before him the Amir would have to observe all the customary honors and protocol. The same was true regarding correspondence between the Amir and a muqati'ji in disfavor.[57]

Another major function of the muqati'ji was the financial administration of his 'uhda. Muqati'jis collected taxes from their subjects and turned them over to the Hakim, after discounting their own share of the tax.[58] On the whole, and at

[54] Yaziji, *Risalah*, pp. 8-9; Isma'il Haqqi, ed., *Lubnan* (Beirut: al Matba'ah al Adabiyyah, 1334 H [1918]), p. 144.

[55] Yaziji, *Risalah*, p. 7; Haydar, *Lubnan*, p. 14; Munayyar, *KTS*, xlviii, 676.

[56] Yaziji, *Risalah*, p. 7; Haydar, *Lubnan*, pp. 37, 40; Munayyar, *KTS*, xlviii, 676.

[57] Yaziji, *Risalah*, p. 7.

[58] The muqati'ji's share was known as *naf'* or benefit. *Ibid.*, pp. 8-9.

the expense of their subjects, the muqati'jis received a favorable treatment in the taxation system, especially since they were exempted from the miri on their own private holdings.[59] The muqati'ji also received gifts from his subjects, particularly the tenant farmers, on ceremonial occasions such as marriages and feasts. These gifts were known as 'idiyyah and consisted of sugar, coffee, soap, or products of the farm.[60] The muqati'jis further put imposts on mills, on local trade, on the crafts, on weighing the silk product, and the corvée.[61]

The muqati'ji's public responsibility included certain expenses. He had to arm his peasants[62] and pay for their upkeep during time of war. His office also required that he keep up a public appearance with signs of authority such as riding horses, keeping servants, and being liberal with his followers. When the government of Mount Lebanon was being reorganized in 1843, a muqati'ji protested over the curtailment of the 'idiyyah, arguing that it was the requirements of honor, not greed, that gave the muqati'ji the right to have more wealth than others.[63]

Kinship and Authority

Authority in the iqta' form of government was hereditary, and the principles determining its exercise and transfer were inseparable from those which governed kinship relations. Kinship relations in the nuclear family were based on the relative equality of brothers and on inequality between brothers and sisters. The family in Lebanese society was patriarchal, and

[59] MAA, MS, no. 2510. See also Hilu papers of September 1811, Patriarchal Archives of Bkirki, (Bkirki, Lebanon) (hereafter cited as *PAB*). Also 'Aynturini, *MTL*, xlvi, 444. For exceptions to this rule see MAA, MS, nos. 2574, 7318.

[60] Dominique Chevallier, "Aux Origines des Troubles Agraires Libanais en 1858," *Annales: Économies, Sociétés, Civilisations*, xiv, No. 1 (January-March 1959); Ma'luf, *TZ*, p. 102.

[61] See document on taxes of Hammana, Abu Shaqra, *al Harakat fi Lubnan*, pp. 175-177; Haqqi, *Lubnan*, p. 180.

[62] Shayban, *Tarikh*, p. 446; MAA, MS, no. 4776.

[63] MAA, MS (number illegible).

the women were subordinate in almost all respects. Thus, female members of the clan shared in social status and title, but not in authority, except in case the male line became extinct, when succession was transferred to the next of kin in the female line. Still, even then authority was not transferred to the female member herself but to her husband or son, as happened with the Shihabis who succeeded the Ma'nis and the Jumblats who succeeded the Qadis.

The principle of relative equality of brothers meant that each one of them was entitled to a share in the inheritance not only of property but also of authority.[64] It was one of the consequential characteristics of the law of inheritance in the iqta' system that it did not basically distinguish between property and authority. However, while the father had the power to favor some of his sons over others, he could not completely disinherit any one of them.[65] To the extent that we can determine from the available sources, the trend was to favor the older two or three sons, or those who were the more capable, at the expense of the others.

The corporate character of kinship in the patrilineal group, on the one hand, and the individualistic basis of holding and exercising authority, on the other, proved incompatible and created conflict among the members of the clan. Let us look at the principle of clan unity and then at the adverse effects which the law of inheritance had upon it. First, the muqata'ah was in the name of the clan even though the clan did not exercise control collectively over it. The muqata'ah was usually a good-sized territory comprising a number of villages ranging from two or three to twenty or more. The subjects who inhabited the muqata'ah were heterogenous in family and religion. The ruling clan, on the other hand, was

---

[64] Shayban, *Tarikh*, pp. 440-443; also Istfan al Bash'alani, "Al Amir Haydar al Lama'i wa 'Asruhu," *Al Manarah*, I-II (1930-1931), II, 369.

[65] It should be noted here that the Druze followed their own customary law, not Muslim law, in personal matters such as inheritance and marriage. Maronites, too, followed the same customary law in the case of inheritance.

cohesive in this respect, forming one kinship group of one religion.

The coherent character of a ruling house was determined by several factors: descent from one male ancestor, the same social status or noble rank, religious identification, and finally the memory of historic unity vis-à-vis other clans and political enemies. These forces which made for unity and coherence in the clan were often symbolized by the presence of an elder known interchangeably as head (*ra's*), or paramount chief (*kabir 'uhdat* or *kabir ismiyat*). The elder, however, had no special political functions or binding authority on the members of the clan; he stood as a moral symbol of unity whose advice was sometimes sought by the members of his kinship group. In some houses, however, the elder was also the actual political head of his clan and enjoyed great power. This was the case among some Druze houses, who also were of the noble title of shaykh, particularly the Jumblats, the 'Imads, and the Nakadis. An instance illustrating this was the agreement among the manasib in 1788 regarding the election of Amir Bashir which was signed by one member for each of the five main Druze houses, whereas the Abillama' amirs signed it individually.[66] Still, the actual political unity of the clan, even among the Druze, could not be considered very strong, as shall be seen.

The forces leading to division and conflict in a clan were stronger than those promoting unity. The root of the conflict was that the clan did not exercise its authority rights collectively or through a single leader, but on an individual basis. Hence the distinction between muqata'ah and 'uhdah: a muqata'ah referred commonly to the whole domain of the clan, whereas 'uhdah referred to the individual muqat'ji's government, which formed only a part of the large muqata'ah. The conflict between the principle of clan unity and the independence of each muqati'ji had its basis in the law of inherit-

[66] See Ma'luf, *TZ*, p. 128.

ance. The law of inheritance affected the iqta' houses in more than one respect. It diminished the wealth and power of the individual muqati'jis and weakened the political unity of the clan.

A comparison of some of the 'uhad between 1711 and 1830 shows the considerable fragmentation resulting from division of authority among heirs. Though not every member of a muqati'ji's house received an 'uhdah, it is clear that potential heirs were not disinherited in favor of one son. In a noble house, those who were not invested with an 'uhdah came under the authority of their ruling brothers.[67] Shayban al Khazin has left a detailed account of how Nadir al Khazin (Abu Nawfal), who died in 1679, divided his large muqata'ah of Kisrwan among his eight sons. The eldest was given one-third of the muqata'ah plus one additional village and the custom house at Juniyah. The next oldest brother received one-third of what was left. Another was given four peasants in each of two villages. A fourth brother was given three villages, and then he was killed by his brothers who shared his holdings. The remaining four sons did not ask for their inheritance during the lifetime of their father, and after his death they received the remaining parts of the muqata'ah of Kisrwan to rule as one joint 'uhdah.[68] Officially the Khazin 'uhdahs were three, exactly as they were originally divided by Abu Nawfal, but actually each had been parcelled into smaller 'uhdahs. The last-mentioned 'uhdah of the four "sons of Abu Nawfal," for instance, was eventually divided into fifteen 'uhdahs, to judge from the miri records.[69]

The Abillama' house started out originally in 1711 with two 'uhdahs, which had become nineteen by the 1830's.[70] The same proliferation of 'uhdahs took place among the Druze clans. 'Ali Jumblat, the first Jumblati muqati'ji, divided his muqa-

[67] Nakad, "Tarikh al Nakadiyyin," p. 12.

[68] Shayban, *Tarikh*, pp. 440-443.   [69] MAA, MS (number illegible).

[70] See miri records, Qustantin al Basha, "Jaridat Tawzi' Mal Kharaj Lubnan al Amiri fi 'Ahd al Amir Bashir al Shihabi," *MQ*, xxxiii (1935), 343-344; Ma'luf, *TZ*, pp. 94, n. 1, and 209.

ta'ah among his five sons, favoring the two older ones.[71] The Talhuq shaykhs in the 1830's had four 'uhdahs; but just how many men held each 'uhdah is not clear. The 'Abd al Malik house had their muqata'ah divided into thirty-three 'uhdahs by the first decades of the nineteenth century.[72]

The muqati'ji's jurisdiction was one of two kinds: he might rule either over a landed estate, or over individual men with no geographical definition of his 'uhdah.

Often the muqati'ji owned a very high proportion of the land of the muqata'ah as his private property, but by no means all. The proportion of land which usually belonged to the muqati'ji in relation to that owned by the peasants cannot be determined with any exactness. Two points, though, are very clear: private property was enjoyed by the muqati'ji as well as by the common people; and his land was far greater than that of the peasants,[73] though by the early nineteenth century the proportion of peasant-owned property was increasing.[74] As can be understood from this, a large percentage of the peasants were laborers on the muqati'ji's land. A peasant without property would cultivate as a tenant a certain plot of land allotted to him by the muqati'ji. The agreement, written or oral, was made for one year but could be renewed indefinitely.[75] The peasant then shared with his lord one-half of the yield.[76]

---

[71] Regarding the Jumblats see Abu Shaqra, al Harakat fi Lubnan, pp. 85-86, 87.

[72] Adel Ismail, Histoire du Liban du XVIIᵉ Siècle à nos Jours, Vol. IV: Redressement et Déclin du Féodalisme Libanais (1840-1861) (Beirut: Matba'at Harb Bijjani, 1958), p. 239.

[73] Nakad, "Tarikh al Nakadiyyin," p. 37; see also Abu Shaqra for the property of the Jumblats, al Harakat fi Lubnan, pp. 91-94; Mashaqah, who was well qualified to speak on this subject, states that in the early nineteenth century the peasants owned one-third of the land while the other two thirds belonged to the a'yan and clergy (see al Jawab, p. 154). A. N. Poliak, basing his account on Volney, states that the class of muqati'jis owned one-tenth of the land, Feudalism in Egypt, Syria, Palestine and the Lebanon, 1250-1900 (London: The Royal Asiatic Society, 1939), p. 58.

[74] See Haydar, Lubnan, p. 692.   [75] Chevallier, Annales, XIV, 45-47.

[76] For details of this, see ibid.

The second major way in which the law of inheritance affected the iqta' institutions was its adverse effects on the political unity of the clan. The relatively equal distribution of property and authority among heirs gave each one of them independence from the others. This rule was thus obviously inimical to the idea of united leadership in the clan, for authority relationship among a number of people is by definition asymmetrical, that is, some must be unequal or subordinate to others, whereas property relationships are not asymmetrical by definition.

While the law of inheritance provided for the independence of each muqati'ji from his kinsmen, the politics of the Imarah made it almost necessary for some members of the clan to impose their will over others. The pressures generated by national politics worked against the established rules of the private integrity of the muqati'ji in his domain. The national politics of the Imarah may be described as the competition among the manasib for influence over the Hakim, particularly with respect to such decisions as might affect the distribution of power and wealth amongst them. A muqati'ji's influence with the Hakim was determined by his following; but since the following of a ruling house was divided among the various members, it was necessary for one who aspired to great influence with the Hakim to force his way among his kinsmen. The subjects themselves were completely dependent on their lords, and any effort to dominate them meant first controlling their respective muqati'jis.

The manasib's stakes in national Imarah policy revolved around the Hakim's favors, which were quite important to them. These favors included some exemption from taxes, partiality toward the Hakim's allies, allocation of land and authority, thwarting of a favored muqati'ji's enemies, and so on. In short, wealth, prestige, and power were involved in the pursuit of national politics.

The demands for clan unity in the national politics of the

Imarah, on the one hand, and the divisive effects of the rules of inheritance on the other, generated a great deal of tension and strife among members of the same clan. In looking at the history of the iqta' houses in Lebanon, we can observe a clear connection between the intensity of strife within a clan and the extent of its participation in the politics of the Imarah. Internal rivalry was considerable in clans which played a vigorous role in Imarah politics and comparatively minor in those houses which were less active. In the latter case, the clan abdicated a great deal of its influence in the country, as was evident in the cases of the Khazin and the Abillama' houses.

The clans active in Imarah politics, on the other hand, were vitally concerned with the problem of unity, and to achieve it they did not hesitate to use violence. Since there were no institutionalized means for realizing political unity in the clan, the tendency was to conspire and/or assassinate contenders among kinsmen. The Jumblats were a prime example of this. Soon after the death of the first Jumblati muqati'ji, a continuing rivalry started among his descendants, who became divided among two main contending parties— those of al Mukhtarah and those of Ba'dhran. The competition for leadership resulted eventually in the assassination of the Mukhtarah group by their cousins of Ba'dhran, who took over the defeated relatives' holdings as well as the leadership of the clan. Then the process repeated itself in the next generation, with the same results.[77] The Jumblats thus were able to maintain united leadership in the politics of the Imarah, putting most of the other clans at a disadvantage. We also witness the same tendency to assassinate rival kinsmen among the Nakadis.[78]

The only restraint on the clansmen against such resort to violence was the Hakim, who punished those responsible.

[77] See Abu-Shaqra, *al Harakat fi Lubnan*, pp. 85-89, 91-93; also Haydar, *Lubnan*, p. 173.
[78] *Ibid.*, p. 174; also Nakad, "Tarikh al Nakadiyyin," p. 15.

However, this source of restraint, while it had to be reckoned with, was not too effective because the only means of punishment the Hakim could use was to send the offender into temporary exile. In practice such periods of exile proved very short, and the Hakim usually granted pardon upon intercession by some of the manasib on behalf of the culprit.

At the same time, the Hakim found in the rivalry among the manasib a valuable political resource which enabled him to interfere in their affairs and prevent them from uniting against him. There are many cases in which the Hakim instigated factious sentiments and pitted one muqati'ji against another and one member of a clan against his kin.[79] He often succeeded in discrediting some of the manasib through these quarrels, after which he further weakened them by punishment for unruliness.[80] In 1796, Bashir II went so far as to enter into conspiracy with the Jumblat and 'Imad shaykhs to destroy the Nakads and even helped them to carry out their plan.[81]

CONCLUSION

The Imarah of Mount Lebanon was a pluralistic political system in which subordination among the actors was conjoined with political supremacy of each in his own domain. The historically derived principle of legitimacy gave the existing institutions and the actors the appearance of being part of the natural order of things. The political institutions of the iqta' system were handed down from generation to generation and represented the central values of a society which revered the past and the ways of its ancestors.

The preceding account has shown how the three constituent parts of the iqta' system stood in consistent relationship to one another, a fact which accounts for the endurance of that

---

[79] *Ibid.*, see Amir Mansur's attempt to raise Kin'an Abu Nakad against his cousins; see below Appendix II.

[80] See Haydar, *Lubnan*, pp. 42, 64, 65.

[81] Munayyar, *KTS*, L, 446; and Haydar, *Lubnan*, p. 183; Shidiaq, *Akhbar*, I, 190.

system for centuries. Both the principle of legitimacy and the institutions were historically derived and were consistent with one another. Similarly, these institutions defined the category of men in whom authority was invested on a perpetual basis. The hereditary right of succession among the muqati'jis clearly consecrated the traditional character of the actors who were separated from other men by inherited titles and styles of life. Thus the actors formed a closed circle not penetrated by any outside elements, for society was divided into separate classes without mobility among them. The actors who were the main beneficiaries of this natural division among men had no interest in changing it, and, as they were constrained by the sense of right and wrong, dutifully conformed to the established institutions. They neither had the freedom to innovate nor attempted to gain a position above the rules of political conduct.

We have also seen in this chapter that the principle of social cohesion under the iqta' system was based on kinship and status. Kinship relations defined the distribution of authority among the actors of each clan, while the actors' superior place and the deference showed them by the common people were functions of their aristocratic status. The subject regarded his lord as part of a natural order superior to his own, and, by tradition, gave his allegiance to those above him. He came under the jurisdiction of his lord from the day he was born and grew up under the latter's auspices. Principles of kinship and status were uniform throughout the whole system, applying equally to the various religious and family groups in society. Thus the unity of the political system was enforced by the allegiance of the subject to his lord, and by the loyalty of the manasib to the ruling dynasty—the Shihabi house.

The iqta' political system, which represented a high degree of consistency in its constituent parts, nevertheless contained certain inherent tendencies in its institutions which generated in it a degree of strain and conflict. Some of the rules of kinship were in conflict with rules of authority, a fact which occasionally led the actors to violate one or the other. The law of inheritance encouraged division of 'uhdahs among heirs of a muqati'ji, whereas the demands of national politics required clan unity.

Similarly with the office of Hakim, the conflict between the principle of hereditary succession and that of election by the manasib greatly increased the intensity of the struggle for power, since the manasib had the right at any time to try to replace one Shihabi amir by another. The fact that the Hakim was the main source of imperative political coordination and balance among the various autonomous chiefs meant that every time election of a new Hakim came up, or the current one was challenged, order in the system was disturbed.

The effects of institutional conflict upon the historical sequence of political change were limited mainly to the impoverishment and diminution in the power of individual muqati'jis and to causing strife among the actors. This rivalry among the manasib, occurring at the same time as their power resources were constantly diminishing, made them more readily receptive to new political forces outside the traditional framework of authority. However, institutional conflicts by themselves did not result in the introduction of innovative political practices but remained within the established rules of the old order.

CHAPTER IV

The Traditional Organization of the Maronite Church

THE SOCIAL COMPOSITION of the Lebanese population, as we have seen, was heterogeneous, made up of two dominant ethnic groups and a number of minorities. In contrast to this social diversity, we have observed that the political institutions of Mount Lebanon were uniform and not differentiated according to social diversity. Regardless of his social or ethnic background, a person in the iqta' political system fitted into a narrow political framework as either a muqati'ji or a subject. There were no other categories in society outside this arrangement.

Under this political organization of society, alternative sources of leadership did not exist. Questions of cooperation or competition, rivalry or unity, war or peace, and control of economic resources and labor were all the exclusive affair of the actors, determined and regulated within their own closed circle. The political culture of the people was historically derived and learned by each new generation by a process of imitation without novelty or creativity. The transmission of the cultural values of the past thus had the effect of enforcing the position of the actors and the order of the system as a whole.

Up until the last few decades of the eighteenth century, political ideas were not in any way derived from the ethnic principle of social composition, for social solidarity was not based on ethnic principles but on kinship and status. Furthermore, there was no intellectual leadership in the system which would be capable of introducing new ideas based on principles uncongenial with the existing political ideas and culture.

During the second half of the eighteenth century in Mount Lebanon, a new source of leadership—cultural and political—

emerged, which gradually but decisively challenged the iqta'
political system. The Maronite clergy who played this role
were not actually a new group, for they belonged to the most
ancient organization in Lebanon—the Maronite Church. The
fact that the Maronite clergy did not assume a significant role
in the political and cultural affairs of Lebanon until the second
half of the eighteenth century was due mostly to the precarious position of the Church in earlier times and to its traditional organization. Reform in the Church and the political
unification of the Maronite lands of northern Lebanon under
Shihabi rule contributed to the emergence of the clergy as an
important force in the political system of Lebanon.

   In the following two chapters we shall look at the history
and organization of the Maronite Church, examine its relations with the iqta' system, and try to assess its cultural and
political role. First, we must look at the traditional character
of the Church and its dependence upon the ruling class. The
next chapter will deal with the movement of reform within
the Church, the changes which took place in its structure,
and its eventual emancipation from the domination of the
political chiefs of the land. Only after the Church had become
a free agent in the system did its impact upon the political
life of Lebanon become far reaching.

CHURCH ORGANIZATION AND CONDITIONS

   For centuries, except for a nominal and intermittent relationship with Rome starting in 1215, the Maronite Church was
almost completely isolated from the Christian world. In the
middle of the fifteenth century, relations with the Holy See
were formally resumed but were limited mainly to the acts
of investiture which each Maronite patriarch solicited after
his election.[1] Franciscan missionaries had been in contact with

[1] For early Maronite relations with Rome, see Salibi, "The Maronite
Church," *Oriens Christianus*, XLII, 92-105. Also Henry Lammens, "Frère Gry-
phon et le Liban au XVe Siècle," *Revue de l'Orient Chrétien*, IV (1899), 68-104.
Also Tobia Anaissi, *Bullarum Maronitarum* (Rome: n.p., 1911).

the Maronites before 1578[2], and they worked toward combating monotheletism and Jacobism among the Maronites.[3] In the latter half of the sixteenth century, the Roman See began to show a more active interest in the Maronites and took steps to bring reform and religious instruction to the Maronite Church. However, the relations between the two Churches were not clearly defined until 1578, when Pope Gregory XIII sent to the Maronites a mission headed by friar Eliano Battista.

The Maronite Church at the time of Battista's visit was small and relatively lacking in organization. It survived under dire economic and political conditions; for centuries it had felt the oppression of the foreign Muslim rulers of the land, as well as the heavy weight of ignorance among its clergy.

Here an attempt will be made to describe the organization of the Maronite Church under these external conditions in the period preceding the middle of the eighteenth century, i.e., before the reform movement succeeded in changing its structure. Such an account, it is hoped, will provide a point of reference with which the later progress of the Church and its important social and political role can be compared.

By the sixteenth century the organization of the Maronite Church had a semblance of hierarchical order, with a supreme head and a number of inferior ranks. However, the Church did not work as a functionally differentiated bureaucracy. It was actually more simple and personal than it appeared, for instance, to Dandini, the second papal messenger after Battista. Dandini observed that the formal aspects of the order were hierarchical, but he also noticed a good many variations in practice.[4]

The formal organization of the Church consisted of a patri-

---

[2] Lammens, "Frère Gryphon," pp. 68-104. Duwayhi, *TTM*, pp. 425-45.
[3] For example, Ibn al Qila'i, who became a Franciscan friar and a missionary to his people, the Maronites. See Salibi, *Maronite Historians*, pp. 23-87.
[4] Dandini, *Voyage to Mount Libanus*, p. 293.

arch, who was the supreme head of the Church, and the bishops, whose number was not fixed but ranged from nine to fourteen at different periods.[5] Below the bishops came the secular priests and monks. The principal of a monastery, the abbot, was not yet a separate office, because in the sixteenth and seventeenth centuries the few monasteries which the Maronites had were usually presided over by one of the bishops.[6]

Relations among these different officers of the Church were highly personal and not formalistic in character. The relationship obtaining between patriarch and the bishops lacked clear definition of function and jurisdiction.[7] The patriarch, for example, might have complete power over some bishops and none among others. There was no rule laid down in writing, nor was there always conformance to custom. Much depended on personal relationships of kinship and acquaintance. Some bishops led quite an independent course of action, even disregarding the patriarch, while others were completely under his control. The patriarch usually acquiesced in this state of affairs and let the strong-minded bishops go their own way.[8] At the same time, although in practice control of the clergy was not always within his reach, the patriarch did not lack a firm idea of his supreme place in the organization. In the

[5] *Ibid.*, pp. 293, 299; also Shaykho, "Al Ta'ifah al Maruniyyah," *MQ*, xvii, 758; also Mas'ad and Khazin, *UT*, ii, 482-487.

[6] Dandini, *Voyage to Mount Libanus*, p. 295. The Church had at that time, and still has, various other clerical ranks than the ones mentioned above. These, however, are ranks related to internal order among the clergy; see Pierre Dib, "Maronites (église)," *Dictionnaire de Théologie Catholique*, ed. E. Amman, x, Part i (Paris, 1928), 122-128.

[7] This condition is also confirmed by the modifications the Maronite hierarchy introduced in the text of the Lebanese Council. The Arabic version of the Council, which was published in 1788, differed from the original Latin version. The change in text is often made to fit the old order rather than to promote consistently the power of one party against another. For comparison between the Arabic and the Latin versions, see Bakhus Fighali, "Watha'iq Tarikhiyyah 'an al Majma' al Lubnani," *MQ*, xlv-xlvi (1951-1952), xlv, 554-556.

[8] See for instance a document written in the seventeenth century, Ibrahim Harfush, "Al Adyar al Qadimah fi Kisrwan," *MQ*, v, 690-691.

early eighteenth century the patriarch gained more power than his predecessors had usually commanded, and tried to resist the reform movement and attempts to limit his authority.

Before the late seventeenth century, the bishops resided with the patriarch in Jibbat Bsharri, where the patriarch generally directed and assigned duties to them as he saw fit.[9] Not all bishops, however, lived under such restrictive conditions, and there were many cases of disobedience among them. Some were able to cut out for themselves dioceses almost like fiefs. One such bishop in the seventeenth century went so far as to prevent the patriarch from visiting his diocese.

The patriarch was not always able to settle disputes among his clergy. Often the clergy raised complaints against their fellows to the non-Christian rulers, and in several councils the Church had to make regulations against resort to temporal rulers.[10] Thus in 1610 the patriarch had to secure an order from the pope threatening with excommunication "all those who prevent prelates from using their authorized powers, and all those who stand in their way or resort to the arms of temporal rulers against the clergy."[11]

Before Pope Gregory XIII opened the Maronite College in Rome in 1584, the clergy, higher as well as lower, had scarcely any learning. "Their priests," wrote Dandini, "are as ignorant as the common people, for they can but only read and write."[12] He mentioned that there were only three or four priests, familiar with theology and philosophy,[13] who had returned from Rome when he made his visit in 1596. Those who were literate could use some Arabic and to a lesser extent read Syriac. Except for the limited contribution toward learning made possible by

---

[9] Tuma al Labudi, "Sirat al Mutran 'Abdallah Qar'ali," ed. A. Rabbat, *MQ*, x (1907), 799. Also Hattuni, *Nabdhah*, p. 145.

[10] Mas'ad and Khazin, *UT*, III, 386-387. For clerical resort to rulers, see also René Ristelhueber, *Traditions Françaises au Liban* (Paris: Felix Alcan, 1918), pp. 216, 217, 218.

[11] Duwayhi, *TTM*, p. 189; also Duwayhi, *TA*, p. 302.

[12] *Voyage to Mount Libanus*, p. 291.

[13] *Ibid.*

the Maronite College, the Maronite clergy continued to be very poorly educated until the middle of the eighteenth century.

Prior to the reform movement, religious office in the Maronite Church was sought by a variety of means including fraud, bribery, and even resort to the backing of powerful rulers.[14] To be sure, the Council of 1580 convened by Battista adopted ordinances regulating the recruitment and ordination of clerics. In the resolutions we read: "Henceforth, no bishop, priest, deacon or others will be ordained or raised to any clerical rank by bribery or other similar means: . . .";[15] also, "everyone who seeks a clerical rank by means of deceit, or robbery, or without the permission of the patriarch or against his will, will be excommunicated and lose his rank."[16] But during that early period these resolutions could hardly be said to have had the effect of law. Even the election of the patriarch was not always free from such means as bribery.[17]

These widespread irregularities were partly the result of the Maronites' practice of permitting the lay population to vote in the elections of the higher ranks of the clergy. The manner of patriarchal election went through various phases from the sixteenth century on. In the sixteenth and seventeenth centuries, the patriarch was elected by the people, the notables, and all the clergy by some sort of popular agreement.[18] Late in the seventeenth century the people seem to have been dropped from the electorate, apparently leaving only the notables and higher clergy.[19] In 1733 the bishops went so far

[14] Duwayhi, *TA*, p. 276.
[15] Bulus Mas'ad, "al Majma' al Maruni al Mun'aqid Sanat 1580," *MQ*, XXXIV, 435.
[16] *Ibid.*, p. 436.
[17] Duwayhi, *TA*, pp. 365, n. 1 through 366. See also Tubiyya 'Anaysi, *Silsilah Tarikhiyyah li al Batarikah al Intakiyyin al Mawarinah* (Rome: Matba'at al Sinato, 1927), pp. 49-50; and Ristelhueber, *Traditions Françaises*, p. 217.
[18] Shayko, "Al Ta'ifah al Maruniyyah," p. 684, and 'Anaysi, *Silsilah*, pp. 33, 37-40; also Ghibra'il, *Tarikh al Kanisah*, II, 382, 383, 391.
[19] A letter from Duwayhi to the Pope, Mas'ad and Khazin, *UT*, III, 29. Also Duwayhi, *TA*, pp. 365, 366; cf. 'Anaysi, *Silsilah*, pp. 41-43, 46.

as to ask the shaykhs to stay out of the electoral body, thus limiting it to themselves.[20] Although the shaykhs recognized the exclusive right of the clergy to elect the patriarch, they continued to influence the results of elections. After the Lebanese Council of 1736, election of the patriarch was regulated by law.

In the case of promotion to the rank of bishop, before 1736 the approval of the patriarch was mandatory. While it was theoretically the right of the patriarch to appoint new bishops, in practice it was not quite clear how bishops were elevated to their offices. As will be seen later, the Khazin muqati'jis could appoint up to four bishops, and other families also could secure the elevation of a member of their clan to the office. The college and/or individual bishops could exert some influence too.

There was no rule defining the jurisdiction of the bishops before the Lebanese Council. Bishops had titles like "Bishop of Damascus," "Bishop of Ba'albak," "Bishop of Hamah," and so on, but this did not mean that the bishop presided over the diocese indicated by the name of the town, or over any diocese for that matter. Damascus, for instance, had only a handful of Maronites; yet there was a bishop designated by that name, who in actual fact presided over a community in Kisrwan. Most of these titles were based on fictions, including the title of the Maronite patriarch, "Peter Patriarch of Antioch."

Before the middle of the eighteenth century, bishops were rarely appointed to particular dioceses, the government and jurisdiction of which became their responsibility. Some of the bishops stayed with the patriarch and helped him manage the affairs of the Church at large and his particular diocese.[21] Others attended to the care of monasteries in which they re-

---

[20] Mas'ad and Khazin, *UT*, ii, 600.

[21] In addition to his responsibility as head of the Church, the Maronite patriarch served one of the eight Church dioceses as an ordinary archbishop would.

sided. Only a few were entrusted with the care of souls, and even these bishops, with pastoral duties, were usually still at the disposal of the patriarch. Only rarely did a bishop have a fixed tenure on a particular diocese; most of them were sent on religious missions by the patriarch as he saw fit, mainly to collect the tithe.[22] This state of affairs, however, did not inhibit some bishops from establishing themselves over certain dioceses in an independent manner like fiefs,[23] as we have seen. The result was a great deal of disputation and trespassing by prelates upon each other's functions or flocks and, in later years, resentment of the patriarch's prerogative in assigning religious duties to bishops as he liked."[24]

The organization of monks in the Maronite Church was no more orderly than that of the Church hierarchy. Before 1700 there was only one order of monks in Mount Lebanon, known as the Antonines. They lived in conditions of complete poverty and had no rules to follow other than vows of celibacy and poverty. Each monastery was separate from the others, with no supreme or central body presiding over the order. Each isolated monastery had its own rules and superior,[25] often a bishop, who lived most of his clerical life with the rest of the monks in the same monastery. During the seventeenth century and part of the eighteenth, a number of monasteries contained monks and nuns within the same premises.

RECRUITMENT TO HIGHER OFFICES

Kin relationship prevailed in recruitment of candidates for the higher clergy. Usually a patriarch raised a nephew, a

---

[22] Labat, Jean Baptiste R. P. (ed.). *Mémoires du Chevalier d'Arvieux* (Paris: n.p., 1735), II, 367; also Ghalib, "Nawabigh al Madrasah," *MQ*, XXII, 27.

[23] For this general account, see the following: Shaykho, "Al Ta'ifah al Maruniyyah," *MQ*, XVII, 758, also XVIII, 972. Also, Dandini, *Voyage to Mount Libanus*, p. 293; Salim Khattar al Dahdah, "Al Abrashiyyat al Maruniyyah wa Silsilatu Asaqifatuha," *MQ*, VII-VIII (1904-1905), VII, 643.

[24] Lewis Bulaybil, "Nabdhah Tarikhiyyah," *MQ*, LI, 280, 294.

[25] *Ibid.*, p. 280.

brother, or a cousin to clerical office. This informal institution lasted much longer than other practices in the Church and continued, though to a lesser extent, after reform. In one diocese, for instance, three out of four known archbishops during the eighteenth century belonged to one family, with nephews twice inheriting the office from uncles.[26] In still another diocese during the same century, one archbishop inherited the office of his brother, and his nephew succeeded him after his death. Even during the nineteenth century, when the kinship basis for recruitment had already been weakened in the church, two dioceses were still monopolized by two families, namely the Khazins and the Bustanis.

Even the office of the patriarchate could sometimes be inherited. At the time when Dandini visited Mount Lebanon, three patriarchs from the same family succeeded each other to the See of Antioch. Dandini wrote:

> I confess, indeed, I had regard to complaints that were made of the former patriarchs for having rendered that dignity as hereditary in their family; as they had already had two brethren that had been patriarchs, the matter was reduced to such a point that the archbishop and abbot of Chsaia [the convent of Qizhayyah] must infallibly succeed his uncle, . . . the archbishopric and abbey of Chsaia must have been given to his brother, who would also be patriarch in his turn, and then the nephews would tread in the same steps.[27]

Dandini wrote this after the death of the second patriarch of the Rizzi family, anticipating the election of the patriarch's nephew, who actually was elected. However, the rest of the

[26] Based on the account given by al Dahdah, "Al Abrashiyyat," pp. 641-647, 1,022-1,029. However, figures for the eighteenth century are not very accurate since at that time division of dioceses was not completed, and because sometimes more than one archbishop held the title to one and the same diocese. See also under Harfush, "Al Adyar," *MQ*, v, 183ff. regarding the family of Muhasib and Dayr Mar Shalita.

[27] Dandini, *Voyage to Mount Libanus*, pp. 299-300.

nephews did not "tread in the same steps," for after the Rizzi case the office of patriarch was not occupied again by members of the same family consecutively. In general, Dandini was quite surprised by the entrenched family relations in the higher offices of the Church. In the two monasteries of Jibbat Bsharri, Qizhayya and St. Anthony, he noticed that the patriarch had two nephews in one monastery, "one of whom was archbishop and abbot of the same monastery and suffragan of the patriarch"; and in the second monastery "he had three other brothers, which [sic] were all three archbishops."[28]

Social status was another criterion, along with kinship, for selecting the higher clergy. Notables were predominant in the higher ranks of the clergy. (The word "notables" is used here in a general sense to refer to the leading families as well as the nobility.) Muqati'ji titles among the Maronites do not date farther back than the seventeenth century, and members of this class did not start to seek religious office before the eighteenth century. Thus any pattern of social stratification can be drawn more fruitfully if limited to the eighteenth and nineteenth centuries. During the eighteenth century the Maronite Church had eight patriarchs, six of whom were members of the notable families. As regards the archbishops (excluding the archbishops of the diocese of Aleppo), fifteen out of twenty known bishops belonged to that class.[29]

The reason for the notables' prominence in Church affairs is not hard to find: it lay in the fact that the Church lacked control over the means of its own administration. The Church itself did not have sufficient revenue to pay the clergy or to provide them with premises where they could freely exercise their religious functions. Its revenue, which came mostly from the tithe and some land owned by the Church, was quite meager. Several patriarchs are said to have left deficits dur-

[28] *Ibid.*, p. 299.

[29] The figures for the archbishops are based on Dahdah's account; see al Dahdah, "Al Abrashiyyat," *MQ*, VII, 641-647, 748-755, 1,022-1,029, 1,099-1,105, and VIII, 151-154, 401-409.

ing their tenure in office,[30] while many bishops had to cultivate the land to make a living.[31] Thus the poverty of the Church made it quite dependent upon the wealthy class for general support, for seats where they could carry on their religious work, and for the establishment and maintenance of new monasteries. In return for these benefits, the notable clans exercised influence over the Church and secured most of the top Church offices for members of their families.

The most notable example of this situation was in Kisrwan, the region that became the most populated Maronite area in which the Khazin house held the most property and influence. The Khazins built monasteries and encouraged the building of village churches. Leading Maronite families such as the Mubaraks, the Muhasibs, and the Istfans and others built their own monasteries, too. Thus one notices that more bishops belonged to these families than to any other family in Mount Lebanon. These monasteries were intended to remain under the control of the builder's family and his descendants.[32] One such patron stated clearly in his will that he had built the monastery as a succor for his family in case of need.[33] The monastery not only provided the members of the family with higher religious office but also brought them revenue from its lands. The Church could not exclude the original patrons from such benefits of office and property. Also, the Church regulation that all of a bishop's wealth and contributions should go, after his death, to the monastery in which he had resided,[34] made the bishops as well as their relatives see to it that anyone who presided over a monastery was appointed from their own family, so that they could continue to benefit from what they considered to be their own property rights. In defense of this right a member of these

[30] Mas'ad and Khazin, *UT*, ii, 600, and iii, 525-526, 528. Also Fighali, "Watha'iq Tarikhiyyah," *MQ*, xlv, 264.

[31] See letter of Bishop 'Umayarah to the pope, in Ghalib, "Nawabigh al Madrasah," pp. 444-445.

[32] See Harfush, "Al Adyar," *MQ*, v, 183-185, 687ff. and n. 1.

[33] *Ibid.*, viii, 347-348.

[34] See Mas'ad and Khazin, *UT*, ii, 604.

clans wrote to the pope: "The monasteries are ours, founded by our fathers and grandfathers, and we will admit to them whomever we want to admit." Then he added, "We remain obedient to the Holy See in all matters religious."[35]

As a result of these conditions, kin relationships were strengthened inside the Church, and those who had monasteries in their names almost monopolized the offices of abbots and bishops. Thus out of twenty-one known archbishops, fourteen came from four clans during the eighteenth century.

THE MARONITE CHURCH AND THE POLITICAL SYSTEM

From the days of the Mamluks, the Maronite Church, as well as the Maronite people, stood in need of protection. This situation defined the political conditions of the Church as it entered the history of the Imarah of Jabal al Druze in the seventeenth century. The protection which the Church sought was generously extended by the Maʿnis, the Shihabis, the Druze muqatiʿjis, and the Maronite muqatiʿjis of Kisrwan. The French government also occasionally extended its diplomatic aid to the Church.

Before the eighteenth century the Maronite Church, while still in Jibbat Bsharri, had no protection from oppression of rulers, unlike the Melkite Orthodox Church which had a legal status in the Ottoman Empire. The Maronite patriarch was neither officially recognized nor covered by Ottoman law. In those days the Maronite patriarchs and clergy in Jibbat Bsharri were directly subject to the governors of Tripoli. The patriarchs had to profess obedience to these governors in person immediately after their election to office.[36]

The Maronite clergy therefore resorted to whatever sources of protection they could reach. They turned sometimes to the rulers of Jabal al Druze and sometimes to the Catholic monarchs of Europe, particularly those of France. In 1647 they were able to procure a letter from the king of France, Louis

---

[35] *Ibid.*, I, 413. A letter from the Khazins to the pope.
[36] Shaykho, "Al Taʾifah al Maruniyyah," *MQ*, XIX, 768.

XIV, in which he promised them protection.[37] Regardless of
the official character of this letter, however, its importance
should not be overestimated as it was not directed toward the
establishment of a French protectorate over the Maronites of
the Ottoman Empire. The French monarch's promise
amounted to a commitment to employ his good offices with
the Ottoman government on behalf of the Maronites for the
alleviation of violent oppressions inflicted by their local Ottoman governors.[38] While French diplomatic intercession was
useful to the Maronites, it was slow in coming when needed.
Paris and Istanbul were both too far from Mount Lebanon
to ward off effectively the oppression imposed on the Maronites by Muslims of the area.

During the second part of the seventeenth century the struggle between the Pasha of Tripoli and the Himadahs for
power over the region caused the Maronites to go through
very hard times. The Pashas of Tripoli, the Himadah clan,
and others raided and looted their lands. During that period
and later under the Himadahs, arbitrary persecution, onerous
taxation, and raids were frequent in the villages and monasteries.[39] To escape persecution and extortions, the patriarchs
sometimes had to hide in caves and other inaccessible spots.[40]
In the seventeenth century, four patriarchs had to flee their
country and take refuge in the country of the Druze; Duwayhi
took flight twice.[41] Later Patriarch Ya'qub 'Awwad (1705-
1733) was able to reach an agreement with the Himadahs
which moderately improved conditions for the Maronites and

---

[37] See text in Ibrahim Aouad, *Droit Privé des Maronites au Temps des
Émirs Chihab (1607-1841)* (Paris: Librairie Orientaliste, Paul Geuthner,
1933), pp. 295-296. French protection was also extended to the Maronite
Lebanese Order of Monks by royal edict, see Ristelhueber, *Traditions Françaises*, p. 293.

[38] See text in Aouad, *Droit Privé*, pp. 295-296.

[39] Duwayhi, *TA*, p. 330, n. 10; also Duwayhi, *TTM*, p. 440; Aouad,
Droit Privé, pp. 96-97.

[40] Ghibra'il, *Tarikh al Kanisah*, II, Part 1, 564; also Duwayhi, *TTM*, p.
16; also Labat, *Mémoires*, p. 419.

[41] Duwayhi, *TA*, p. 375; also Hattuni, *Nabdhah*, p. 113.

their clergy; but this was only a temporary and slight respite from oppression.

It would be a mistake, however, to consider all the ills which befell the Maronite clergy as the work of the non-Christian rulers of their country. Sometimes the patriarch was just a helpless figure among his own people. In 1609, for instance, the Maronite muqaddam of Bsharri forced the patriarch to flee his seat at Qannubin and seek refuge in the country of the Druze; and having been unable to win the support of the Maronite people of Bsharri, the patriarch could not use religious sanctions against the muqaddam.[42] In another instance a muqaddam of Bsharri looted a monastery in his district and killed one of its monks.[43] As discussed earlier, the clergy themselves sometimes raised complaints to Muslim rulers against each other and thus brought great suffering upon themselves.[44]

These difficult conditions in Jibbat Bsharri caused the patriarchs to leave the fifteenth-century see of the Church at Qannubin monastery and take up residence in Kisrwan in the Imarah of Jabal al Druze. Patriarch Yusuf Istfan (1766-1793) took permanent residence in Kisrwan, a practice followed by the succeeding patriarchs until 1809, when Patriarch Yuhanna al Hilu (1809-1823) returned to Qannubin. Hilu's successor, Patriarch Yusuf Hubaysh (1823-1845), started the tradition still in force to this day, by which the patriarch takes residence in northern Lebanon in the summer and in Kisrwan during the winter.

The transference of the patriarch's seat to Kisrwan reflected the growing influence of the muqati'ji house of that region, the Khazins, over the Church. The Khazins had a special interest in making Kisrwan the seat of the patriarchs. The rise of the Khazins in Kisrwan under Fakhr al Din II opened that region to Maronite colonization, and by the beginning of the eighteenth century the whole district had become almost

---

[42] Duwayhi, *TA*, p. 301.   [43] *Ibid.*, p. 315.   [44] *Ibid.*, pp. 335-336.

completely Maronite territory. The encouragement which the Khazins gave Maronite peasants to settle in their region, and their assistance to and protection of the clergy, gave Kisrwan the largest Maronite population in Lebanon for almost the entire eighteenth century. Kisrwan also became the center of Church life even before the establishment of the patriarchal see in the region, since it had the largest number of churches, monasteries, priests, monks, and bishops during that period. At least four dioceses had their archbishops residing in Kisrwan during the eighteenth century, in addition to the bishops.[45] The seat of the Lebanese Order of monks, one of the most flourishing orders, was also in Kisrwan in the monastery of al Luwayzah and that of Tamish. Thus to have the patriarchal see also in their muqata'ah would add to their influence among their subjects.

The Khazins, being the rulers of Kisrwan and the most illustrious and powerful Maronite house at that time, exercised a kind of protectorate over the Church. At first the clergy were more than happy to be sponsored and supported by a Maronite house, not only because they had been in a condition of bondage under the Matawilah, but also because the Khazins were faithful Maronites and, like the other muqati'jis of Jabal al Druze, were genuinely concerned about their subjects and looked after their interests. In a letter to the pope in 1657, the patriarch described the Khazin protectors in these words:

> Prince [i.e Abu Nawfal al Khazin] of all the Catholics in Mt. Lebanon and the Orient, protector of the Church: its patriarch, bishops, monks, priests, churches, monasteries, and the faith of Christians in these regions. He shields the Maronite community and church from the ills which are visited upon them by rulers and others.[46]

[45] The dioceses of Damascus, Ba'albak, Beirut, and sometimes Tripoli. Some archbishops of Aleppo resided in Lebanon.
[46] Mas'ad and Khazin, *UT*, I, 231.

The clergy under the Khazins were subject to the iqta'
principle of government. The Khazins extended their protection to the Church and in return expected the Church's recognition of their patronage and certain other benefits. The iqta'
principle was clearly demonstrated in the appointment, in
1763, of some archbishops to monasteries within the Khazins'
'uhdah. The archbishop had to submit a statement confirm-
ing his consent to the iqta' relationship, which reads as follows:

As regards their honors the sons of Shaykh Kattar [al
Khazin] we shall do their bidding and stand in their service; we shall also do their favor in whatever they require
us to do. In return they[47] will extend to us their aid and
protection and preserve us in all matters corporeal.

As to the shaykhs, their cousins, we shall behave ourselves
in a way to be always equally in their favor and subject of
their approval, as God and our conscience command.

We also promise their honors, Shaykh Najd and his
brother Shaykh Khaz'al in the name of God and our Lady
the Virgin Mary that under all conditions and in all their
dealings with us, good or bad, we should never rise above
them to seek justice from higher authorities. We trust in
the mentioned shaykhs and they will be our protection,
support and shield us from evil in all times, to the exception
of all other men.[48]

The exchange of benefits was undertaken in a practical manner according to the iqta' practice. A cleric received office with
the approval of the Khazins. He benefited from the privileges
of that office whether a principal or a bishop. Also, the cleric's

[47] In the Arabic text, the first sentence is written in the plural form
whereas the second is written in the singular, which may mean that there
was only one son to Shaykh Khattar. In the translation the plural form was
followed in both cases for the sake of consistency.
[48] Mas'ad and Khazin, *UT*, ii, 604.

authority became sanctioned and respected among the people by virtue of the Khazins' political authority over him. A bishop or any other Church prelate who stood in a special relationship to the Khazins was given due respect even by non-Christian muqati'jis, a fact which helped build up the prestige of the Church.

On their side, the Khazins used the clergy's prestige among the people to add an element of religious support to their civil authority. In the way of material returns the Khazins received special benefits and revenues from these monasteries, called *'awayid*.[49] They also obtained benefits of the type they regularly received from their peasants, for instance, a measure of coffee and sugar and the like from every nun or monk whom they permitted to join a monastery under their control.[50]

The Khazins' influence over the Church was not limited to monasteries under their control but extended to the entire Church organization. They influenced the election of the patriarch and his later behavior in office, and they had power to choose three archbishops for three dioceses in Kisrwan. The Maronite shaykhs of the houses of Khazin, Hubaysh, and a few others from Jibbat Bsharri formed a part of the electoral body which, before the nineteenth century, chose a patriarch along with other Church prelates.[51] When, in 1670, Istfan al Duwayhi was elected by the bishops and some of the notables of Jibbat Bsharri[52] without the approval of the chief Khazin at the time, Shaykh Abu Nadir al Khazin, the latter objected to the election and refused to recognize its legitimacy. For this reason Rome delayed in sending the Pallium in confirmation of the election of al Duwayhi; and the newly elected

---

[49] *Ibid.*, p. 596, see letter no. 11. For a detailed list of these benefits see statement written in 1780, Ghalib, "Nawabigh al Madrasah," *MQ*, xxii, 21, n. 1.

[50] Mas'ad and Khazin, *UT*, ii, 597, 592, 599, 601.

[51] 'Anaysi, *Silsilah*, p. 46.

[52] Duwayhi, *TA*, pp. 563-566, also Ghibra'il, *Tarikh al Kanisah*, ii, 505-506.

patriarch, embarrassed and perplexed by the problem, had to appease the Khazin muqati'ji by visiting him and asking his forgiveness and approbation.[53]

Starting early in the eighteenth century, the Khazins made a concerted effort to impose their control more effectively over the Church. They tried to make the patriarchs leave their seat in Jibbat Bsharri and settle permanently in Kisrwan; but as the patriarchs did not give up Qannubin for good until the middle of the century, the Khazins managed to bring the bishops to Kisrwan for the periods of patriarchal elections. Thus in 1704 they succeeded in making the bishops convene in Kisrwan for the election of a new patriarch, but not entirely without opposition. The election which took place then elevated to the See of Antioch the archbishop of Aleppo, Bishop Jibra'il al Blawzawi. The archbishops of Aleppo at that time were the protégés of the Khazins and resided in Kisrwan. The successor of al Blawzawi was elected at Qannubin under the strong pressure of the French consul of Tripoli, who wanted to curb the Khazins and demonstrate his influence over the Church. The rest of the patriarchs of the eighteenth century were elected in Kisrwan.

In 1733 a bishop from the Khazin family was elected patriarch for the first time, and another Khazin bishop, Tubiyya al Khazin, contested the election which followed and had himself elected by illegal means. However, as the pope cancelled the latter's election, he was instead made a patriarchal secretary. After the death of the patriarch who was appointed by the pope, Tubiyya al Khazin finally was elected to the See of Antioch in 1756.

The Khazins' influence in the Maronite Church also determined the choice of three archbishops[54] and possibly other

---

[53] *Ibid.*; and Duwayhi, *TTM*, p. 13. Similarly Patriarch 'Umayrah's election; see Harfush, "Al Adyar," *MQ*, v, 688, n. 5, through p. 691.

[54] Yusuf Khattar Ghanim, *Barnamaj Akhawiyyat al Qiddis Marun* (Beirut: al Matba'ah al Kathulikiyyah, 1903), II, 303; also Mas'ad and Khazin, *UT*, III, 397, 538. See also letter from Archbishop Jirmanus Farhat to Shaykh Sirhan al Khazin in *MQ*, LI, 329.

ordinary bishops on different occasions. The family's prerogative in choosing prelates started in the middle of the seventeenth century and lasted for just about a hundred years. The dioceses concerned, namely Damascus, Aleppo, and Ba'albak, were almost like fiefs of the Khazin house. The Khazins had the right to name the candidate, and the patriarch made the appointment formal.[55] Sometimes the Khazins could also raise archbishops to the dioceses of Beirut and Tripoli,[56] thus controlling almost completely the appointments of the archbishops and bishops. When one of these archbishops tried to shake off the influence of the Khazins, they did not take kindly to the display of independence; for instance, in 1737 the Khazins resorted to violence to intimidate the archbishop of Aleppo into obedience and iqta' tutelage.[57]

In matters related to the administration of the Church affairs, the Khazins also shared in decision-making with the higher clergy.[58] Khazin signatures appeared on Church decrees and orders alongside those of the patriarch and bishops, apparently to give the Church orders effectiveness and political sanction.

Although the Khazins imposed their influence over the Church, the Church enjoyed more freedom under their protection than it had in earlier periods. The same could be said for the activities of the Church in the rest of the Shihabi Imarah. At no other time in history did the Maronite Church flourish as it did during the eighteenth and nineteenth centuries in Kisrwan and Jabal al Druze. But the muqati'jis' policy toward the Church was practical: they provided the Church with their protection and the Church paid them in return with moral and material support. For instance, through its relations with the pope and its good offices with the French

---

[55] Al Labudi, "Sirat al Mutran," *MQ*, x, 799.   [56] *Ibid.*
[57] See Mas'ad and Khazin, *UT*, ii, 527, 530, 531; cf. *ibid.*, iii, 520-521, also i, 469.
[58] See for instance, Ghibra'il, *Tarikh al Kanisah*, ii, Part 1, 564; also Harfush, "Al Adyar," *MQ*, v, 688, n. 5 through 691.

consuls, the Church was instrumental in securing for the Khazins a French royal edict making Abu Nawfal al Khazin and his sons after him French consuls in Beirut, and bequeathing on him French citizenship and honors.[59] This office greatly increased the influence and prestige of the Khazins, not only with the Maronites but also with the Imarah chiefs. The patriarchs also interceded with the pope to give the Khazin rulers titles of honor and medals to enhance their standing among the Catholic population. In one of these letters Patriarch al Duwayhi states the policy of the Church very clearly in this respect:

> We submit to the attention of your Holiness that the Khazins are the notables of our community, and that the Popes before your Holiness used to bequeath to them a golden icon and a chain of silver.
>
> Now Shaykh Abu Nasif [al Khazin] has passed away and has been succeeded by his son Khalid. We wish that you honor him with the same signs which his father and grandfather enjoyed before him in order that the Maronite community shows greater deference toward him and that he becomes more obedient to your Holiness and more concerned about the interests of the Maronite community.[60]

Influence in the Church was also important to the Khazins with respect to the judicial authority which the clergy held in some civil and personal matters. A preponderant influence over the Church meant for the Khazins a measure of control over the judicial power in their country. The Khazin muqati'jis' gain from supporting the Church included pecuniary compensations every time they raised a cleric to one of the monasteries or higher ranks of the clergy. But the Church also benefited materially from the Khazins' practice of in-

---

[59] Duwayhi, *TTM*, pp. 233-234, also Mas'ad and Khazin, *UT*, i, 230-232. See also Ristelhueber, *Traditions Françaises*, pp. 138-139, 140-141, 158-159.
[60] Mas'ad and Khazin, *UT*, iii, 49.

creasingly alienating their property and turning it into mort-main (waqfs).[61]

The non-Christian rulers of Jabal al Druze left the Maronite Church to its own affairs in a remarkable demonstration of religious freedom and respect. Before the nineteenth century, the Shihabis did not interfere in the business of the Church except when the higher clergy sought their aid in keeping order within the organization. For instance, the patriarch and the bishops appealed to the Shihabi rulers to help bring recalcitrant clerics into line or to settle disputes among the clergy themselves. The Druze muqat'jis also respected the freedom of the Maronite Church. The alliance, or convergence of interests, of the muqati'ji class and the clergy continued unabated until the end of the eighteenth century. The unity of interest between the clergy and the muqati'jis, Druze and Maronites, will be discussed further in another context.

As for the Shihabi and Abillama' houses, who changed to Christianity from Sunni Islam and the Druze religion respectively, their interests in Church affairs did not increase after the conversion. None of them ever sought religious or clerical office as did the Khazins.

There can be no doubt that the condition of the Maronite Church and Maronite community in the early Ottoman times was quite humble. The community lived in a state of isolation and bondage and had no social or political influence in the life of Mount Lebanon. The parochial nature of the Church organization prevented it from playing an effective role in the life of its own adherents or in the country as a whole.

The structure of the Church organization, as has been clearly shown, was inadequate to build up solidarity and group identity among the Maronites. Furthermore, the traditional organization of the Church was no longer even capable to meet the spiritual needs of the community. The claims that

[61] See Shahin al Khazin, "Awqaf al 'A'ilah al Khaziniyyah 'ala Dhatiha," *MQ*, v (1902), 115-122.

some Maronite writers in recent times have made regarding the power and prestige of the clergy before the eighteenth century[62] are not merely exaggerated but completely unfounded. Survival of the Maronites as a separate religious group would have been seriously imperiled had conditions continued much longer without change.

As a second major conclusion, we have seen that the financial dependence of the Church upon the wealthy ruling class made it dependent in administration as well. So long as the means of administration remained in the hands of the temporal leaders, the Church could not be considered master of its own house. If the Church was to act freely and effectively in the community, the conditions determining its existence and functions would have to change.

The reform movement in the eighteenth century served to fulfill the need for change. The Church gradually appeared as a growing organization with new forces driving toward a position of influence and leadership in the affairs of the country. In the following chapter we shall turn to the reform movement and its cultural and political consequences.

[62] See, for instance, Aouad, *Droit Privé*, pp. 18, 26, 89, 102; also Wajih Khury, "Hawl al Qawanin al Fardiyyah 'ind al Ta'ifah al Maruniyyah fi Zaman al Umara' al Shihabiyyin," *MQ*, xxxii (1934), 203; also Ferdinand Tyan, *The Entente Cordiale in Lebanon* (London: T. Fisher Unwin, Ltd. [1916]).

CHAPTER V

The Reform Movement and the
Church Bureaucracy

As WE have now seen, one of the striking facts about the Maronite community, unlike the Druze, is that it had an organized Church, the structure and goals of which were distinct and separate from every other organization, political or economic. However, the tutelary relationship which the Church had with the ruling class limited its contribution to the social and political life of the country. Eventually, the influence of Rome and internal developments in the Maronite community resulted in far-reaching changes in the structure and role of the Church organization. These changes, referred to here as reforms, had the effect of redefining the Church's position vis-à-vis the ruling class and the clergy's role in the cultural and political life of Lebanon. The course of the reform movement in the Maronite Church, and its results, will be the subject of this chapter.

Reform in the Maronite Church started with the efforts made by Rome about two decades after the Council of Trent (1545-1563), a fact which may indicate the effects which the Council had on the revival of Church life and on the Maronites. In 1578, Pope Gregory XIII sent the Jesuit monk Eliano Battista to the eastern Mediterranean with the special mission of strengthening the relations of the Maronites with Rome and reforming their Church and religious practice.

Battista started the course of reform in the Maronite Church by undertaking two steps: the education of the clergy and the organization of the Church hierarchy. With his efforts a college was opened in Rome in 1584 for the education of the Maronites who planned to become clerics. It was the second school opened by the popes for the eastern sects; the first was started in 1577 for the Greeks. The Maronite college continued in operation until 1799 when it was sacked by the occupying forces of Napoleon.[1]

As for reform of the Church organization, Battista convened the first of a number of councils for this purpose. He tried to regulate the relations of various Church offices in accordance with fixed laws laid down in the text of the council. Three other councils were held in the Church in the last two decades of the sixteenth century. There is no consensus among Church historians about the total number of councils held over the next two and a half centuries; estimates range from thirteen to seventeen.[2] Of those mentioned, fourteen can be considered certain; and the rest, which are much in doubt, can easily be ignored.[3] Only four out of these fourteen were confirmed by the popes, and all four of them were held with the supervision and active participation of papal messengers or delegates. But this fact should not discourage the historian from considering the other ten councils, for they provide us with a truer picture of the actual organization and practices of the Maronite Church through the ages.

The periodicity of Church council meetings clearly indicates that the eighteenth century was the era of reform. The first Maronite council was held in 1580 and the last in 1856. Between these two dates, three councils were held in the last two decades of the sixteenth century, one in the seventeenth, eight in the eighteenth, and two in the nineteenth century. The first three showed the impact on the Maronites of the initial Roman effort to revive Catholic sects in the east. Their aim was to strengthen ties with the Roman see, establish true Catholic practices and creed, educate the clergy, and put some

[1] See Pierre Raphael, *Le Rôle du Collège Maronite Romain dans l'Orientalisme aux XVIIᵉ et XVIIIᵉ Siècles* (Beirut: Université de Saint Joseph de Beyrouth, 1950), pp. 53-63.

[2] See Bulus Mas'ad (ed.), *Al Majma' al Baladi* (Beirut: al Matba'ah al Kathulikiyyah, 1959), p. 2 (hereafter cited as Mas'ad, *MB*).

[3] Ignored here are the councils attributed to Patriarch Musa al 'Ikkari in 1557, Patriarch Yusuf al Rizzi in 1596, and Patriarch Istfan al Duwayhi. Regarding these councils, see Mas'ad, *MB*, p. 3.

order into the Church organization. The major measures of discipline which the popes wanted to inculcate into the Maronite Church concerned the hierarchical order in the Church organization. Efforts were made to impose the authority of the higher offices over the lower ones, to regulate the pattern of clerical recruitment, and to differentiate the functions of various offices.

Although the reform movement started with the mission of Battista, it took a century and a half thereafter for the spirit of reform to catch on among the Maronites themselves. During the eighteenth century a struggle started among the higher clergy between the forces which pushed for change and rationalization of the Church organization and the conservatives who wanted things to remain as they were.

Many social and religious factors, as will soon be seen, converged to make the eighteenth century the major period of reform. The eight councils which were held during this century took place within a period of fifty-four years, between 1736 and 1790. This short period witnessed the most violent disturbances and intense conflict that ever appeared in the ranks of the Church. New needs created by the sweeping reforms of the Lebanese Council contributed still more to this conflict. As the Lebanese Council produced the most comprehensive and authoritative statement of reform in the Maronite Church, an historical account of the origin, purpose, and circumstances of the Council will be given here.[4]

In 1734 the newly elected patriarch, Yusuf al Khazin, and the Church prelates, bishops, and heads of the Lebanese Order of Monks[5] held a meeting to settle some of their disputes. As they were not able to reach agreement, however, they appealed to the Holy See to send a papal delegate to Mount Lebanon to preside over a Church council and help solve the

---

[4] In recent years there have been new changes made in the constitution of the Church.

[5] Lewis Bulaybil, "Nabdhah Tarikhiyyah 'an al Rahbaniyyah al Lubnaniyyah," ed. Antonius Shibli, *MQ*, LI (1957), 277.

conflicts in the Church.[6] The prelates asked specifically for Yusuf al Sim'ani, a Maronite clergyman and scholar in the service of the Holy See in the Roman Court, because of his familiarity with the language and the customs of his people. This opportunity was immediately taken up by the Congregation of Propaganda as an occasion for a thorough reform in the Church. Before al Sim'ani left for Lebanon, the Propaganda, with his aid, laid down the entire substance and form of the council,[7] taking into consideration, however, some resolutions of previous Maronite councils.

In September 1736, al Sim'ani arrived in Mount Lebanon to find the Church prelates divided into two groups. On one side were the protagonists of reform, supporting al Sim'ani. At their head were Bishop 'Abdallah Qar'ali and Bishop Tubiyya al Khazin, the European missionaries in Lebanon and Syria, and Tuma al Labudi, the principal general of the Lebanese Order of Monks. On the opposing side were the patriarch, Yusuf al Khazin, Bishop Ilias Muhasib, and Bishop Hanna Istfan. The patriarch was backed by Shaykh Nawfal al Khazin, who was at that time muqati'ji and French consul in Beirut, and by some other members of the Khazin house.

The papal delegate, al Sim'ani, then appealed to the temporal powers to counter the Khazins' opposition. As an Apostolic delegate, he had access to two sources of temporal power, the Shihabi Hakim of Jabal al Druze, and the French consul general in Sayda. Before the council meeting, the Apostolic delegate happened to visit the Hakim in Dayr al Qamar on a special, unrelated, matter of business. He took the opportunity presented by this visit to ask that the Amir use his influence with the patriarch to get more cooperation from him. The Hakim actually did send a letter to the patriarch, the bishops, and the Khazin shaykhs asking them to obey the

---

[6] Ghibra'il, *Tarikh al Kanisah*, II, Part 1, 579; also [Yusuf al Sim'ani], *Tarikh al Majma' al Lubnani*, published in *UT*, II, 494 (hereafter cited as TML).

[7] Mas'ad, *MB*, see Preface. Dib, *Dictionnaire de Théologie Catholique*, X, Part 1, 80.

Apostolic delegate.[8] But according to the political rules of the time, the Amir could not do more, for he had no right to interfere with the prelates or to take action against any of the shaykhs' subjects without the latters' intercession.[9]

Al Sim'ani also appealed to the French consul in Sayda, who was the superior of Shaykh Nawfal al Khazin, the consul in Beirut. The French consul reproached Shaykh Nawfal al Khazin for his opposition to the Apostolic delegate and brought home to him the implications for his position as consul if he persisted in his policy.[10] At that point, Shaykh Nawfal had to moderate his stand and he then tried to mediate differences existing between the patriarch and his opponents. In any case, the stalemate which had been holding up the council meeting was overcome and the convocation began on 27 September 1736.

Discussion in the meetings was restricted. What the Lebanese Council amounted to was the presentation of the prepared text to the delegates; very minor points were modified as a result of deliberation. At the conclusion of the sixth and final meeting, all those present signed the document. It was clear that al Sim'ani had succeeded in bringing the Maronite clergy to external conformity, but had failed drastically in winning their confidence and goodwill. Many were later heard to comment that they had signed the Council text to oblige the Apostolic delegate and the French consul.[11]

Al Sim'ani, however, was determined to see some of the reforms immediately implemented before his return to Rome. Therefore he proceeded to carry out the Council resolutions himself, starting with separation of the mixed monasteries.

---

[8] Al Sim'ani, *TML*, p. 483ff.

[9] Patriarch Istfan (1766-1793), when engaged in a later dispute with Rome, claimed that Amir Mulhim had sent ten soldiers and forced the patriarch to agree to al Sim'ani's terms. See Fighali, "Watha'iq Tarikhiyyah," *MQ*, XLV, 265, in a letter from Monsignor Jirmanus Adam to the pope, based on the conversation of the former with the patriarch.

[10] Sim'ani, *TML*, p. 497.

[11] Shayban, *Tarikh*, pp. 524-525.

He could not finish the task, though, for his assumption of executive authority irked the patriarch and brought the two into open hostility again. The patriarch ordered al Sim'ani to stop all action and interference in the affairs of his community. Then he sent a circular letter to all the monks and prelates admonishing them not to respect any measure taken by the delegate, and he absolved those whom al Sim'ani had suspended.[12] The patriarch finally raised the matter directly with the pope, but lost his case as the Lebanese Council was confirmed by the pope in 1741. The Council resolutions thus became the formal constitution of the Maronite Church. Implementation, however, was gradual and took over a century to be realized.

Traditional attitudes and unfavorable environment made the implementation of the Council resolutions very difficult, not to mention the hostile attitude of the Maronites toward the manner in which the Council was conducted. There were inherent problems in the reorganization plan set forth by the Council, and these baffled the reformists in the Church as well. The Holy See, however, persisted in its request that all the reform measures should be put into effect. This steadfast policy on the part of Rome encouraged those who were interested in reform to continue the effort, and for the next fifty years the Church was engaged in a relentless struggle. As a result, seven councils were held within the short time span of fifty-four years following the Lebanese Council, all of which revolved on the measures introduced by that Council. The effect of this endeavor was to apply the reform measures gradually, instead of immediately as al Sim'ani had wished.

The Lebanese Council did not aim at the destruction of the autonomy of the Maronite Church; it simply intended greater rationalization of the Church's organization. To combat this modernizing trend, the conservative forces in the Maronite Church appealed to national pride and the history of

[12] Sim'ani, *TML*, pp. 528-529.

their Church. They declared that their duty was to preserve the legacy entrusted to them by their fathers and grandfathers. National pride and opposition to Latinization are still lively issues in the Maronite Church to this day.[13]

The Causes of Reform

The preceding historical synopsis of the reform effort may leave the impression that what took place in the Church was solely due to the desire of Rome to revive Catholicism in the East. This is partly true, but not the whole picture. For a comprehensive understanding of the causes of reform, one also has to take into account developments in Mount Lebanon which created new needs in the community not met by the old parochial organization of the Maronite hierarchy. The Maronites' population expansion into distant places and their intermixing with non-Maronites and non-Christians, the growth in numbers of the clergy and the increase in Church property and revenue, the ideas of Western-educated clergy, and the freedom enjoyed by the Church under the Shihabis, were all factors determining the outcome of the encounter between East and West in the Maronite Church.

During the sixteenth and seventeenth centuries, the conditions in the Church as well as in the Maronite community militated against any attempts to improve the organization of the Church. In the first place, the Maronites were watched carefully by the Muslim masters of the land, and any ostentatious demonstration of contact with the Franjis (Franks) was bound to bring upon them considerable misfortune. All contact with the Western world then passed through the Muslim town of Tripoli which formed the gate to the Maronite hinterland. In the second place, the Maronite community, at that

---

[13] See Mas'ad, *MB*, Preface. The controversy during the second centennial of the Lebanese Council is an example of this; see Mikha'il al Rajji, "Hawl al Majma' al Lubnani," MS (mimeographed), personal copy of the author; cf. Bulus Mas'ad, *Al Rad 'ala Mikha'il al Rajji* (Aleppo: al Matba'ah al Maruniyyah, 1937).

period and well into the seventeenth century, formed a small group of people who lived together within a very limited radius. Almost all relations among them were local and personal. Thus they could hardly be expected to feel the need for rationalization of the Church structure. Much of the opposition to reform came from the fact that the new rules and regulations went contrary to established practice and seemed to the people and clergy to have no *raison d'être*. Third, at that time the Maronites themselves could not be considered wholly committed to Catholicism. Strong local feelings of independence and incomplete understanding of the Catholic faith tended to limit their relations with Rome.

By the eighteenth century new developments led to a different phase in the efforts toward reform. First, the number of Maronite clericals educated in Rome had increased and their mission in Mount Lebanon started to give results after more than a century of work. However, distance, the hazards of the trip, and absence of a preparatory school in Mount Lebanon made it impossible for as many students to go to Rome as the Holy See would have liked. Nevertheless, in 1685, when the centennial of the College was celebrated in Rome, twenty-four graduates were honored by the College for their distinguished services. Three of these had become patriarchs, one of them Syrian Catholic and the other two—Jirjus 'Umayrah (1633-1644) and Istfan al Duwayhi (1670-1704)—Maronite. Twelve others had become bishops, and nine were honored for their distinguished learning and services to the community. These graduates of Rome introduced the first seeds of learning to Mount Lebanon and prepared for the literary revival in the Arab world which germinated in Lebanon. While a number of them became oriental scholars in Europe, many of the students went home to serve the flock and to teach village children. In Lebanon their mission consisted of preaching and writing religious and historical works for the clergy and the lay population.

During their educational sojourn in Rome, the students of the Maronite College acquired new abilities, new habits, and new ideas which they introduced to Mount Lebanon. Many of them determined upon missionary work; as one of them stated on the eve of his departure from Rome, "I want to extend the scope for the Catholic faith as much as I can . . . after my return home."[14] From the careers which they followed it is clear that missionary work in educating both the flock and the clergy in Mount Lebanon was the major activity of this early group of students.

The outlook of the new generation of clergy and their plans for advancement were bound to clash with the existing practices and structure of the Church. The cleric quoted above, Monsignor 'Umayrah, later wrote a letter to the pope describing the obstacles confronting the religious worker in the Maronite Church and foreseeing the clash which was to erupt a couple of decades after his death. He stated in his letter that the need for workers was great, for the crop was plentiful but the workers few. He mentioned the hardships to which a bishop was exposed, such as oppression from non-Christian rulers and lack of reverence from his own people. Then he described the chains shackling the modern cleric in a traditional Church:

> I feel weary and unable to fulfil the duties of my episcopal rank. . . . I cannot devote time to the needs of souls in a state of peace of mind, nor am I able to write or translate religious books from Latin, for I am obliged to tend to my land and other occupations not worthy of the noble rank of my office, instead of the episcopal duties and responsibilities. . . . All these things and similar ones make me impatient and anxious, and my mind is perplexed.

He did not even have the episcopal costume in which to conduct mass, he added.[15]

[14] Ghalib, "Nawabigh al Madrasah," *MQ*, xxii, 345.
[15] Letter published in Ghalib, *ibid.*, 444.

Monsignor ʿUmayrah suggested one way to improve this sad state of affairs, namely for the bishop to have a fixed salary which would enable him to attend to the duties of his office without distraction. He turned to the Holy See to aid the Church in this objective. In later times, though, other bishops with similar problems focused on the reorganization of their Church hierarchy, instead of turning to the Holy See, to provide for the livelihood of Church officers.

The migration of Maronites from northern Lebanon to Jabal al Druze was another factor contributing to the reform movement. As we have seen in Chapter II, the Maronite population grew very rapidly during the eighteenth century; they spread out into new territories to the south in Kisrwan and Jabal al Druze. The religious needs of the more widely dispersed community required priests and bishops to live among their flock wherever they happened to be. In staying with the people, away from the patriarchal see, the prelates and priests felt it was necessary for them to have a measure of autonomy in their relations with the patriarch. The new situation induced the Church prelates to attempt changes in the order of the Church.

Another factor which called for the reorganization of the Church was the growth of the orders of monks. The relations between the orders and the Church hierarchy needed regulation if the increasing conflicts between them were to be ameliorated.

The issues leading to most of the conflict in the Church institutions were primarily the following, though there were others as well. First, the question of decentralizing the Church administration: autonomy was sought for archbishops and priests to serve the more distant Maronite communities. This was a question of jurisdiction. The Maronite patriarchs had previously followed the practice, no doubt the result of the community's humble beginnings, of personally conducting most of the Church affairs, with the bishops acting simply as officials who could be sent on missions and various errands. Few bishops could complain about this state of affairs when they could not see in the Church structure any alternative choices or other prospects open for them within a small and poor community. Before the seventeenth century there was hardly a Maronite community in Mount Lebanon that could afford to support a bishop of its own; and in Jibbat Bsharri where most of the Maronites lived, the patriarch was in charge.

As the community grew in size and importance, however, new conditions presented greater possibilities for the bishops. They could serve in several dioceses, especially in Kisrwan and Jabal al Druze, and make some living in that way. Continued subservience to the patriarch was greatly resented. Complete dependence on the head of the Church raised administrative problems for the bishops who served the flock and for their priests as well. In the first place the patriarch, as has already been mentioned, did not appoint a bishop to a diocese with a fixed tenure. The frequent changes in duties prevented the bishops from devoting their attention to one definite group of the community and also made it impossible for them to secure a steady flow of revenue from their parishes. These conditions caused much annoyance among the clergy.

A second difficulty stemming from the inadequacy of the old organization was the problem of the holy oil, an item necessary for the priests and prelates to carry out their functions. The practice had been for each archbishop and priest to go to the patriarchal see for the oil,[16] for which the patriarch exacted a certain price. This was one of the sources of his revenue. By the eighteenth century it was obvious that this custom was getting increasingly impractical. It took a priest several days to reach the patriarchal see every time he went for the oil, and as a consequence he had to leave his district unattended.[17] The view of the proponents of reform was that this practice should cease and that the function of

[16] Sim'ani, *TML*, p. 487.
[17] *Ibid.*, p. 488.

blessing the oil should be turned over to archbishops who would distribute it to the priests and monks. The issue was finally resolved in the Lebanese Council in favor of the reformists. A papal bull later confirmed the Council resolution: the patriarch was to distribute the holy oil to the bishops without any charge whatsoever. The patriarch agreed to this, but not without bad feeling.

The above issue was related to the question of the episcopal sees and decentralization of administration. As was mentioned earlier, a major reform item was the establishment of separate and defined dioceses with a Church-owned episcopal see in each. The Holy See was strongly on the side of the reformists on this question and looked very critically at the unusual prerogatives of the patriarch by which he could act as he wished regarding the bishops and their functions.[18] When this issue came up at the Lebanese Council, Patriarch Yusuf al Khazin reacted violently. Even after he had signed the Council resolutions with the rest of the delegates, he refused to acquiesce in al Sim'ani's attempt to restore one of the bishops to his diocese in accordance with the new rules. He told al Sim'ani that the flock was his and he would do with it as he liked.[19]

The new division of functions and definition of jurisdiction among the Church prelates had repercussions in the Church which were not unforeseen by the Lebanese Council. It was now clear that in order to function, a rational organization must have salaried personnel. For a long time this was the most difficult question standing in the way of Church reform. The difficulties stemming from this problem exposed the weaknesses of the Lebanese Council. For the Council was a blueprint more appropriate for the condition of the Church in European countries than in Mount Lebanon. The bureaucratic structure planned by the Council was too expensive for a subsistence economy like that of Mount Lebanon.

---

[18] See papal bull in Mas'ad, *MB*, p. 106.   [19] Sim'ani, *TML*, p. 510.

It was clear that the Maronite clergy would not and could not follow *in toto* the Council's resolutions regarding the income of patriarch and bishops. But after the reorganization of the Church, neither could they keep the earlier means of finance, for the Council struck at the foundation of the old order when it canceled some of the existing sources of the patriarch's revenue. This situation caused much confusion and friction among the higher clergy. In 1769 a number of bishops met, without the permission of the patriarch, and decided to send him a memorandum asking that each archbishop should live in the diocese which was in his name and have a fixed salary.[20] The patriarch's answer was quite cynical: he replied that he had not tampered with the bishops' income, for he had left it as it was since the days of Saint Marun (d. 707). This was probably true, but it was in complete disregard of recent developments and the Lebanese Council. The bishops then sent their complaint to the Holy See. The Pope exerted new pressure on the patriarch and issued an order in which he fixed the income of the patriarch and that of his bishops.

As suggested earlier, one of the causes for reform, and a problem which was discussed in the Lebanese Council, was the Lebanese Order of Monks. The monks disliked the fact that the patriarch had a great deal of power over their activities. On the other hand, the patriarch, and the bishops and priests as well, were unhappy about the monks' encroachments on their domain in providing service to the parishes. The monks were popular among the people and drew them away from their regular priests. The priests complained to their superiors and the latter curbed the monks' activities. As a result, the Lebanese Order of Monks was among the most active and enthusiastic supporter of al Sim'ani and the reform movement.[21]

[20] Ghibra'il, *Tarikh al Kanisah*, II, Part 1, 629.
[21] Bulaybil, "Nabdhah Tarikhiyyah," *MQ*, LI, 318.

SOME IDEAS OF REFORM

The ideas of the reform movement represented an outlook entirely new to the Lebanese scene at that time, and by their very nature they undermined the traditional institutions upon which the Church rested. The first thing which attracts the attention of the historian is the existence of two markedly opposed attitudes among the clergy. On one side were those who stood for new ideas and for progress, and on the other their conservative opponents upholding the traditional ways of their predecessors.

The historian Shayban al Khazin, who was closely connected with the internal affairs of the Church, illustrated clearly the split between the modernists and the conservatives, having himself been associated with the latter. From the day the bishops spread out and began to take up residence away from the patriarchal see, he wrote, the modernists claimed that such separation meant freedom[22] and spiritual growth; but in fact it proved to be the heart of the trouble and was causing the destruction of the community. Naturally, he continued, other Christian communities would follow the steps of destruction like the Maronites.[23] Shayban was obsessed with a feeling of deterioration in the Church and in the political institutions of the country. Decline in the Church, he thought, was the result of the freedom given to the bishops.[24] Its symptoms were free expression of views and constant disagreement among the prelates. The deterioration of the social order according to the views of Shayban will be discussed later in another context.

Shayban al Khazin was an experienced man and well informed on the affairs of his country. He showed a degree of insight rare in Mount Lebanon during his time, yet his fears in this case were not as serious as he imagined them to be.

---

[22] ". . . *itlaq al hurriyyah*. . . ."
[23] Shayban, *Tarikh*, p. 521.
[24] *Ibid*., p. 451.

For under the impetus of reform the Church showed much activity, intellectual venture, and enterprising spirit. The struggles, conflicts, and fights generated by the introduction of reform and by the new demands of a growing community distressed Shayban al Khazin and many others like him who were inclined toward tranquility and security.

The argument between modernists and conservatives was also sharply drawn in a polemic between Bishop 'Abdallah Qar'ali, one of the leading reformists of the Maronite clergy, and another monk. He wrote:

> You will perhaps object and say that one should adhere to the old and established, not to the new and modern; but this will not serve your purpose, for those who enter the monastic life have a choice of the way they want to live after the permission of their superiors. . . . The new law is not incompatible with the rites of the Church.[25]

Emphasis on achievement values defined the new outlook and undermined the old. The concept of merit was advanced as the basis of recruitment and promotion to Church offices. In particular this was directed against the practice of filling offices through kin relationships, which, as we have seen, was prevalent in the Church. The advocates of the new outlook sought legitimization of their ideas from the scriptures. Resolution 17 of the Council of Ghusta, 1768, reads:

> As is stated in the Holy Book kin relationship does not lead to the glory of God. . . .[26] Offices and ranks in the Church should not be subjected to inheritance by blood relations, but rather on the basis of merit which is more suitable to the glory of God and for the interest of the faithful.[27]

Measures were also taken at the Council of Ghusta to insure that those who presented themselves to be ordained were really

[25] Mas'ad and Khazin, *UT*, II, 410-411.
[26] Rashid al Khury al Shartuni (ed.), *Al Majami' al Maruniyyah* (Beirut: al Matba'ah al Kathulikiyyah, 1904), p. 37.
[27] *Ibid.*, p. 27.

qualified. A board of examiners was set up, but for various reasons it could not function for long, and the archbishops took over its function.[28]

Freedom of the Church from interference by commoners, nobles, and rulers was another principle advocated by the reformers. For example, a group of villagers who had been incited against the Council of Ghusta by one of the recalcitrant bishops who did not attend the meeting, went to the Council to plead the bishop's cause. In answer to their intrusion, the delegates issued a statement threatening the villagers with excommunication if they meddled in affairs strictly under Church jurisdiction. Then they made clear to the people that Church affairs were not subject to inheritance and that the Church was not the property of individuals, that the Council was not meeting to discuss private cases but to deliberate and decide on public matters, and that "equality in what belongs to the public causes no harm to anyone."[29] The Church was thus a free and independent organization in the view of the reformists, and anyone who caused an outside element to encroach on its freedom committed a great sin subject to severe penalty. If temporal rulers interfered in a Church decision and forced the clergy to settle a matter or pass a judgment, it was maintained, that judgment would be considered nullified. The same applied to promotion to clerical office effected under threat of force.[30]

THE ORDERS OF MONKS

The orders of monks represented one of the most remarkable achievements of the reform-minded clerics. Not only did they play a leading role in the reform movement, but they also established and supported a new, relatively progressive organization which occupies an interesting part in the history

---

[28] See letter of Archbishop Mikha'il Fadil to the monks, Bulaybil, *TRLM*, LI, 530.

[29] *Ibid.*

[30] *Ibid.*, pp. 21-22, 24; Ghibra'il, *Tarikh al Kanisah*, II, 578.

of Mount Lebanon in general and the Maronite Church in particular.

There were three orders of monks in Lebanon: the Native Lebanese Order, the Aleppine Lebanese Order, and the Order of Mar Ashiʻia, all of which started around 1700. The Native Lebanese Order was by far the most important of the three. These orders were formally organized hierarchies enjoying autonomy within the Church, but not independence. They all came under the authority of the patriarch, and in certain respects under the archbishops. The monks led a collective type of life in their monasteries and were completely under the jurisdiction and supervision of the abbot. They were not allowed to have any private ownership of property or independent personal commitments outside the order.

The orders were very wealthy corporate bodies. One estimate (a rather liberal one) in the mid-nineteenth century had them occupying "nearly a fourth of the entire surface of the Mountain."[31] Whether this was very close to the truth or not cannot be determined; but what was doubtless true is that in just a century's time from their founding, the orders of monks had become one of the largest propertied sectors of Lebanese society.

Cultivable land is scarce in Mount Lebanon, and the population was growing fast by the second part of the eighteenth century. As collective bodies the organizations of monks were able to cultivate lands that the peasants with their meager means could not bring under cultivation. Propertyless peasant children, and disinherited ones, found refuge and economic security in the monasteries.[32] This explains the fact that the Lebanese Order of Monks, in contrast to the Church hierarchy, was predominantly constituted of clergy with peasant backgrounds. Moreover, the monks not only worked on the land

[31] Colonel [Charles Henry] Churchill, *Mount Lebanon: A Ten Years' Residence from 1842-1852* (London: Saunders and Otley, 1853), III, 88-89.
[32] See Faris Yusuf al Shidiaq, *Kitab al Saq 'ala al Saq fi ma Huwa al Fariaq* (Paris: Benjamin Dupart, 1855), passim.

but also in crafts such as printing, an art they introduced to Lebanon.

The monks acquired property in various ways. It should be remembered that when the Lebanese Order started, they had nothing to build upon and the patriarch gave them two dilapidated monasteries which they were to live in and rehabilitate. By the middle of the nineteenth century the Order (both divisions) possessed some fifty monasteries with a large amount of property attached to them. The entire monastic body in Mount Lebanon had about eighty monasteries for monks and nuns.

The major means to this wealth was labor. The monks were organized workers. Starting with but little at first, plus donations from the faithful, they used their savings for the purchase of more land. Living on very little themselves and with few social commitments requiring expense, the monks could use the product of their collective work to augment their wealth. Moreover, they were the recipients of social benefits. They were paid, for instance, for their religious services and for the education of children. Most of this compensation for the monks' work was not in cash but in land; a village would ask the monks to teach the children and in compensation the village as a whole granted them a plot of land as their own property.[33] The monks could also draw income from the gifts the faithful regularly made to them on special occasions and feasts. Furthermore, they were able to procure many indulgences for their monasteries and churches from the pope.[34] These indulgences attracted to the monasteries large numbers of the common folk.

Donations of waqfs (mortmain) by various people among the faithful, especially the Khazins and other propertied families,[35] increased the wealth of the orders and the Church.

[33] See some of these contracts between villagers and monks in Bulaybil, *TRLM*, LI, 529; LII, 551.

[34] *Ibid.*, pp. 297, 305-306, 526, 538-539, 700-701, 702.

[35] Hattuni mentions seventeen monasteries turned into waqfs, six of

Many also donated land and other material rewards in return for prayers for the dead.

As for the muqati'jis, they also were very favorably impressed by the organizations of monks. The monks demonstrated to everyone that they were hard workers and could actually increase the country's productiveness and hence the revenue of the muqati'jis. Thus various Druze and Maronite muqati'jis like the Shihabis, the Abillama's, the Nakads, and the Khazins encouraged the agricultural activities of the monasteries. Business dealings between the monks and the muqati'jis became very complex in the late eighteenth century, when the monks started entering into tenancy relationships with the muqati'jis. The muqati'ji would ask them, like the peasants, to cultivate his lands and in return to share in the produce. In addition, some of these tenancy contracts had wider terms which stipulated that land reclaimed by the monks' labor would become the order's property after a period of time, usually ten years. The muqati'jis, it seems, were so interested in the monks' reclamation of lands that they gave them land on very easy terms, such as exemption from paying miri on reclaimed land.

Another reason why the muqati'jis encouraged the activities of the monks was the resulting flow of labor into their regions; the security which the Maronite peasants felt in the neighborhoods of monasteries induced them to settle by convents. The monks could also provide employment for these peasants, as they were unable to cultivate all their property by themselves. For these reasons many of the muqati'jis preferred to see monks serving their subjects rather than the village secular priest, for the secular priest, as an individual working by himself, was not the productive force the organization of monks was. Therefore, the ruling families often supported the

which were for the interest of the donors, and the rest for other people; Hattuni, *Nabdhah*, pp. 263-264. See also Shahin al Khazin, "Awqaf al 'A'ilah al Khaziniyyah 'ala al Tawa'if al Laji'ah ila Lubnan," *MQ*, iv (1901), 973-978; *ibid.*, *MQ*, v, 115-122.

monks against the pressures of the Church hierarchy, which resented the monks' encroachment on the domain of the secular priest.[36]

Early in the eighteenth century the clergy, especially the Lebanese Order of Monks, started to become active in the religiously mixed areas like al Matn, al Shuf, and Iqlim Jazzin. The Shihabis, as well as the other muqati'jis, encouraged their economic venture in those regions. But this encouragement went beyond economic support and reached the point of actually building up the prestige of the monks among the people. Written orders went from the muqati'jis to their Maronite subjects commanding them to obey the clergy in religious matters. One of these orders, written in 1772, was sent to the

> shaykhs of the people of Zahlah and our people [*nasna*] in the Biqa'. . . . We inform you that we have issued a decree to the respected brother 'Ammanu'il al Rishmawi that he may choose for his monks a place to build a church to serve you in matters of your religion. We want you to show obedience to them and would not permit any action against them or opposition.[37]

In another case concerning a contract between a muqati'ji and the monks, similar conditions were stated. The muqati'ji declared:

> Whoever in those regions is one of our followers will also follow the monks in matters of their religion, make themselves serviceable to them, and respect their property. No one shall ever oppose them in any way. They will also be permitted to ring bells. . . .[38]

The orders of monks became politically and economically integrated into the iqta' system. They were given complete

---

[36] See the decree of the Abillama' muqati'jis to the people of Zahlah in Bulaybil, *TRLM*, p. 506, n. 2.

[37] Letter reproduced in Bulaybil, *TRLM*, LI, 506-507.

[38] *Ibid.*, p. 499.

protection for their organization, property, and religious practices. Another contract reads:

> They will have from us the right of protection. Our influence will also be made available to uphold their authority and integrity. We shall also remove whatever is obstructive and against their laws, whether it is caused by us or others. . . . In case anyone complains against their association, we would not listen to his complaint or suit, but shall stand in their aid [i.e., the monks] and close ranks with them.[39]

The importance of this willingness on the part of the muqati'jis to share their authority with the monks in religious and personal matters should be underlined. It clearly indicates that, for a certain time at least, the religious and political elements in the country were complementary and supported each other.

Relations between the monks and the muqati'jis, however, did not long continue to be very friendly and conducive to the interests of both parties. By the late eighteenth and early nineteenth century the muqati'jis were starting to look with jealousy on the growing wealth and extensive land held by the monks. At times they tried to take back the land which they had turned over to the monks, and this caused friction and litigation.[40] The monks in turn were getting weary of the various taxes imposed on them by the muqati'jis, and tried to seek the help of the Hakim against the powers which the muqati'jis had over them. Thus in 1812, for instance, the principal-general of the Lebanese Order of Monks secured an order from the Hakim in which the latter deprived the muqati'jis of the right to levy taxes on the Order's monasteries, and authorized the abbots to collect and forward the

[39] Contract between Amir As'ad and Amir Faris Shihab on the one hand, and the principal-general of the Lebanese Order of Monks and his secretaries on the other; reproduced in Bulaybil, *ibid.*, pp. 685-686.

[40] Hilu papers of 1817, 1819, PAB; also Bulaybil, *TRLM*, LII, 354-355.

miri to him.[41] The loss to the muqati'jis here was one of both prestige and finance since they had traditionally deducted a certain amount of the tax for themselves. The amount which the muqati'jis had previously kept then reverted to the monasteries' funds.

The impression made by the economic activities of the monks on some of their countrymen is well illustrated by the following story of an attempt to purchase land from the Matawilah in the south. The abbot of Dayr Mashmushah of the Lebanese Order used a middleman to convince a Matawilah family to sell a field which the monks wanted. The middleman told the Matawilah family that "the monks are good in heart and simple people; if you sell them this field and then later decide you would like to have it back, they would not hesitate to sell it back to you." But the owner objected, "These black ones give cause for fear, for they never entered into a place which they later quitted."[42] However, hard pressed for money, the owner sold the field to the monks, who still own it to this day.

Church Bureaucracy and the Political System

From the start, reform of the Church organization struck at the root of tutelage to the notables and muqati'jis. Acquisition of the means of administration such as episcopal sees, along with monasteries, land, churches, and regular income, plus the greater degree of discipline within the hierarchy, helped to free the Church and give it more independence and organizational integrity. With the lessening of the Church's economic dependence upon the ruling families, political dependence diminished as well.

Before discussing the growing independence of the Church, something should be said about the climate of opinion within

[41] Bulaybil, *TRLM*, LII, 542, and LIII, 202. For other instances see Hubaysh papers, MSS, nos. 2280, 8075, PAB.
[42] *Ibid.*

the Church regarding its relations with the political system. From the seventeenth century, ideas about freedom from temporal rulers had been entertained by members of the higher clergy. This tendency had its strongest early expression in the ideas and actions of Patriarch Jirjus 'Umayrah (1633-1644), although he was too early to see his ideas realized. Ideas aimed at freeing the Church from temporal influence were also aired in the Council of Hrash convoked by 'Umayrah's successor, Patriarch Yusuf Halib. The most forceful statement reflecting the growing feeling of independence from temporal leaders was formulated in the Council of Ghusta in 1768. The tenth rule of the Council read as follows:

> Whoever, clerical or laic, resorts to temporal rulers in Church affairs, or solicits their aid to gain a Church office, or in any other matter that comes under Church jurisdiction, will be put outside the Church laws and will immediately bring upon himself the penalty of excommunication and the divine curse, as is stated in the Lebanese and other Church councils. The same shall apply to those who aided and abetted him in whatever way. We [who are meeting in this council], too, for the sake of strengthening and supporting the freedom of the Church and to put an end to these harmful doubts common in our community, will add further appropriate penalties.[43]

Similarly, in the two councils held in 1818 and 1856, further strong statements were made on this subject.

The establishment of Church-owned episcopal sees and fixed income for the clergy were two measures incompatible with the privileges of the notables. In earlier times members of the leading families were entitled to Church offices by virtue of their ownership of monasteries and influence over the Church. Reform in the Church deprived them of these privileges and of their traditional influence in the Church.

---

[43] See text in Shartuni, *Al Majami' al Maruniyyah*, p. 21.

Thus the strongest opposition to al Sim'ani and his reform efforts came from these families, namely the Khazins, the Muhasibs, and the Istfans, all of whom possessed some monastery or other and claimed a disproportionately high number of bishops and archbishops. Archbishop Ilias Muhasib, whose family apparently never failed to place one of their numbers as archbishop or abbot in their monastery, led, with Patriarch Yusuf al Khazin, the group of conservatives against al Sim'ani's reform measures.[44]

The Khazins resented seeing the Church, which they had protected and strengthened, free itself from their domination. Two nineteenth-century Khazin historians made sharp remarks about the degeneration of the Church after the reform movement and criticized the measures of al Sim'ani in particular, refusing to admit that the modern and formalistic rules which he introduced to the organization of the Church could apply to "a small and insignificant sect like ours [i.e., the Maronite sect]."[45] In 1809 when the newly elected patriarch, Yuhanna al Hilu, established residence in Qannubin, the official but earlier abandoned see, the Khazins objected to the move and tried to get the patriarch to return to their muqata'ah. Shaykh Bisharah al Khazin, who had been urged by the Holy See to help implement reform in the Church, wrote to Rome objecting to the patriarch's move. Immediately after the conclusion of the Council of Luwayzah in 1818, he complained to the Holy See that the bishops made it impossible for the patriarch to restore his see to Kisrwan. Then, expressing his impatience with the reform measures taken at the Council, he claimed that the arrangements made by the Church prelates were "no good at all."[46] The Khazins' irritation and sense of loss were clearly demonstrated in Bisharah's letter; he further charged that the prelates had removed a

---

[44] Dib, *Dictionnaire de Théologie Catholique*, x, Part 1, 81; see also Sim'ani, *TML*, ii, passim.

[45] Shayban, *Tarikh*, pp. 514, 516.

[46] See letter in Mas'ad and Khazin, *UT*, i, 609.

Khazin cousin of his from office as abbot of a convent in Kisrwan,

> although we have in our possession title-deeds signed by al Sim'ani which confirm that the mentioned convent belongs to our family . . . they [the prelates] are also planning to put under their charge other monasteries which belong to our family. We hope that your fatherly concern would move to redress the wrongs that have taken place.[47]

Both the Khazin and Hubaysh houses put strong pressure on the Council of Luwayzah to maintain their property claims in the Church.[48]

Struggle between the Khazins and the reformed Church organization took sharp form again in 1845, when the prelates were faced with the candidacy of a Khazin to the office of patriarch. They had to choose between Bulus Mas'ad, a commoner and graduate of 'Ayn Waraqah College with higher education in Rome, and the aristocratic but less educated Bishop Yusuf al Khazin. A contest ensued among the bishops who were divided between the two parties. When Yusuf al Khazin was finally elected, he went to Qannubin to appease the popular discontent against him in Jibbat Bsharri.[49] However, agitation flared up again in protest against the idea of forcing a Khazin patriarch on the people.[50] The people were also disturbed by the new patriarch's alleged friendly relations with the Druze.[51]

The success of Yusuf al Khazin in the election was enhanced by the interference of the French consul in Beirut, Eugène Poujade, and the political turmoil which was then spreading over Mount Lebanon between the Druze and the

[47] *Ibid.*, p. 610.   [48] *Ibid.*, ii, 588.

[49] See regarding these events Hubaysh papers, MSS, nos. 7616, 7626, PAB; also Ghibra'il, *Tarikh al Kanisah*, ii, 768-769.

[50] Eugène Poujade, *Le Liban et la Syrie 1845-1860* (Paris: Librairie Nouvelle, 1860), pp. 127-185.

[51] Poujade, *Le Liban*, p. 186.

Maronites.[52] The French consul, as well as some of the prelates, believed that election of a Khazin would be more advantageous in this tense situation since the Khazins traditionally had had good relations with the Druze muqati'jis and especially the Jumblats.[53]

However, the vulnerable position of the iqta' houses and the clergy's opposition to them was demonstrated again when Mas'ad was elected to succeed Yusuf al Khazin as a patriarch in 1854. Mas'ad encouraged the peasantry in their struggle against the muqati'jis and iqta' privileges and continued the efforts of the Church to free the Christians from Druze domination.

While the reform movement on the whole was undermining the notables' supremacy over the Church, the clergy, with their Western education and outlook, were acquiring a new view of their role and place in society. Monsignor 'Abdallah Qar'ali, one of the founders of the Lebanese Order of Monks and the greatest legal mind in the history of the Maronite Church, was a good example of the changing attitude of the clergy and their relations with the notables. An interesting and revealing story is told of him which illustrates this point.

As archbishop of Beirut (1724-1742), Qar'ali placed the penalty of temporary excommunication upon a Khazin shaykh who had committed a transgression. This action upset the whole Khazin house, who realized that a threat of this nature against one of them was in principle a threat against their social status as a whole. Pressure was put on the archbishop to withdraw his stand and absolve the shaykh, but to no avail. Thereupon the penalized shaykh, armed with the support of his whole family, went to the archbishop with every intention of intimidating him into submission. The first remark the

[52] *Ibid.*, pp. 182-185.
[53] Hubaysh papers, MSS, nos. 7616, 7626, PAB; also Poujade, *Le Liban*, pp. 127-159. See also Yusuf al Dibs, *Tarikh Suriyyah* (Beirut: al Matba'ah al 'Umumiyyah, 1905), VIII, 783-784.

shaykh uttered was an indication of the disparity of their social ranks. "A man of your status and place," he said, "dares
act toward a man of my status the way you have acted?" The
archbishop, however, was not perturbed. He ended up con-
vincing the shaykh to submit to his authority and in addition
imposed on him a pecuniary penalty.[54]

The Church's freedom from the aegis of the ruling class
was reflected in the recruitment of its higher officers. Looking
at the Church elite in historical perspective, we can notice
that there was a marked difference in recruitment patterns
between the eighteenth century and the nineteenth. For example, out of a total of eight patriarchs who occupied the
office in the eighteenth century, six were members of notable
families. As for the archbishops (excluding the archbishops
of Aleppo), fifteen out of twenty known bishops belonged to
the same class. By way of contrast, in the nineteenth century
we find that two patriarchs out of a total of six were notables;
while of the seventeen archbishops, seven only came from that
class.[55]

Relations between the Church and the two converted Maronite houses of Shihab and Abillamaʿ were somewhat different
and should be treated separately from the situation concerning the Khazins. In spite of their central position within the
political system, these two houses did not show as much interest in the Church as did the Khazins. None of them had
ever tried to enter the clerical profession, and their activities
in Church politics were fairly limited. On the other hand,
like the rest of the muqatiʿjis of Jabal al Druze, the Shihabis
and Abillamaʿs found their initial encounter with the Maronite clergy favorable and encouraging. They contributed, in
terms of economic and social support, to the advancement of
the Church establishment within their domains.

[54] An eye-witness account by Qarʿali's secretary, Tuma al Labudi; see
Labudi, "Sirat al Mutran," *MQ*, x, 801-802.

[55] The identification of archbishops for these periods is based on Dahdah's
account; see Dahdah, "Al Abrashiyyat," *MQ*, vii, 641ff., and viii, 151ff.

As for the Shihabi Amir, the head of the political hierarchy, his relations with the Church were marked by mutual respect. Following the traditions of their predecessors, the Ma'nis, the Shihabis granted protection and freedom to the clergy in their lives, property, and religious practices.[56] The political institutions of the country gave the Church another guarantee of liberty in that the Hakim could not extend his authority directly over the subjects of the muqati'jis, and, as a consequence, the Hakim could not have oppressed the clergy even if he had wanted to do so.

Nevertheless, the Shihabi Hakim as supreme head of the country was bound to become involved in Church affairs to some extent.[57] At first this involvement came at the invitation of the Church itself. The Shihabis' tolerant attitude and the confidence they inspired among their subjects encouraged the Church to approach them for arbitration in disputes among the higher clergy. The Holy See, in fact, frequently took advantage of the Amir's responsiveness to its requests to ask his intervention in imposing order and reform in the Church.[58]

Not only Rome but also the Maronite higher clergy turned to the Shihabis to help settle their differences. The clergy's access to the Shihabis was first achieved through the muqati'jis of the Maronite faith; but later, during the second part of the eighteenth century, they dispensed with intermediaries. The clergy approached the Shihabis mainly for three general purposes: they brought forward matters of interest to the community; second, they sought the support of the secular authorities and particularly the Shihabi Amir in their own disputes;[59] and third, the higher clerical authorities tried to

[56] See written statement given by Bashir I to Bishop Butrus Makhluf, Ghalib, "Nawabigh al Madrasah," *MQ*, xxii (1924), 110.

[57] See for example Mas'ad and Khazin, *UT*, ii, 579; also Bulaybil, *TRLM*, liii, 334.

[58] Mas'ad and Khazin, *UT*, ii, 566-580, and Hattuni, *Nabdhah*, p. 208. Also letters reproduced in Muzhir, *Tarikh Lubnan al 'Am*, i, 387. Hilu papers, 15 February 1817, PAB.

[59] For instance, see Shayban, *Tarikh*, pp. 514, 526. Also Yusuf As'ad

secure the aid of the Amir to bring into line some of the re-calcitrant subordinates.[60] As a rule the policy of the Shihabis was on the side of the Church authority; that is, they stood for order in the Church and backed the higher authorities in cases of disorderly conduct on the part of the lower-ranking clergy. The same applied to the role they played vis-à-vis the Holy See and the Maronite hierarchy: they supported the Holy See in most cases. The Shihabis were responsive to the requests of Rome because of their desire to have friendly re-lations with European powers. Second, the Shihabis favored the reform movement and the establishment of order in the Church. Third, particularly in the early nineteenth century, the Shihabis needed the Holy See as a check on the ambitious activities of the Maronite Church.

However, either because of the political rules of the game in Mount Lebanon, or because they did not like religious mat-ters to assume too much importance in what was essentially a secular government, the Shihabis played a very restrained role in the affairs of the Church.[61] There was also, of course, a limit to the extent to which the Church itself would permit interference in its affairs. On many occasions, in fact, the intercession of the Shihabis or other chiefs went unheeded by the Church. It did not pay al Sim'ani, for instance, to enlist the aid of Amir Mulhim Shihab; on the contrary, it aroused the anger of the Khazins to see the papal delegate appeal over their heads to the Amir. Shaykh Nawfal al Khazin pro-tested to al Sim'ani that in going to the non-Christian tem-poral ruler, he was flouting the customs of the country and violating the rules of the Church.[62] Again in 1817, the com-

---

Daghir, *Lubnan: Lamhah fi Tarikhihi wa Atharihi wa Usarihi* (Juniyah: Matba'at al Mursalin al Lubnaniyyin, 1938), pp. 392-393.

[60] See Yusuf Ziadah, *Al Qada' al Maruni wa 'Alaqatuhu bi al Shar' al Rumani* (Juniyah: Matba'at al Mursalin al Lubnaniyyin, 1929), pp. 72-74.

[61] See Mas'ad and Khazin, *UT*, II, 569-570.

[62] Sim'ani, *TML*, p. 509.

bined efforts of Amir Bashir Shihab, Shaykh Bashir Jumblat, and the apostolic delegate did not succeed in making the patriarch move an inch away from his stand concerning the Council of al Luwayzah.[63]

CONCLUSION

With Patriarch Yusuf al Tiyyan (1796-1808), a new relationship between Church and state began to develop in Mount Lebanon. This period was marked by the Church's venture into the political arena on its own. The religious establishment had grown so much that the clergy was no longer willing to be relegated to a secondary place in society. By the end of the eighteenth century, the Church had become the largest, the most organized, and the wealthiest organization in the whole of Mount Lebanon. Its interests as an organization became entwined with those of the political system. It was obvious that the Church was in a position to take the initiative in relations with the state to its advantage, as will be seen later.

There can be no comparison between the fortunes of Patriarch Istfan al Duwayhi (1670-1704), for example, and those of Patriarch Yusuf Hubaysh (1823-1845). Al Duwayhi had to hide in caves and seek refuge in the country of the Druze to the last day of his life. Hubaysh was a national and religious leader, received with full state honors whenever he visited the ruling amir. He would be welcomed with popular acclaim in the villages on his route; and near the palace, music would play at his appearance, and a squad of soldiers would salute him while the Amir went out to the palace court to receive him.[64]

To summarize, reform in the Maronite Church was stimulated and advanced by the Roman See starting in the late six-

---

[63] Mas'ad and Khazin, *UT*, ii, 579. For Patriarch Hilu's resistance to the interference of Bashir in Church affairs, particularly in matters of clerical promotions, see Hilu papers, MSS, nos. C 127, 267.

[64] See Bulus Qar'ali, "Al Batriyark Yusuf Hubaysh: Kalimah fi Siyasatihi al Ta'ifiyyah wa al Dawliyyah," *Al Bayraq* (Beirut), 24 October 1949.

teenth century and greatly accelerating in the eighteenth. Social developments in the Maronite community, such as population expansion and migration and better education, made reform an urgent question in the eighteenth century. In effect, the reform measures rationalized the Church bureaucracy and envigorated its religious and social role.

Reform in the Maronite Church had a serious and lasting effect on its position vis-à-vis the ruling aristocracy. By organizing its affairs, the Church was better able to untangle itself from the temporal powers. When the Church established its own sees, monasteries, and fixed salaries for its clergy, it acquired control over the means of its own administration, thus depriving the muqati'ji class and other notables of their former powers over it. The achievement of financial independence had a marked effect not only on its course of action, but also on its recruitment of clergy. While in the eighteenth century the higher clergy belonged to the more influential class of notables, in the nineteenth the proportion of commoners in the higher Church offices was much greater than that of the notables.

The independence of the Church gave rise to competition for prestige and power between the clergy and the a'yan. The muqati'ji class were not pleased with the appearance of an organized and powerful body in the country relatively free from their control. The clergy in their own turn disliked the outmoded pretensions which the muqati'jis continued to display in their dealings with the Church and their financial exactions.

The emergence of the Church as a well organized and free agent in the system made it possible for the clergy to pursue their ideas and goals, which were not the same as those of the actors in the traditional system. In their new role, as we shall see, the clergy showed leadership in political affairs as well as ability to articulate and advance the new communal values of the Maronite people.

CHAPTER VI

Ideology and Communication

THE SLOW PACE of change in the iqta' system of Lebanon was aggravated by the absence of rational and innovative agencies for political socialization. Ideas and traditions were transmitted from father to son by imitation in the family and neighborhood. The effect of such a learning process was to preserve the cultural and political values of the past and promote a strong feeling of dislike for deviation and the unfamiliar.

For new political ideas to appear in such a system there had to be a cadre of men who could articulate them, relate them closely to the interests and aspirations of the people, and be reasonably free to spread them. The one group who could and did fulfill these conditions in Lebanon was the Maronite clergy. The clergy were the only learned men in Lebanon, deriving their ideas both from their contact with Europe and from the history and beliefs of their own community. In addition, the clergy belonged to an elaborate Church organization and monastic orders, and thus not only possessed the means of spreading ideas but also the relative freedom and strength to pursue their goals unobstructed.

In this chapter we shall be concerned with tracing the Maronites' image of themselves as a people as reflected in writings of their intellectual leaders, particularly with respect to the Maronites' beliefs regarding their origin, ethnicity, values, struggles, and place in history. Maronite ideology and the ways in which it was developed by the clergy had serious implications to the iqta' political system, which rested on beliefs and values basically different from those preached by the Maronite clergy.

No analysis will be attempted regarding the historical truth or falsehood of the Maronites' views; it is only the way they interpreted life around them and their self-image that concerns us here. Thus the following will focus on ideas which were held as beliefs by the Maronites, the communication network through which they were propagated, and the way they served to undermine the iqta' political system.

THE FOUNDERS OF MARONITE IDEOLOGY

The Maronite people may be considered a national group. They reflect distinctive ethnic characteristics, a single religion, and a long history; for centuries they lived in one compact area and once had a distinct language (of which they kept some vestiges in their religious books) and memories up to the recent past. In addition to this, they once enjoyed a political history and life of their own, the memory of which they translated into a national myth. The Maronite Church, the most enduring and stable organization in the history of the Maronite people, played a significant role in preserving, developing, and propagating the ideas of nationhood. This national tradition was recorded mostly by the clergy, in the form of popular poetry, chronicles, treatises, and religious books. The Maronite view of the history of Lebanon enjoys a certain coherence and purpose which to this day dominates the most commonly accepted interpretation of Lebanese history and constitutes the basis of Lebanese nationalism. As Kamal Salibi has observed, the early Maronite historians wrote history not as a scholarly pursuit but "as an expression of national pride."[1]

Ibn al Qila'i

The first Maronite writer who represents a coherent view of the values of the Maronite community is Jibra'il Ibn al Qila'i (d. 1516), Maronite bishop of Cyprus. The life and works of Ibn al Qila'i have many qualities which recommend him to the attention of the historian. Born in Mount Lebanon, he was educated by the Franciscan friars, whose order he eventually joined after he had been sent by the friars to study in Rome.

[1] Salibi, *Maronite Historians*, p. 15.

Thus he was the first Maronite to receive a European education.[2] He returned as a missionary to his people, who were then in the throes of a religious struggle between Catholicism and Jacobism,[3] and immediately took the lead in combating Jacobite missionaries. He preached Catholicism, wrote the history of the founder of the sect and the history of the Maronite people, and traced the early relations between the Maronites and the Church of Rome. Although Ibn al Qila'i sometimes wrote in prose, his favorite medium was popular poetry, *al zajaliyyah*. He relied mostly on oral tradition as well as religious manuscripts in Lebanon and Rome.

Ibn al Qila'i describes Mount Lebanon as the national home of the Maronites. When the Arab Muslims occupied Syria, he explains, the Maronites were already living in Lebanon and held out against occupation by sheer might. They were faithful adherents of the Church of Rome and obedient to their patriarch, who lived among them in the Mountain. They were strong warriors and defenders of the faith, and they made their country a haven for every oppressed person. The idea of Mount Lebanon as a homeland was not vague or general. Ibn al Qila'i defined it in geographic terms, comprising the mountain and coastland extending from al Shuf in the south to Bilad 'Akkar in the north.

Ibn al Qila'i relates the history of his country and people as a song of heroism, *Madihah*, recounting the rise and fall of the Maronites. Ibn al Qila'i tells the story to teach his people a lesson—to emulate the glorious past and avoid the causes of decline. In the time of their glory, the Maronite chiefs, prelates, and people were all united in one struggle to preserve their home, lives, and beliefs. Virtue, courage, and religious

[2] *Ibid.* Salibi gives the most comprehensive account of Ibn al Qila'i. For Ibn al Qila'i's ideas, see his poem (*al zajaliyyah*, a poem composed in the vernacular Arabic) entitled "Madihah 'ala Jabal Lubnan," published in Bulus Qar'ali, *Hurub al Muqaddamin: 1075-1450* (Bayt Shabab, Lebanon: n.p., 1937). Also summary of the poem in 'Aynturini, *MTL*, XLVI, 541-552.

[3] The Jacobites are an old Christian sect who believed in the single holy nature of Christ.

orthodoxy, he says, characterized that period. Fortified in their mountains and united in the faith, the Maronites had little to fear from Islam in their long drawn-out struggle. Orthodoxy and heroism in war against Islam were the two major commitments of the Maronite community as seen by Ibn al Qila'i.

The manner in which Ibn al Qila'i interprets the events of the past gives a clear idea of how central is the concept of true Catholic faith in the lives of the Maronites. The *Madihah* is an epic of the struggle of a nation not only against an enemy from the outside but also against decadence from within, namely heresy. The Maronites continued to prosper and be victorious in their war against Islam for as long as they remained orthodox. For example, as Ibn al Qila'i sings their victories:

> [Then] thirty thousand warriors
> Descended from the mountains like rain,
> And the Moslems, out on a stroll,
> Found death waiting on the battlefield.[4]

However, these victories did not last long before the seeds of heresy crept into the heart of the Maronite land and gave rise to schism and moral turpitude. The Maronites started to stray from orthodoxy under the influence of two Jacobite monks. Heresy, in the poet's opinion, led to military defeat:

> King Barquq heard of that;
> He sent soldiers with banners
> to lay siege in Mount Lebanon.
> The country was internally split,
> And its inside was soiled with heresy.
> Its ruler was puffed up with pride,
> And it lacked both loyalty and faith.[5]

As a result of their defeat on the battlefield, the Maronites fled from Kisrwan to the northern parts of their country in

---

[4] Salibi, *Maronite Historians*, p. 70.
[5] *Ibid.*, pp. 72-73.

Jibbat Bsharri, where they were concentrated in the days of Ibn al Qila'i. The amir of the Maronite country, awed by the disaster, summoned the patriarch and asked him to go to Rome and seek indulgence from the pope to redress the wrong that had taken place and atone for the Maronites' disbelief. Thereupon the patriarch visited Rome in the year 1215. (This is the date, it is believed by Maronites, when the Maronite patriarch was summoned to attend the fourth Lateran Council of the Catholic Church.) The interpretation which Ibn al Qila'i gives this patriarchal trip which united the Maronites with the Church of Rome is heavily weighted with the struggle of his community, its suffering, religious turpitude, and hope of eventual redemption with the help of Rome.

In the picture presented by Ibn al Qila'i, the Maronites were ruled by their princes and muqaddams and by their religious prelates who shared political power with the lay leaders and participated in their election to office. Ibn al Qila'i, however, gives us no idea of what the Maronites of those days expected of their ruler, aside from being true to the Catholic faith and courageous in war.

Ibn al Qila'i died in Mount Lebanon fighting Jacobite heresy, which made great inroads into the Maronite community during his lifetime. Though he did not live to see his efforts succeed in purging the country of Jacobism, his memory and influence were enduring, and his epic, *Madihah*, with its images and ideas, was sung long after him by Maronites young and old.

Patriarch Istfan al Duwayhi (1629-1704)

The Maronites who studied at the Maronite College in Rome were intellectually overshadowed by the figure of Patriarch Istfan al Duwayhi. Al Duwayhi was more of a historian than Ibn al Qila'i and showed interest in historical events per se. But he was also much interested in the history of the Maronites and particularly in demonstrating their unbroken orthodoxy and association with the Roman See. Unlike Ibn al Qila'i, he was neither a propagandist nor a missionary obsessed with the idea of saving his nation and the souls of its men. He was a man of responsibility, being the head of the Maronite Church. Al Duwayhi's works include a book on the history of the Maronite community[6] in which he is mostly concerned with the image of the patron saint of the sect and its early leader, Patriarch Yuhanna Marun, and with the early history of the community in Mount Lebanon. A major theme of the book is the perpetual orthodoxy of the Maronites and their early connections with the Church of Rome. His second book is a general Middle Eastern chronicle[7] in which he devotes much attention to events affecting the Maronites and to their local history.

There are some shifts of emphasis in the themes which al Duwayhi dealt with, compared with those of Ibn al Qila'i's epic. In al Duwayhi's works, the Maronites' long heroic struggles with Islam are toned down. This is perhaps due to the fact that at the time in which he lived and wrote, the Maronites were under direct Muslim rule and enjoyed less freedom and independence than they apparently had in earlier times.

Nevertheless, the common Maronite theme that the community's history is a continuous struggle to maintain national and religious identity in a dominant Muslim environment preoccupies al Duwayhi, too. The first Maronite patriarch, he tells us, escaped from Syria and took refuge in Lebanon because of persecution by Melkites. He and the Maradah of Lebanon joined causes. Little is known historically about the Maradah except that they were a warrior group placed in Mount Lebanon by the Byzantine emperor in the seventh century to harass the Arab conquerors of Syria.[8] For al

---

[6] Istfan al Duwayhi, *TTM*.   [7] Istfan al Duwayhi, *TA*.

[8] On the Maradah, see Adel Ismail, *Histoire du Liban du XVIIᵉ Siècle à nos Jours*, Vol. 1: *Le Liban au Temps de Fakhr-ed-Din II (1590-1633)* (Paris: Librairie Orientale et Américaine, G.-P. Maissonneuve–M. Besson. Succ., 1955), 169-189.

Duwayhi, as for Ibn al Qila'i before him, the Maradah and the Maronites were one and the same people. Identification with the Maradah was an important national tradition among the Maronites, and even in recent times skepticism on this point has wounded Maronite feelings. In 1902 the Jesuit historian Henry Lammens received a letter from the Maronite historian Archbishop Yusuf al Dibs in which the Maronite prelate strongly protested that Lammens, who had always been a friend to the Maronites, should throw doubt on the ethnic origin of the community. In the same letter he wrote a concise account to prove that the Maradah and the Maronites were the same people.[9]

Al Duwayhi reflected the popular Maronite belief that in the past the Maronites had been powerful fighters who resisted Islamic assaults on their mountain and collaborated with all outside expeditions against Islam, such as the Crusades.[10] He was acutely aware of their lonely lot in the Orient where they were the only major Catholic community. In a letter to a Roman cardinal, al Duwayhi sought comfort through confession: "We are the only people in all the East who hold fast to the orthodox faith," adding, "We are surrounded by heretics and nonbelievers who hate us to the point of death because we are united with you."[11] The Maronites were pleased to receive condolences and sympathy from no less a personage than Pope Leo X himself, who described them as "roses among thorns." The Maronites never forgot that appellation and took pride in it for generations—as did their historians and clergy and men like Jirjus Baz, the Maronite layman who rose to the highest position of power in the Imarah.[12]

Very curiously, though, al Duwayhi had very little to say about the Imarah of Jabal al Druze and its significance for

[9] Yusuf al Dibs, "Al Maradah wa al Mawarinah," *MQ*, v, 914-923.
[10] See Letter in Aouad, *Droit Privé*, pp. 297-298.
[11] Letter published in Mas'ad and Khazin, *UT*, III, 33.
[12] In a letter to Rome in 1804 in which Baz discusses the affairs of the community with the Holy See, Bulaybil, *TRLM*, LII, 325-327.

his Church and people. Not only was he on many occasions a well-received refugee in the Imarah, but also the Maronites who lived in the Imarah were on an equal footing with the Druze. The Khazins, who participated in the government of the Imarah, appear in his writings simply as a Maronite notable house lauded for their achievements and efforts to advance the interests of the Maronites.

To Duwayhi the Druze were still an alien people, and similarly the Imarah as a political order was a concept not yet integrated into the communal history ideology of the Maronite people.

Yusuf Marun al Duwayhi (d. 1780)

For the middle of the eighteenth century another Maronite cleric, Yusuf Marun al Duwayhi, gives us an idea of the Maronite self-image in history. Yusuf al Duwayhi was a priest of the patriarchal see and former assistant to the archbishop of al Batrun. He studied at the Maronite College in Rome and then returned to Lebanon, where his strong views on clerical matters and Church politics stood in the way of his promotion to higher clerical positions. Like Patriarch Istfan al Duwayhi, he opened a school for children and left all his money to it.

Yusuf al Duwayhi had read earlier Maronite writers such as Ibn al Qila'i, Ibrahim al Haqilani,[13] Mirhij Namrun al Bani,[14] and Istfan al Duwayhi. His own account is particularly interesting for its coherence and the strong national sense it reflects.

In his treatise called "On the Prestige of the Maronite Community,"[15] the same themes which we have already noticed

[13] A Maronite student of the Maronite College; see Raphael, *Le Rôle du Collège*, pp. 87-92.

[14] Also studied in Rome and wrote a treatise on the origin of the Maronites, in Latin, *ibid.*, pp. 105-108. See his book on the Maronites in the Vatican Library under: Antonio Fausto Naironi, *Dissertatio de Origine nomine ae religione de Maronitarum* (Rome: n.p., 1679).

[15] Incorporated in its original form in al 'Aynturini's history; see 'Aynturini, *MTL*, 556-570.

recur: the Maronites are a national community bound by one religion, they are the same as the people known in history as the Maradah, Mount Lebanon is their national home, and their history is characterized by a ceaseless struggle to maintain their own identity in the midst of a hostile environment. In his view the Maronites remained politically independent until 1609,[16] and then the rise of the Maronite Khazin house into prominence in the Imarah made up somewhat for their losses elsewhere.

Al Duwayhi's presentation has the distinction of being concise and complete. Not only does he give an account of the origins, beliefs, and history of the community, but he also provides the reader with a complete list of temporal and religious heads of the community to his day. There is reason to doubt the historical truth of his claim that the community enjoyed political unity and stability for all these centuries, but what interests us here is the image he had of his people and the national pride the Maronites continued to show.

It is curious that Duwayhi does not dwell on the century in which he lived nor does he attempt to define the relations which the Maronites then had with the Imarah of Jabal al Shuf. Among the ruling class in the Imarah, he singles out the Maronite house only—the Khazins, who obviously enjoyed the greatest prestige in the community. His exclusion of the Imarah from consideration in the history of the Maronite people, many of whom lived and prospered under the iqta' system, indicates that the Maronite intellectual then identified with Maronite ideology rather than with the iqta' order of society.

Yusuf al Duwayhi died in 1780, after the Shihabis had united north and south Lebanon under their rule; yet he made no reference to this important event in his treatise. This might have been because he finished writing his treatise sometime in

---

[16] This date and the event it refers to are left completely unexplained.

the period between May 1742 and March 1743,[17] that is, before the unification took place. We do not have anything from his pen after that date to indicate whether he modified his views or not.

One may draw the following conclusion regarding the Maronite world-view up to the middle of the eighteenth century. There is a strong sense of ethnic unity and pride in the history and political integrity of the community. The early integration of some Maronites, lords and subjects, into the Imarah political system of Jabal al Druze did not affect the clerical outlook of the Maronite self-image. The community continued to be viewed as a unit apart from its relations with the Imarah. This would suggest that the Maronite intellectual nurtured political ideas alien to those upon which the iqta' system of the Imarah rested.

Antonious Abi Khattar al 'Aynturini (d. 1821)

Al 'Aynturini and his contemporary, Shayban al Khazin (1750-1820?), to be discussed later, were the first lay Maronites to write on Maronite and Lebanese questions. Al 'Aynturini was a hereditary shaykh presiding over the village of 'Aynturin in Jibbat Bsharri. In the last decade of his life he rose to political prominence in his region and participated in the revolt of the Maronites against Amir Bashir II. With the failure of that revolt he was captured and tortured, and died soon after in 1821.

Although al 'Aynturini was a lay writer, his history, *Mukh-*

---

[17] It is almost certain that this is the date of the treatise, for in his treatise Yusuf al Duwayhi included a list of the Maronite patriarchs from the days of Patriarch Yuhanna Marun, the founder, to his own day. The last patriarch he mentioned was Yusuf Dargham al Khazin (1733-1742); also, he noted that Patriarch Khazin had died, but did not mention the name of his successor, Sim'an 'Awwad, referring to the latter as Bishop 'Awwad. This should mean that by the time he finished writing his treatise, 'Awwad had not yet been elected patriarch. The time span between the death of Patriarch Khazin, 13 May 1742, and the election of 'Awwad on 16 March 1743, then, must be the period in which Duwayhi finished writing his treatise.

tasar Tarikh Jabal Lubnan,[18] is a continuation of the ideological tradition of his clerical predecessors. He was familiar with their writings and used some of them[19] in addition to other Maronite and Muslim works. In preparing his history he was helped by the principal of 'Ayn Waraqah College, Bishop Yusuf Istfan, a prelate learned in the affairs and history of his community. The latter played a role similar to that of al 'Aynturini in the abortive revolt against Bashir II and met a similar fate.

The Maronite world-view of al 'Aynturini is essentially the same as that portrayed by the clerics, who were his instructors. He sums up the history of the Maronite people as a struggle against a hostile environment. Al 'Aynturini's contribution is more than repetition of the same convictions of earlier times; he provides us with an idea of the changing attitude of Maronite writers toward the Imarah of Mount Lebanon.

Al 'Aynturini's account is the first we have of Maronite views after northern Lebanon became united under Shihabi dominion. He dwells in some detail upon the historical circumstances which brought about the unity, particularly the revolt of the Maronites of northern Lebanon against their Matawilah lords. It is in connection with this event that the Imarah begins to loom large in the Maronites' own account of their history. The Maronite people of the north rebelled against their lords, expelled them, and sought Shihabi rule. The then ruling Shihabi, Amir Mansur, did not show sufficient interest, but the contender to the office, Amir Yusuf Shihab, responded to the Maronites' desire and eventually became their first Shihabi Hakim. Among the Shihabi Hakims, Amir Yusuf and his sons after him enjoyed the loyalty of the Maronites as did no other Shihabi.

---

[18] Published by Father Ighnatius Tannus al Khury, in *al Mashriq*, XLVI-XLVII.

[19] 'Aynturini used the whole treatise of Yusuf al Duwayhi, as was previously mentioned, and wrote a summary in prose of the *Madihah* of Ibn al Qila'i, as well as other writings such as those of Bishop Jirmanus Farhat.

There can be little doubt that it was not until after Amir Yusuf united northern with southern Lebanon that Maronite historians began to reflect a sense of identification with the Shihabi Imarah. Maronite partisanship toward Amir Yusuf Shihab and his descendants was as strongly expressed in 'Aynturini's writings as it was in the attitude of the common people. Thus al 'Aynturini's version of the community's history takes into account the Imarah and its ruling class, regardless of their ethnic background. He was not unaware of the ethnic differences separating the major ruling houses from the Maronite community, but what is important is that his views show a change in Maronite political attitudes. His people were starting to regard themselves as part of a political order larger and more encompassing than their own community. From the beginning, Shihabis at the center of the system provided the Maronites with an object for identification. Loyalty to the Shihabi dynasty, particularly the Yusuf Shihab line, was more evident in Maronite views of the Imarah than was any other aspect of the system. On the whole, al 'Aynturini took cognizance of the political exchange between Maronites and Druze, yet stayed short of considering the two groups as one people.

Al 'Aynturini's account is a nineteenth century one, as he wrote in the last sixteen years of his life, before his death in 1821. If, therefore, we accept his views as representative of the way the Maronites in northern Lebanon thought of themselves and the world, important conclusions should follow. The main one is that even by the early nineteenth century the Maronites of northern Lebanon had not significantly changed their world-view or reached new ways of thinking which would include non-Maronite people in their political life as a community. They seem to have preserved a sense of distinctness as a community quite separate from the Druze.

It is possible that the tragic end of their champion, Amir Yusuf Shihab, and the change of government to another

Shihabi line put them on a course of conflict with the Druze early in their newly established relations with the Shihabis. This view gains more ground when we know that the Maronites constituted the major force of opposition to Amir Bashir Shihab II, the rival and successor of Amir Yusuf, for the first three decades of his rule. The world-view of al 'Aynturini reflects the attitude of the Maronites of northern Lebanon more than it does that of the south, where the Maronites had been living for a long time under the iqta' system of the Imarah. The integration of the Maronites of the south into the Imarah system was more complete, and their condition is represented more in the writings of Shayban al Khazin and Tannus al Shidiaq than by 'Aynturini, as we shall soon see. Nevertheless, the ideology and new national spirit was generated among the northern Maronites; and under the system of communications established by the Church, it affected and stirred those of the south into national awareness.

In the 1820's the relations of the Maronites with Bashir II changed from hostile to friendly, and Bashir relied on them more than he had earlier. By the 1840's the Maronites in the Imarah had gone through such a change of fortune that they were quite openly challenging the political supremacy of the Druze in the Imarah. The attempt to reach a Maronite outlook which would assimilate the Imarah into Maronite communal life and history came from the pen of a cleric from Kisrwan, Bishop Niqula Murad.

Bishop Niqula Murad (d. 1862)

Murad was a graduate of the Maronite College of 'Ayn Waraqah and entered the service of a Maronite muqati'ji before he joined the clerical profession. He rose to prominence in the Maronite community when he was still a priest and was chosen by Patriarch Hubaysh for important political missions in Istanbul and Paris.[20] Then he was made patri-

[20] Yusuf As'ad Daghir, *Batarikat al Mawarinah* (Beirut: n.p., 1958), pp. 88-89.

archal deputy in Rome and was elected bishop in 1843. Bishop Murad was also very active in the civil war in Mount Lebanon between the years 1841 and 1845.

In his treatise *Notice Historique sur la Nation Maronite*, which he wrote on his political mission to seek the French government's support against the Ottomans, Murad affirms that the Maronites were always Catholics, the first Catholics in the East. Ethnically, they are the Maradah who defended Christianity against the onslaught of the Muslims in Syria and preserved their mountain independent and pure of all heresy. Again the Maronite self-image as a people with a distinct and separate character from their neighbors is strongly reflected in the thinking of Bishop Murad: Catholics in the midst of schismatic Christians and nonbelievers, "roses among thorns," these are the Maronites of Lebanon.

Murad wrote at a time when it was the official policy of the Church to support and uphold the cause of the Shihabis and their restoration to the government of Lebanon. Bishop Murad himself was appointed by the patriarch to fight for the cause of Lebanese unity under a Maronite Shihabi amir. His official duty at the outbreak of the civil war in 1841 was to campaign in Europe for the Maronite cause, and his mission started in Istanbul and then moved to Paris and London. Thus his writings form part of a nationalist effort to justify a Christian Imarah for the whole of Lebanon. For this purpose he had to base his argument on two points: that a Christian Imarah existed in the past, and that non-Christian communities in Mount Lebanon, including the Druze, were a small and inconsequential minority.

The first argument constitutes Bishop Murad's major contribution to nationalist ideology. He was the first Maronite to lay down the modern Lebanese nationalist thesis: the political unity of the whole of Mount Lebanon under the Imarah. In this argument he also extends his line of thought to the earlier times of the Ma'nis and claims that the history of Lebanon as a united polity dates back to their period. No mention is made of the religion of the Ma'nis or the iqta' leaders who ruled the country under them. However, when he treats of the Shihabi Imarah, Murad is more confident. With the Shihabis converted to the Maronite faith, together with the Abillama' house, he could claim that the Hakim of Mount Lebanon was always a Maronite under the Shihabis and that the country's ruling aristocracy was Maronite, too.

Having demonstrated to his own satisfaction that Lebanon was ruled for a long time by a Christian Hakim and aristocracy, Murad did not find it difficult to argue that the Druze were an undeserving minority rebelling against the legitimate rulers of the country. The idea that the Maronites are superior to the Druze is clearly reflected in his writings. The Druze are a small, minor group in the country, he argues, and they are quite insignificant compared with the Maronite population. He draws a chart to demonstrate the numerical superiority of the Maronites.[21]

Matawilah	
All Christians	Druze mixed with 40,000 Christians

The Druze, in his opinion, are inferior in all respects. They are religiously confused and socially backward, generally lazy with no skills or trades other than tilling the ground. It is interesting to notice here how national images have become

[21] Niqula Murad, *Notice Historique sur l'Origine de la Nation Maronite et sur ses Rapports avec la France, sur la Nation Druze et sur les Diverses Populations du Mont Liban* (Paris: le Clère, 1844), p. 48.

reversed—it is now the Druze who are peasant laborers, rather than the Maronites. Except for a few of them who have intimate contacts with the Maronites, Murad goes on, the Druze can neither read nor write. Besides, they are dependent upon the Maronites, for "they cannot live without the Christians of the country who are familiar with all the occupations prevalent in Europe."[22]

Most significant yet in all Murad's ideas is that he brings to their natural conclusion the earlier Maronite writings. The bearing of Murad's argument is this: that being a national group with their own history, the Maronites should also form a state. The Maronites, he argues, have had their own government for a very long time and therefore should continue to have it. All the disturbances and events which have taken place in Lebanon to deprive the Lebanese of their natural government, the Imarah of the Shihabis, are illegal. As for the Druze of the Lebanon, he seems to relegate their place in the polity to a dependent minority.

The government which he was trying to convince the European powers to reestablish in Lebanon was an independent one and, he argued, should continue to be so. With almost complete disregard of the true history of the Imarah, Murad maintains that the Amirs of Lebanon were independent and did not have to pay tribute to the Ottomans except in recent years, and even then, not as a sign of political tutelage but as a means to ward off the dangers of the Ottomans' increasing aggressiveness. The history of the Imarah he views as a long struggle by the Amirs to keep their country's independence from the Ottomans. Like many of Murad's other theses, this one is without historical foundation but very suggestive regarding the Maronites' self-image at that time. Some of these views, like the identification of the Imarah with the whole of Mount Lebanon and the unity of Lebanon under one independent government, first of the Ma'nis and later of the

---

[22] *Ibid.*, p. 22.

Shihabis, remain the basis of the modern version of Lebanese nationalist ideology.[23]

Shayban al Khazin (1750-1820?)

So far we have discussed developments in Maronite ideology which reflected the political and national views of the clergy, and it would be important to show here how these views differ from those of the Maronite actors who were an integral part of the iqta' political system. If different ideologies were entertained by the actors and by the clergy, then the success of the clerical views would have serious implications for the position of the traditional actors, Druze as well as Maronites. We shall therefore take into account here the only two accounts by laymen which we have left to us and contrast them with the political views of the clergy. One of these two accounts was written by a muqati'ji, Shayban al Khazin, and the second by a Maronite notable descended from political and administrative assistants to the Imarah Hakims, namely Tannus al Shidiaq (1791-1861).

The first thing to draw the attention of the reader in Shayban's account[24] of the Imarah is that he differs in his approach from the other Maronite writers who have been discussed thus far. His major focus is on the political affairs of the Imarah as a secular government, whereas the religious orientation and Church history assume a secondary role in his mind. In a sense he can even be considered anti-clerical, for he is critical of the clergy and seems angry at the growing wealth of the monasteries and their waqfs, which, he claims, was one of the causes of the decline and impoverishment of his own house.

[23] For instance, Michel Chebli, *Une Histoire du Liban à l'Époque des Emirs (1635-1841)* (Beirut: Imprimerie Catholique, 1955); Hitti, *Lebanon in History*; Muzhir, *Tarikh Lubnan al 'Am*; Isma'il, *Histoire du Liban*. For the Lebanese nationalist party, the Kata'ib, see Jamil Jabr al Ashqar, *Al Harakah al Kata'ibiyyah* (Beirut: Matba'at al 'Ummal al Lubnaniyyah, n.d.).
[24] See Tarikh Shayban, published in *UT*, III.

The main object of his attention is the Imarah and its ruling houses, in whose sphere everything else revolves. Whatever events are discussed, they are viewed in terms of their relationship to the Imarah, including developments in Jibbat Bsharri and other Maronite regions. The major concern and struggle of the Imarah government, as he presents it, is to keep the influence and power of the Ottoman State at a distance from the political affairs of Mount Lebanon. In the Imarah the Druze, Maronites, and even Shi'i chiefs are all engaged in the political game indifferently of their religion. An actor is viewed with respect to his ability to influence events, not because he belongs to one or another particular community. Politics and government, in his view, are the exclusive privilege of the aristocracy, with the clergy and the people as subjects.

Shayban not only represented the secular outlook of Maronite chiefs in the Imarah of Jabal al Druze but also reflected the spirit of his day, that is, the beginning decline of the old order of the iqta' political system. In his discussion of his family and other ruling houses, he foresees the downfall of the iqta' system. Destruction, he warns, is on our threshold, and in many parts it has already taken place and soon will spread to the rest.[25]

Shayban's analysis of the system is a criticism of the institution of succession, in his iqta' house and in other houses which he thought shared the same conditions as his own, such as the Abillama's and the Himadahs. He expresses a belief in an iron law of governance, namely, that of single united leadership. All animate life, he says, from bees to flock animals to men, angels, and even the devils, must have a head to rule over their collectivities. Shayban's view of politics is one of a pluralistic polity like the muqati'ji system in Mount Lebanon. For one man to rule over all is impractical—not even Moses

---

[25] Shayban, *Tarikh*, p. 447.

with his divine source of authority could rule without dividing his men into small groups with a chief over each.[26] Thus
Shayban is satisfied with the division of power in Lebanon
between the Hakim and the muqati'ji houses, though he
grumbles at the increase in the Amir's power and the growing division and weakness in the muqati'ji houses.

It is clear from this that Shayban's political world-view differed greatly from that of the Maronite clergy. The focus of
his attention was not the Maronite community and its struggles for independence, but the lords of the Imarah and their
relations, thus depicting a secular political outlook. Another
strain in Shayban's thought was his keen awareness of decline—decline in the political power, wealth, and prestige of
the muqati'ji houses. The good order in his view was the
kind that prevailed in the early history of his family, when
political power was concentrated in the hands of a few
muqati'jis in each house, who could rule effectively and check
the ambitions of the Hakim.

Tannus al Shidiaq (1794-1861)

Our second secular writer is Tannus al Shidiaq. Al Shidiaq
was a descendant of a Maronite family whose members distinguished themselves in the service of the amirs of Lebanon.
He himself was occasionally employed by the Hakims and
the manasib in various political capacities. Although he was
educated by the clergy at 'Ayn Waraqah, Shidiaq did not lose
sight of his family's traditions in the Imarah. His attitude
toward the Imarah was like that of Shayban, different from
the clerical outlook dominant in northern Lebanon. More
than Shayban, he was concerned distinctly with a single political community, the Lebanese community, not with religious
groups or ruling houses. As Albert Hourani observes:

> His specific subject is Lebanon itself. He sees Lebanon not
> simply as a territory unified and ruled by one princely fam-

[26] *Ibid.*, p. 449.

ily, but as a whole structure of families each with its own sphere of authority, and all intricately balanced and connected with one another.[27]

Al Shidiaq has a coherent concept of Lebanon as a pluralistic society geographically and politically united. He looks upon geographic Lebanon in two ways: one as a national homeland, the other as the geographic limits of the Imarah. In the first case he refers to Phoenician Lebanon as consisting of the mountain range plus the coastal towns, a concept closer to present-day Lebanon than any other view current in his days. His second idea of Lebanon is one strictly corresponding to the boundaries of the Shihabi Imarah, particularly under Bashir II.

Historically, to a great extent al Shidiaq assimilates the Maronite world-view with the concept of the Imarah of Jabal al Druze. He traces the history of the Lebanese people to the time of the Phoenicians and calls the sea coast towns Phoenician towns. Thus he is the first to introduce into the Lebanese national ideology the "Phoenician" concept, which acquires stronger expression later in Lebanese nationalist ideas. He also draws from the clerical world-view, and though he does not mention Yusuf al Duwayhi among his sources, he actually copied from the latter's treatise and followed the list of Maronite chiefs name by name in the same order given by al Duwayhi. For him as for the others, the Maronites are the Maradah, an orthodox Catholic sect who lived in Mount Lebanon and fought the Muslim Arabs from the seventh century on. Similarly, he asserts that the Maronite community preserved its unity and continuity through the ages.

In spite of the fact that al Shidiaq presents a synthesis of the clerical and the secular outlooks here, his main concern is actually with the ruling class of the iqta' system. He devotes most of his two volume history to the news and activi-

[27] Bernard Lewis and P. M. Holt (eds.), *Historians of the Middle East* (London: Oxford University Press, 1962), p. 233.

ties of the iqta' lords and clearly views politics as the exclusive and natural privilege of the ruling houses regardless of their religious background.

Shidiaq's attitude is that of a "citizen" of the Imarah, a secular political outlook. He represents the Maronite who, without being unaware of his particular community's heritage, looks at that heritage as a part of a larger whole—Lebanon under the Imarah political order. It is this sense of national unity, perhaps, which prompts him to point out that Mount Lebanon is a holy place for both great religions, Christianity and Islam.[28]

Yusuf Karam (1823-1889)

Between 1841 and 1861 the Shihabi Imarah and the iqta' political system broke down. This period was also marked by a civil war between the Christians and the Druze. During this time of civil strife the Maronite world-view found its most vivid embodiment in the person of a young Maronite leader who emerged out of the wreckage of the old system. That leader was the national hero Yusuf Karam.

Karam was born of a family of small shaykhs in the Maronite stronghold of Ihdin in Jibbat Bsharri. His father, Butrus Karam, was the first in his family to hold the 'uhdah of Ihdin, and Shaykh Abi Khattar al 'Aynturini was Yusuf's grandfather on his mother's side. Like all the children of his generation, Yusuf received his education from the clergy in his village. His Arabic was excellent and he could speak and write in French. Early in his life he showed aptitude for leadership and desire for ruling. Before the death of his father he started to compete with his elder brother to inherit the 'uhdah of Ihdin. Yusuf also managed to attract attention to himself during the Qa'immaqamiyyah period in the whole region of Jubayl and Jibbat Bsharri. He was chosen by the people of these regions to represent them and seek redress for their con-

---

[28] Shidiaq, *Akhbar*, 1, 6.

dition from the government.[29] He was deeply involved in the civil war and Lebanese politics even after the settlement of 1861.

In 1860, Karam was the only Christian leader to emerge who really could offer something for the people. Unlike the war of 1841-1845, in 1860 the conflict was mostly religious, and the old ruling class of the Imarah including the Shihabis and the Abillama's showed no leadership at all. As a result, the advent of Karam aroused the Maronite population and he gained a considerable following. Witnessing his popularity, in 1860 the Ottoman government's conciliatory commission recognized Karam's leadership and appointed him as the Christian governor for a short period.

There are two points worth noting regarding this episode. One is that for the first time in Mount Lebanon a relatively young man of no high rank or position could aspire to the highest political office. In the second place, a new popular leadership had emerged in Mount Lebanon that had no precedent under the iqta' system. Karam's devoted following was made up of Maronite people all over the country, not just of the subjects of a muqati'ji. He was particularly attractive to the young generation of men who followed his leadership and command.[30] He himself seems to have believed that he was something of a new type of leader in the country and expressed this feeling when he wrote that he was leaving behind him "for my dear countrymen a secure way . . . putting ahead of their eyes new principles and new traditions to follow. . . ."[31]

The Lebanese civil war in 1860 had reached such magnitude that only a settlement imposed by the international powers could reestablish peace and order again. But for Karam, who was stimulated by popular acclaim, nothing less than becoming

[29] See Butrus Karam, *Qala'id al Murjan fi Tarikh Shamali Lubnan*, Vol. I (Beirut: Matba'at al Huda al Lubnaniyyah, 1929); Vol. II (Beirut: Matba'at al Ittihad, 1937), II, 221.

[30] Hattuni, *Nabdhah*, p. 365.

[31] Karam, *Qala'id*, II, 214, 217.

the national ruler of his country would do. When it became understood that under the Mutasarrifiyyah system no Lebanese would be allowed to occupy the office of governor, Karam turned against the new arrangement. For his opposition to the newly appointed Ottoman governor, he was sent into exile in Istanbul but soon returned to lead the forces of discontent among the Maronites and to fight the new governor. Again he lost and was sent once more into exile in Algeria; then he moved to France and other parts of Europe, seeking in vain permission to return home. He died an exile in Italy in 1889.

Karam personified the intractability of the Maronite nationalist goal: a Maronite Imarah in a country formed of various national and religious groups. He himself believed that non-Christians would be willing to accept a government under him, perhaps falsely encouraged by overtures from the Matawilah who stood united with the Maronites throughout the period of civil war. His extreme nationalism and determination to become Hakim in a situation thoroughly adverse to his aspirations brought defeat and frustration.

With respect to his ideas, Karam represented the line of thought laid down by Bishop Murad. However, in his later years and as a result of his observations of Europe, he started to draw from the current ideas of European thinkers and to meet, by a different route, the ideas of Ottoman liberals who were residing in European cities. Here, however, we shall be concerned only with his early ideas and how they came about as a result of the Lebanese intellectual climate.

First, Karam was very keen about the idea of authority drawn from the people. He justified his bid for power by the support the people gave him and by the ideas of Maronite nationality, namely the independence of Lebanon and the supremacy of the Maronites. In his expression of this national sentiment, Karam rose to the status of a full-fledged national leader, writing: "Every leader (*ra'is*), ecclesiastical or civil, is face to face with death every moment of his life, but the life and development of the people continuously marches with the ages and produces leaders all the time."[32] He had no doubt that he was the chosen leader of his people and strongly aspired to be at the head of the country. In the early part of his career the clergy, too, supported him, rejoiced at his successes, and felt sorry for his failures.[33]

In line with Murad and other Maronite writers discussed above, Karam believed in the historical independence of Lebanon. From the time of the Muslim conquest of Syria, he maintained, Lebanon was able to preserve its autonomous status. In the Ottoman period the Lebanese paid a fixed tribute as a means to keep the Ottomans from interfering in the internal affairs of their country. When he talked about Lebanon, he meant the whole of the Imarah, ignoring the historical division between north and south Lebanon. Karam regarded himself as the champion of this independence and on this ground criticized the constitution of 1860, which, he argued, violated this long-established Lebanese independence and deprived the Lebanese of their traditional way of defending themselves against Ottoman aggression. By this he meant, of course, their political system of self-rule, under a ruling family from among the Lebanese themselves.

Like Murad, Karam thought of the Imarah as a Christian government. In the Imarah which he aspired to head, the Druze would have been relegated to a secondary position. Although the Druze emerged as the military victors in the civil wars of 1841-1845 and 1860, Karam was not willing to concede to them any political prominence, nor even the right to rule the mixed areas where they had always had their home and political bastion. The political division of Lebanon, whether communal or geographic, was totally unacceptable to him, and he strongly repudiated the Qa'immaqamiyyah system which divided the country between 1843 and 1860. The

---

[32] *Ibid.*, I, 233.
[33] Hattuni, *Nabdhah*, p. 375. Also al Dibs, *Tarikh Suriyyah*, VIII, 726-733.

Lebanese could not afford to be divided, for if they were, they would not be able to withstand the oppression of their powerful neighbors whom they had successfully resisted throughout history. Lebanon is the land of refuge for the minorities of the East, he maintained, and by saying this he perhaps also included the Druze. But the Druze were a minority in Lebanon and to give them political power out of proportion to their numbers would have been dangerous and unfair. The Maronites occupied all important fields of public activity and constituted three-fourths of the entire population, he claimed; Druze political precedence would have been an unbearable anomaly. His unwillingness to admit that the Druze were still a strong power, stronger than their numbers suggested, was at the root of his frustrations as a political leader.

Karam represented the Maronite nationalism of the northern Lebanese in its strongest temper. Not only in his life career but also in his writings he formulated the idea of Maronite nationalism. The Maronites, he wrote, "are the sons of one homeland, and the members of one Church, and they have one nationality."[34]

To summarize and conclude, the study of writings by the Maronites shows that they were strongly aware of themselves as a distinct group with their own history, religion, and national character. They were religiously devoted to the territory of Lebanon with which their early struggles, victories, and defeats were identified. Though they viewed themselves as an independent people with their own rulers, no clear statement emerges in these early accounts as to the necessity of having a state of their own, though by implication they wished to have Maronite rulers. Not until the first part of the nineteenth century was such a claim made, interestingly enough at the time the clergy had become increasingly active and influential in the affairs of the Imarah. This view was held by Bishop Murad and, as we shall see later, by the

[34] Karam, *Qala'id*, ii, 212-213.

Church as a whole. In the early period as well as later on, the clergy were the bearers of Maronite ideology, and they were also the first to develop the nationalist theme of a Maronite State.

THE COMMUNICATION OF IDEAS

As we have seen from the preceding section, the clergy in Mount Lebanon were the bearers of the community's world-view and from them it was disseminated to the lay population over the centuries. It is perhaps this fact which gives the Maronite clergy what recent Maronite writers call "profoundly popular" and "essentially national" character.[35]

The role of the Maronite clergy in maintaining the faith, the identity, and the solidarity of the Maronites in the face of adverse conditions of both political and intellectual opposition in Ottoman Syria, cannot be underestimated. Threats to the continued cohesive sense of identity among the Maronites came from several sources. Hostility toward the Maronite Church was shown by ancient Churches in the Levant as well as by new missionaries from the West, Catholic and Protestant. In order to preserve its flock, the Maronite Church had to fight against all these outside influences, not only the Jacobites of Ibn al Qila'i's days, but even against Catholic missionaries, who claimed to aid the Church but aimed at converting the Maronites into the Latin order. The fight against Protestant missionaries in the nineteenth century was no less intense. Finally, the Maronites had to cope with the threat to their faith and lives from the dominant Muslim environment in the midst of which they lived.

How, then, was the Church able to undertake such a formidable task as preserving the community's faith and sense of unity? Second, how did the Maronite national ideology advocated by the clerical intellectuals become dominant during the first half of the nineteenth century? What means did the

[35] Aouad, *Droit Privé*, p. 7.

Church have to achieve successfully these goals? The answer is evident: the Church had an extensive organization and an active clergy. Let us turn then to a review of the various activities which emanated from the Church and contributed to the rise of communal consciousness among the Maronites.

In the preceding chapter concerning the reform of the Church organization, it was shown how, as a result of the population movement, the Church had to reorganize its structure to meet the people's need for pastoral care. Decentralization made it possible for distant villages to have their own priest no matter where they happened to be. We have also seen how decentralization brought better religious services to the Maronite flock when it became possible for the bishop to have a special diocese in which he could reside. Bishops were the best educated clerics in the Church and *ipso facto* the most learned men in the entire country. Gradually, over the years it became possible for them to raise the standards of religious life. Reform in the Church also improved the quality of service which the priest could offer and imposed better discipline among the people. These efforts left a marked effect upon the behavior of the Maronites in their relations with the clergy. The people's respect for the clergy and the influence of the latter upon them impressed many observers and travelers in the eighteenth and nineteenth centuries.[36]

The priest in the village was a symbol of the continuous presence of religion and the Church. He conducted mass and the personal ceremonies like marriages, baptisms, and funerals; he taught children the catechism, reading, and writing. He was of central importance in the handling of family problems and regularly acted as a consultant for his flock.[37] He also had authorization to settle marital cases and to waive the law

---

[36] Volney, *Travels Through Syria and Egypt*, II, 20-21, and Churchill, *Mount Lebanon*, III, 83. Also Henry Harris Jessup, *Fifty-Three Years in Syria*, 2 vols. (New York: Fleming H. Revell Co., n.d.), I, 158.

[37] Churchill, *Mount Lebanon*, III, 83.

in minor questions such as marriages between first cousins.[38] The central importance of the priest in the village was described by Colonel Charles Henry Churchill, who lived about ten years with the Lebanese. (Unfortunately, his anti-clerical and anti-Catholic prejudices strongly weighted his judgments.) Churchill wrote:

> In fact, in worldly as in spiritual, nay, in all family matters, amongst Maronites, the priest rules supreme. Constantly prowling about from house to house, not an incident, however trivial, escapes his vigilance. . . . No Maronite peasant dares to marry without getting the consent of the priest. . . . Custom and ancient usage have made it hereditary throughout the entire population; and, lest education might in the least degree dissipate the *prestige* which time has so thoroughly implanted in the breasts of these simple people, the very school-books which are placed in the hands of their children are carefully compiled so as to increase the natural awe with which they regard their spiritual guides.[39]

In 1844, for example, there were 1,205 of these priests in Mount Lebanon[40] among a population of about 250,000 Maronites, or a ratio of roughly one priest for every two hundred lay Maronites.

While the priests revived the faith of the people and gave them religious education, in their turn they received instruction and help from the archbishops of their dioceses. It was these bishops with their prestige and education who succeeded in converting to the Maronite faith the two top families in Lebanon, the Shihabis and the Abillama's, whose conversion added strength and prestige to the Maronite community in Mount Lebanon. Educated clerics like Bishop Yusuf Istfan (later patriarch), the priest Mikha'il Fadil (later bishop and then patriarch), and some others of the higher clerics of the

[38] Daghir, *Batarikat al Mawarinah*, p. 80.
[39] Churchill, *Mount Lebanon*, III, 83.
[40] Murad, *Notice Historique*, p. 46.

154

monk orders were responsible for the proselytization of the Shihabis and Abillama's.[41]

The Shihabis were originally Sunni Muslims, while the Abillama's were Druze. Both houses were of the rank of amirs. Proselytizing began with the Shihabis in the middle of the eighteenth century, and later during that period the Abillama's also started to change their faith, a process which continued with the latter throughout the nineteenth century. The first act of conversion took place in 1754 among the sons of the ruling line of Shihabis, the sons of Amir Mulhim. These conversions, it is sometimes suggested, were made for political reasons, that is, to meet the growing political importance of the Maronites. This seems a rather far-fetched explanation. During the middle of the eighteenth century the Maronites had no political power to compare with that of the Druze, who constituted the real ruling class. The Maronites of north Lebanon were also outside the Imarah at that time and were suffering from the oppressive rule of their Himadah overlords. The Shihabi who would most likely have been suspect of such a maneuver, Amir Yusuf Shihab, was not one of the converts;[42] and although he remained Muslim he received unswerving support from the Maronites, even against the Maronite Amir Bashir Shihab II.[43] Furthermore, the conversions of the Shihabis and the Abillama's were then politically harmful with respect to their relations with their subjects and the Ottoman government, and they maintained the utmost secrecy about their new faith and religious practices. However,

---

[41] Shidiaq, *Akhbar*, II, 31, 38, and Antonius Shibli, "Nabdhah Tarikhiyyah fi Tanassur Ba'd al Umara' al Lama'yyin," *MQ*, XXVIII (1930), 431-434; 'Isa Iskandar al Ma'luf and Salim al Dahdah, "Tanassur al Umara' al Shihabiyyin wa al Lama'yyin fi Lubnan," *MQ*, XVIII (1920), 543-552.

[42] Pierre Dib contends that Amir Yusuf was Maronite; see Pierre Dib, *L'Église Maronite*, Vol. II; *Les Maronites sous les Ottomans, Histoire Civile* (Beirut: Imprimerie Catholique, 1962), 170.

[43] We can now conclusively maintain that Bashir was a Christian who followed, off and on, the Maronite and Latin rites. PAB, Tiyyan papers, 227, 228; also France, Ministère des Affaires Étrangères, Correspondance Consulaire, Tripoli, 7 June 1807.

in the case of the Abillama's a possibility remains that their conversion was motivated by the personal relations which they maintained with the Shihabis.

It was the intellectual and educational advancement of the Maronite clergy that was the positive factor in these conversions, for the men who succeeded in winning the new believers had a Western education, the best in Lebanon. Two other indirect reasons may help account for their success. First was the fact that Lebanon was politically autonomous and its people enjoyed religious liberty; and second, the Shihabis' religious isolation from the Sunni Muslim world, in the midst of Maronites and Druze, may have made it easier for them to change religion.

The monks also played an important role in the rehabilitation of religious life in the Maronite community. Every monastery with its monks proved to be an active religious center in the community. They were particularly important in distant and difficult places in the mixed areas which the priests usually avoided. A look at the areas where they carried out religious services shows their concentration in the religiously mixed regions, a fact which indicates the monks' missionary importance. In mixed areas of al Shuf and Jazzin they served in fifty-five places, whereas in Kisrwan, the region with the most homogeneous and numerous Maronite population, they served in only eleven places. In another mixed area, al Matn, monks were active in twenty-five localities, and in twenty-six in Bilad Jubayl and al Batrun, districts where the Maronite population was mixed with Matawilah and once ruled by them. In many of these centers where they carried out their mission, the population had been quite ignorant about the teachings of their religion before the monks' arrival.[44]

The monks were popular among the people. They also contributed in their own right to the migration movement,

[44] Regarding the cases of Qartaba and Wadi Shahrur, see Bulaybil, *TRLM*, LII, 551.

for the peasants went to live in the vicinity of the monks' monasteries because of the security and work which the latter provided.[45] Another attraction which the monks possessed lay in the linguistic factor, for they stressed Arabic in their services, whereas the priests leaned heavily on Syriac liturgies and prayers. The use of Arabic made the monks more intelligible to the peasants than was the regular priest, and consequently more popular. The monks made a major contribution to the Church in introducing the Arabic language into its mass and other services, and the founders of the Lebanese Order, like Qar'ali and Jirmanus Farhat, were pioneers in the advancement of the Arabic language.

There were two other ways by which the Church hierarchy and the orders of monks stimulated religious life among the people and increased clerical influence: papal indulgences and religious societies. The popes and the Maronite patriarchs bestowed a number of indulgences on churches and monasteries. Though the regular Church hierarchy benefited from these indulgences and from special powers to absolve sinners, it was the Lebanese Order which was granted the larger number of indulgences for its churches and places of worship. In 1734 the pope bestowed for the first time a number of indulgences on the Lebanese Order; then he expanded them in 1775, 1779, and 1786. Aside from the indulgences, special powers of redemption were conferred on eleven of the Order's churches in 1779.

The indulgences, the monks' asceticism, and their use of the Arabic language made them very popular among the peasant population of Lebanon, who flocked to their churches and monasteries from distant places. Once when the Church prelates tried to limit their activities because they encroached on the regular organization, the monks suspended all their activi-

---

[45] See Antonius Shibli, "Al Zira'ah wa al Sina'ah bayn al Ruhban," *MQ*, xxxi (1933), 863-864. This applies to Melkite Catholic monasteries too, like the monastery of Mar Ilias in Zahlah; see Munayyar, *KTS*, L, 199, n. 1.

ties and refused to offer any religious services to the people for several days, to demonstrate to the higher clergy the extent of their popular support. The excitement of the people forced the Church to rescind its orders,[46] thus yielding to the monks in the contest of strength.

Religious Societies

The Church and the monks also founded religious societies for the lay population, the most important of which were the following: Sharikat al Habal Bila Danas,[47] Sharikat al Wardiyyah, Sharikat al Qiddisin, Jam'iyat al Mursalin al Injiliyin, and other smaller ones. Sharikat al Qiddisin was founded in 1725 and al Wardiyyah around the same period; the latter was put under the jurisdiction of the patriarch in 1732.[48] Both of these societies were popular. The society of al Mursalin al Injiliyin was founded in 1840 as a means to counteract the Protestant missions in Lebanon and was entrusted to three clerics who were graduates of 'Ayn Waraqah. The three clerics, Yusuf al Rizzi, Yuhanna al Sayigh al Islambuly, and Yusuf 'Atiyah, were well known for their good education and skill in oratory. The Wardiyyah and the Mursalin al Injiliyin were directed by the patriarch and his bishops while the others were mainly directed by the monks, who also took an active part in the first-mentioned two societies. But though these associations were supervised and guided by the clergy, with the exception of al Mursalin they were under the direct leadership of lay people. The minutes of one chapter of the Society of al Habal Bila Danas in the village of Zuq Mikha'il shows that these societies were highly organized, with regular meetings, officers, and records.[49]

[46] Bulaybil, "Nabdhah Tarikhiyyah," p. 296.

[47] A comprehensive account of the organization and condition of this fraternity is available in Yusuf al Dibs (ed.), *Kitab Qawanin Akhawiyyat al Habal Bila Danas* (Ihdin, Lebanon: al Matba'at al Lubnaniyyah, 1865).

[48] Ghibra'il, *Tarikh al Kanisah*, II, 574-575; see the text of the papal message in this regard.

[49] Manuscript of the minutes, read with the permission of its owner, Father John Naffa' of the Church of Our Lady of Lebanon, Chicago.

No comprehensive account can be given of the membership of these societies or their size. However, some figures are available and may give an idea of the relative size of membership. For instance, in 1727 the Lebanese monks were able to recruit in al Qati' (see Fig. 1) 1,200 members for the Society of al Wardiyyah in fifteen days.[50] The chapter of the Society of al Habal Bila Danas in the village of Zuq Mikha'il in 1838 had forty members.[51] Members were common folk, and some came from the upper classes.[52] Amir Haydar Abillama' himself was known as the Father of al Wardiyyah.[53]

The Printing Press

In addition to all these activities, the Church controlled the printing presses and the schools. The press up to the late nineteenth century was the exclusive possession of the clergy, whether Maronite or Protestant. The Maronites had their first printing press in Lebanon in 1610 and later acquired two more presses, those of Mar Musa al Habashi and Tamish; the Melkite Catholics acquired theirs in 1733, and the Melkite Orthodox in 1751.[54] Still, printing facilities were very limited, and the Maronites themselves depended on Rome more than on their own printing presses. For instance, in 1830 the clergy had printed in Rome 1,750 copies of a liturgy book.[55] Printing output increased in the second part of the eighteenth century and considerably more so in the first part of the nineteenth.

The books printed in these presses were almost all religious, like the Psalms (which also served as a reading text in schools), prayer books, the Gospel and Epistles, and certain

[50] Bulaybil, "Nabdhab Tarikhiyyah," p. 296.
[51] Naffa' manuscript.
[52] *PAB*, Hubaysh papers, 3213. Haydar, *Tarikh Ahmad Basha al Jazzar*, p. 240, n. 1.
[53] Kerr, *Lebanon in the Last Years of Feudalism . . .* , p. 36.
[54] See Hitti, *Lebanon in History*, 456-457, and Lewis Shaykho, "Usul Fan al Tiba'ah," *MQ*, iii (1900), 78-79ff.
[55] See Bulaybil, *TRLM*, liii, 200, and Bulaybil, "Nabdhah Tarikhiyyah," *MQ*, li, 309-310.

books of the Bible.[56] The influence of the press around the end of the eighteenth century, though still limited, sufficiently impressed Volney to write that among the Christians

> this influence of the press is so efficacious, that the establishment of Mar Hanna alone, imperfect as it is, has already produced a sensible difference among the Christians. The art of reading and writing, and even a sort of information, are more common among them at present, than they were thirty years ago.[57]

Volney also observed:

> Unfortunately their output [the presses] has been of that kind, which long retarded the progress of improvement, and excited innumerable discords in Europe. For bibles and religious books being the first which proceed from the press, the general attention was turned towards theological discussion whence resulted a fermentation which was the source of schism of England and Germany, and the unhappy political troubles of France.[58]

His presentiment of the effect of the propagation of religious books came true half a century later.

School System

No less effective was the school system in spreading Maronite ideology and clerical influence, for the school system was entirely clerical and almost all Maronite. Great credit should be given to the Holy See for spreading education among the Maronites. As can be recalled from the previous chapters, the Maronite College at Rome was opened as early as 1584 and continued until it was closed in 1799. Though there was some tradition of literacy in Karshuni and Syriac

---

[56] *Ibid.*, also Bulaybil, *TRLM*, LII, 563-564. Volney, *Travels Through Syria and Egypt*, II, 196-199.
[57] *Ibid.*, p. 454.
[58] *Ibid.*

among the Maronites before this period, education and schools did not go back to an earlier period.[59]

The first record we have of a Maronite school is that of Huqa in Jibbat Bsharri, opened by Patriarch Yuhanna Makhluf in 1624.[60] In 1670, Patriarch Duwayhi moved the school from Huqa to Qannubin where he put the school under his direct supervision and participated in the teaching.[61] The clerics who studied in Rome and returned to Lebanon made a large contribution to the spread of schools and the religious mission in Mount Lebanon during the seventeenth and eighteenth centuries, as we learn from the biographical account of these students written by Patriarch Duwayhi and from later accounts.[62] After his return from Rome, Duwayhi himself opened a school in his village, Ihdin. Another seventeenth-century Maronite school was that of Zgharta, also in Jibbat Bsharri, opened by a graduate of the Maronite College who later turned it over to the Jesuits. Two years after the Jesuit order was dissolved in 1773, the school returned to the bishop of Ihdin under whom it continued its work until the nineteenth century.[63] It is not known how many students these seventeenth-century schools generally had, though it is likely that much depended on the teacher who happened to be in charge. When Istfan al Duwayhi was running the school of Qannubin, about sixty students were in attendance, quite a large number for that time and place.[64]

Of the seventeenth-century schools, only the Zgharta school continued in operation through the nineteenth century. Other schools, however, were started in the eighteenth century, and

[59] In 1578, Battista wrote that those who could read and write among the Maronites could be counted on the fingers. See Shaykho, "Al Ta'ifah al Maruniyyah," *MQ*, xviii, 679.

[60] Duwayhi, *TA*, pp. 320, 322.

[61] 'Aynturini, *MTL*, xlvii, 28.

[62] See Shaykho, "Al Ta'ifah al Maruniyyah," *MQ*, xix, 141-146, 293-302, 625-630.

[63] Regarding the school of Zgharta, see 'Aynturini, *MTL*, xlvii, 30; also Mas'ad and Khazin, *UT*, i, 472-525.

[64] 'Aynturini, *MTL*, xlvii, 28.

some of the best go back to this period, like 'Ayn Waraqah (1789)[65] and that of 'Ayntura. Eight other lesser schools were opened by the clergy in the second part of the eighteenth century in Jibbat Bsharri, Kisrwan, and the mixed areas. In the early years of the nineteenth century, additional schools were opened of which the most important were Kfarhay (1811), Kfayfan (1808), both in Bilad al Batrun; and al Rumiyyah (1818), Mar 'Abda Harhariya (1830), and Rayfun (1832) in Kisrwan. About twenty-seven other smaller schools were opened in various places during the eighteenth and nineteenth centuries. In addition to this, in eight monasteries the monks taught classes of children from neighboring villages.

As for the Catholic missionaries, the Jesuits opened and directed the schools of Bikfayya (1833) and Ghazir in 1843, and two smaller schools in Beirut and Zahlah. The schools of Zgharta and 'Ayntura were directed by both the missionaries and the Maronite clergy alternately.

The clergy bore almost all the burden of the school system. While the Lebanese Order (native) was responsible for the opening of seventeen schools and the Aleppine Order for six, the rest were opened and directed by the Church hierarchy. The major schools like 'Ayn Waraqah, Mar 'Abda Harhariya, Rumiyyah, and Rayfun were directly under the supervision of the patriarch. The clergy were also aided in their educational enterprise by a few members of the Maronite aristocracy, who sometimes contributed land for schools. Greater support, however, came from the villagers themselves, who would invite the clerics, especially the monks of the Lebanese Order, to open schools in their villages. The peasants contributed land and property usually sufficient for the maintenance of a teacher, while the monks would provide the teacher and in turn gain the property for their establishment. Also many of

[65] See Khayrallah Istfan, *Zubdat al Bayan aw Khulasat Tarikh umm Madaris Suriyyah wa Lubnan: 'Ayn Waraqah* (New York: Syrian-American Press, 1923). Although it was started in 1789, the college was not put into operation until 1797 by the joint efforts of Bishop Yusuf Istfan and Patriarch Yusuf Tiyyan.

the clerics, bishops, and priests bequeathed their property and worldly acquisitions to the benefit of schools or for the opening of new ones, as is clear from the documents left from that period.

With the exception of the few best schools, all the rest were merely concerned with teaching the three R's and the Church catechism. At 'Ayn Waraqah, Mar 'Abda, Rumiyyah, Kfarhay, and Kfayfan, subjects ranging from calligraphy to literature, logic, philosophy, theology, and European and oriental languages were taught. However, there was no vocation in Lebanon for those who learned these more advanced subjects other than the clerical profession. Thus it was in that profession that the fruits of this higher education were felt most. Almost all the higher clergy who played an important part in the political life of Lebanon in the first half of the nineteenth century were either graduates of the Maronite College of Rome, like Patriarch Tiyyan, or of 'Ayn Waraqah, while the following were some of the politically important clerics who graduated from that college: Bishops Butrus al Bustani, Yusuf Rizq, Yusuf Ja'ja', and Niqula Murad; and Patriarchs Yusuf Hubaysh, Yusuf al Khazin, and Bulus Mas'ad. Those who did not want to join the clergy had virtually no opportunity to use their educational advantages. To find new scopes and opportunities which their education merited, they had to make a break with their culture, as is borne out by the case of As'ad al Shidiaq, and Butrus al Bustani,[66] who adopted Protestantism.

Literacy and arithmetic were all the education that the average Lebanese really needed during the Imarah period. It was the knowledge of reading, writing, and arithmetic that raised some Maronites to positions of political importance as aides and secretaries to the Hakim and sometimes to the Ottoman Valis in Syria. It was these skills, too, especially arithmetic, which were needed by the people in their everyday life. In

---

[66] Not to be confused with Archbishop Butrus al Bustani.

a book left by a Maronite shaykh to his son, the writer ends every page with the same advice: the boy should give his undivided attention to arithmetic and to his mulberry trees.[67] Calligraphy was particularly important and much desired, because of the value put on it by the Amir and the aristocracy, who always needed scribes. Faris al Shidiaq, in his criticism of clerical education, became particularly annoyed over the emphasis put on calligraphy and the ruler who encouraged the people's interest in it. Noting this excessive interest, he wrote, "The people used to prefer good calligraphy to all the other manual arts. They considered him who excelled in it above his equals in virtue."[68] But in spite of Shidiaq's criticism, education in literacy was useful to the people, and the education provided in the superior Maronite schools of Lebanon was the best available.

There is no clear account available which indicates the number of students in these schools during this period. However, one can assume that not many had sixty students at one time like Duwayhi's school.[69] Usually, a very small number of young boys went to school on a regular basis. For instance, 'Ayntura had only eight students in 1736,[70] and in 1858 the number had increased to about a hundred.[71] Some of these schools provided scholarships for a small number of students, which took care of their living expenses and education; the school of Kfarhay, for example, provided for twelve students.[72] Bishop Niqula Murad tells us that in 1844 each of the four main schools in Lebanon had about twenty-five students.[73] Hattuni's estimate of the total number of students in Kisrwan

---

[67] Shibli, "Al Athar al Matwiyyah," *MQ*, LIV, 526, 531, 652.

[68] Faris al Shidiaq, *Kitab al Saq 'ala al Saq*, p. 17.

[69] Dayr Sayidat al Luwayzah is said to have had at one time eighty students; see Ghalib, "Tagrir al Sayyid . . . ," *MQ*, XXVIII, 579, n. 2 through to p. 580.

[70] *Ibid.*, p. 578.

[71] M. H. "Sahifah min Tarikh Lubnan fi al Qarn al Tasi' 'Ashar," *MQ*, XXI (1923), 828.

[72] Daghir, *Lubnan*, p. 160.

[73] Murad, *Notice Historique*, p. 18.

at the time he wrote his book in the 1880's was about four hundred.[74] Another indication of the number of those who went to school can be gathered from the number of those who graduated. We are told, for instance, that about fifty students graduated from 'Ayn Waraqah, between 1789 and 1818.[75] Between 1808 and 1874, 260 students graduated from Kfayfan.[76] These figures clearly show the limited number of persons these schools could teach.

Nonetheless, for a small mountain country of the Asian-Arab part of the Ottoman Empire, these achievements by the Maronite Church were still extraordinary. They instilled in the people a consciousness of themselves as a community and strengthened their ties with the Church organization through missionary work, religious organization, religious societies, and education.

We can now sum up the three significant developments within the Church which contributed to the rise of Maronite feeling in the early nineteenth century. First, the Church was emancipated from its subservience to the iqta' houses. Second, the bureaucratic structure of the Church was reformed, which enabled it to control the means of its own administration and to carry out extensive activities in large areas covering all of Mount Lebanon. Finally, progress in the education of the clergy had its effect on the capacity of Churchmen for leadership and in their emergence as the creators and promoters of Maronite national ideology.

In reviewing the development of Maronite ideology from early times to the nineteenth century, we have observed how Maronite communal ideas gradually came to define the community's revolutionary attitude toward the iqta' system. The outlook of the clergy, it was seen, differed basically from that of the secular writers of the ruling class, and their ideas chal-

[74] Hattuni, *Nabdhah*, p. 27.
[75] Duwayhi, *TTM*, p. 266.
[76] Butrus Sarah, "Dayr Kfayfan," *MQ*, xxvi (1928), 891.

lenged the iqta' system in its entirety. It challenged the system's principle of legitimacy, the position of the traditional actors, and the institutions governing authority relationships. Identification with the national community became the new source of legitimate authority. Political cohesion and integration no longer depended on kinship ties, status, and personal loyalty to the iqta' houses, but on a communal basis. The source of legitimate authority in the communal system was the nation—the symbol of solidarity and collective sentiments of a historic ethnic group. The leaders' claims to positions of authority in such a system rested on their active sharing in the national sentiment and values. Moreover, the right to leadership was no longer granted freely and exclusively to the hereditary actors; on the contrary, these were challenged by a rising generation of peasant leaders. In the following chapters, we shall see how these principles became the political goals of rebellious Maronites who were trying to reorganize the political institutions of the Imarah on the communal basis of Maronite ideology.

The ability of the Church to transmit new ideas among the people was enhanced by its control of the major means of communication in Mount Lebanon. The presence of the clergy in every village and town, their contacts with the people in churches, at feasts, and on social occasions, were conspicuous. In addition, the clergy's contact with the people through the Maronite school system, the only system of education in the country, and through religious societies, had definite effect upon the spread of new ideas. Traditional actors in the iqta' system could not counter these activities because their traditional role did not extend to undertaking tasks of this kind, and because they lacked education and an educated corps of people, similar to the clergy, to carry out a counterpropaganda campaign. Their resort to force in the last stages of the conflict was conclusive evidence of their inability to cope with the new situation through similar means.

CHAPTER VII

The Office of Mudabbir

THE hereditary chiefs in the iqta' system of government, as we have seen from Chapter III, exercised their political functions directly and in person without the aid of administrative staff. The Hakim, however, had a small number of assistants and servants to help him carry out his daily administrative work. Of these, the only office to which important administrative and political authority was delegated was the mudabbir, the Hakim's secretary. The relations which, over time, developed between the mudabbirs and the manasib reflected certain basic conflicts in the system, between delegated and constituted authority. In the following chapter we shall examine these relations with a view to determining the extent to which conflict contributed to instability and change in the system.

The difference between delegated and constituted authority should first be made clear. Constituted authority is defined in terms of the principle of legitimacy which obtains in a society, and those actors whose rights to command are drawn from this principle are the holders of constituted authority. A person with delegated authority, on the other hand, is one who draws his power from the legitimate actors, not directly from the society's principle of legitimacy. Thus the source of authority, rather than functional differentiation, is considered here the main distinction between the two types of authority.

The authority which the mudabbir enjoyed in the Imarah was delegated to him by the Hakim and he had no independent claim to authority by himself. As an aid to the Hakim, the mudabbir naturally acquired great influence with the manasib by virtue of his strategic position in the system. Therefore, as we shall see, the role played by the mudabbir in the politics of Mount Lebanon is of considerable significance in our study.

The office of mudabbir went back to the early Ma'ni period and was also known in the Ottoman vilayets. The word "mudabbir," meaning literally "manager," was a special Lebanese term for what was more commonly known as *kakhya* or *kikhya*, both of which are corruptions of the Turkish *ketkhuda*.[1] Actually "mudabbir" and "kakhya" were interchangeable terms in Lebanese usage. In the Ottoman vilayets, the *ketkhuda* was the Vali's chief administrator.[2] Military and financial affairs did not fall within his jurisdiction, according to Gibb and Bowen.[3] His actual powers could be large or small according to his personal ability.

Under the Imarah, the office varied from time to time in its functions, since it was never clearly defined. The mudabbir was an administrative factotum who acted as scribe, financial controller, political advisor, regular administrator, and military commander.[4] All these functions are known to have been centered in the hands of mudabbirs at one time or another. By the middle of the eighteenth century the office of mudabbir was increasingly confined to higher matters of state, while other officers like the scribes and financial controllers were left in charge of writing and handling accounts. Although the mudabbir was always a key figure in the administration, his political importance became increasingly evident during the second part of the eighteenth century.

The term "administration," as it will be used here, refers to the management of the Hakim's work; in other words, administrators were the Amir's household officials. Under the Imarah, as in the feudal system in Europe, there was no bu-

---

[1] Gibb and Bowen, *Islamic Society*, I, Part I, 201.

[2] Asad Jibrail Rustum, "Syria under Mehemet Ali" (unpublished Ph.D. dissertation, Department of Oriental Languages and Literatures, University of Chicago, 1923), pp. 76-77. Also Edward William Lane, *The Manners and Customs of the Modern Egyptians* (London: Everyman's Library, J. M. Dent & Sons Ltd., 1954), p. 114. Also Ibrahim al 'Awrah, *Tarikh Wilayat Sulayman Basha al 'Adil*, ed. Qustantin al Basha (Sayda, Lebanon: Matba'at Dayr al Mukhallis, 1936), pp. 266 and n. 1.

[3] *Islamic Society*, I, 201.

[4] Muzhir, *Tarikh Lubnan al 'Am*, I, 357, 361.

reaucratic organization for the execution of policy. Officers appointed by the Hakim, like the qadi and the mudabbir, were, strictly speaking, servants of the Amir assisting him in carrying out his business. The powers they enjoyed were delegated to them by the Hakim himself. Since daily government was discharged by the muqati'jis, no administrative apparatus was necessary; nor would the manasib have permitted any such system to develop.

Our knowledge of the Amir's administration during the early part of the Shihabi Imarah is sparse and can only be inferred from scattered references. Even the office of mudabbir, as to its duties and limitations, was not discussed in the chronicles.[5] In view of the great importance of the office for the political history of the Imarah, it is curious that the mudabbir has as yet received hardly any attention in studies on the history of Lebanon.

THE OFFICE OF THE MUDABBIR AND THE IQTA' SYSTEM

There are two aspects to our examination of the role of the mudabbir, which overlap to a considerable extent. The first has to do with one of the ethnic communities living under the iqta' system, the Maronites, from whom mudabbirs were recruited; and the other relates to the strains in the itqa' political institutions resulting from the mudabbirs' actions. Since, therefore, the mudabbirs were Maronites, and the Maronites the group who eventually challenged the iqta' system, we must look at the effects of the office of mudabbir upon both the Maronite community and its political fortunes, and the iqta' political system per se.

The integration of the Maronite people into the Imarah of Jabal al Shuf at the beginning of the seventeenth century started because of the particular services which the Maronites

---

[5] The only account we have in some detail pertains to the administrative staff of Amir Bashir II during the last decade of his rule. See Rustum Baz, *Mudhakkirat Rustum Baz*, ed. Fu'ad Afram al Bustani (Beirut: Manshurat al Jami'ah al Lubnaniyyah, 1955).

could offer the Druze. These were mainly of two kinds: as laborers who cultivated the land, and as scribes who handled the accounts and business of the ruling families. As they settled in Jabal al Druze, these Maronites offered their services and received protection as subjects. The fact that they were accepted as subjects and treated on an equal basis with the Druze and Muslim communities meant that the Maronites could acquire land as property owners and share in political duties like everyone else.

The most striking development which helped the Maronites become an integral part of the Imarah political system came as a result of the Shihabi Hakims' reliance on Maronite scribes as mudabbirs, and the eventual entrance of those Maronites into the ruling class. After some years of distinguished service as mudabbirs, a number of Maronite individuals were enfeoffed by the Hakim and made hereditary muqati'jis on a par with the rest of the muqati'jis. While it is not true that all Maronites who served as mudabbirs to the Hakim were raised to the ruling class, it is a fact that all those Maronite houses who were of the manasib achieved their status after service as mudabbirs. The history of Maronite muqati'ji houses confirms this statement. The first Maronite muqati'ji houses, the Khazins and the Hubayshes, were employed as scribes and mudabbirs by the Ma'nis and were then enfeoffed by them after decades of service. The rest, like the Khuris, the Dahdahs, and the Dahirs, were raised to the rank of muqati'ji for the same reasons by the Shihabi Hakims during the eighteenth century.[6]

There was, however, another category of Maronite shaykhs who did not acquire their muqati'ji rank through administrative service, namely the shaykhs of Jibbat Bsharri and Bilad al Batrun. These were the original village shaykhs who were

---

[6] The Khuris may have been an exception since they had received favors from the Shihabis in 1711 before they were made mudabbirs. However, it is not clear what the political significance of those favors was, and there is reason to doubt that the Khuris rose to the muqati'ji rank at that period.

confirmed in their positions after Jibbat Bsharri was incorporated into the Shihabi domain. They never really enjoyed full privileges and power in the Imarah of Jabal al Druze and, unlike the muqati'jis of Jabal al Shuf and Kisrwan, could be removed by the Hakim.

Under the Shihabis the Maronites practically held a monopoly over the office of mudabbir and other administrative jobs. Not until the last decade of the eighteenth century, when the struggle started between Amir Bashir II and Amir Yusuf (and his sons after him), were the Druze brought in. At the start of his career as Hakim, Bashir began to employ Druze as mudabbirs. The reason for his policy of recruiting individuals from the Druze community was related to the fact that he was almost entirely dependent on the Druze manasib, particularly the Jumblats, for his accession to the office. While the Druze seem to have had no fears or objections to the Maronites' hold on the office before the last two decades of the eighteenth century,[7] their attitude began to change as they saw their political prerogatives increasingly threatened by the growing powers of the mudabbirs. Nonetheless, the tenure of the Druze mudabbirs during the first few years of Bashir's rule proved to be too short to amount to anything politically.[8]

There were good reasons why the Hakims, particularly the Shihabis, chose their mudabbirs and administrative officers from the Maronite community and not the Druze. Political considerations came first. The most powerful muqati'jis under the Shihabi Imarah were Druze, and as we already know, the muqati'jis were fairly independent of the Hakim. Their political interest lay in maintaining such measures of independence as they enjoyed and in keeping constant vigilance against possible extension of the Amir's powers. They were thus pre-

---

[7] Shayban, *Tarikh*, p. 506.

[8] Regarding their short period of service, see Haydar, *Lubnan*, pp. 149, 181, 194, 195; also Salim Khattar al Dahdah, "Al Amir Bashir al Shihabi al Kabir al Ma'ruf bi al Malti," *MQ*, XXII (1924), 571.

cluded from being political advisors or servants to the Amir, since they were not in a position to offer him free and un-prejudiced advice or to be personally attached to him. The Amir needed individuals who would owe all their political prestige to him and would be personally loyal. The Maronites could fulfill these conditions. They were loyal subjects whose well-being depended on the protection and freedom given them under the Imarah, and very few among them enjoyed independence similar to that of the Druze muqati'jis. Being a part of the system, the Maronites were also well informed about the political life and institutions of the country.

Another factor which favored the Maronites in being se-lected for administrative posts was their literacy. We have already seen how the advancement of education was spear-headed by the Church as early as the seventeenth century. The most valuable asset for a person in acquiring an admin-istrative job was good calligraphy.[9] The Hakim, as well as the muqati'jis, needed scribes to write down accounts and handle correspondence. Catholics, Jews, and Copts fulfilled these functions for the Valis in Syria and Egypt. Muhammad 'Ali, for instance, sent to Syria for some Melkite Catholics who excelled in calligraphy and gave them lucrative positions in his administration.[10] The traveler Volney noticed the politi-cal significance of the education provided by the clerical schools in Mount Lebanon:

> The most valuable advantage that has resulted from these apostolical labours is that the art of writing has become more common among the Maronites, and rendered them, in this country, what the Copts are in Egypt; I mean, they are in possession of all the posts of writers, intendants, and kiayas [kakhyas] among the Turks [i.e., Muslims] and

[9] See for instance 'Aynturini, *MTL*, xlvi, 445; Mashaqah, *al Jawab*, p. 28. On the importance of calligraphy, see Shibli, "Al Athar al Matwiyyah," *MQ*, liv, 652.
[10] Rustum, "Syria Under Mehemet Ali," pp. 75, 76.

especially of those among their allies and neighbours, the Druze.[11]

There may have been other reasons for the fact that the Maronites were favored for offices in the administration, but these seem the most pertinent. However, conditions peculiar to Mount Lebanon made the office of mudabbir more important politically for the Maronites than was true for other Christians serving in the same administrative capacity under Ottoman Valis in Syria and Egypt. Under the Imarah a secular spirit pervaded in the political practices, and therefore the Maronites were not in a precarious position because of their religion. In contrast to this, in the cities where they, and other Christians, worked for Valis, no sooner would they have made some progress than they would be removed and persecuted by their employers.[12] Another contributing factor, not found outside the Imarah, was the fact that the Maronites were part of the political life and government of the Lebanon, unlike Christians in the other parts of the Ottoman Empire, who were dhimmah people. Thus only in Mount Lebanon was it possible for the Maronites to use administrative office to augment the political power of their community.

Up to the last few decades of the eighteenth century, the effect of recruiting mudabbirs from among the Maronites was to integrate the community more fully into the Imarah political system. But the increase in political power which this office brought the community made political conflict inevitable between the Maronites and the Druze manasib who were the main custodians of power in the system. In order to understand this aspect clearly, we shall look first at the career of certain Maronite mudabbirs who rose to positions of

[11] Volney, *Travels Through Syria and Egypt*, II, 32. In the same vein see Tannus al Shidiaq, *Akhbar*, I, 102, and Faris al Shidiaq, *Al Saq 'ala al Saq*, p. 17.

[12] Regarding the fate of these individuals see Duwayhi, *TA*, pp. 348-350, and Mas'ad and Khazin, *UT*, III, 55. Also Shayban, *Tarikh*, 391, 393-394, and 'Aynturini, *MTL*, XLVI, 445-446, and Tannus al Shidiaq, *Akhbar*, I, 102.

great influence, and then examine their changing relations with the manasib and the consequences for the iqta' institutions.

THE MUDABBIR SHAYKH SA'D AL KHURY (1722-1786)

Shaykh Sa'd al Khury was the first mudabbir to rise to a position of prominence under the Shihabis. When Amir Mulhim Shihab stepped down as the Hakim of Mount Lebanon, his two sons were still children. The elder, Muhammad, was physically defective, and the next, Yusuf, was only about six or seven years old. In 1761, Amir Mulhim died, but after he had appointed a Maronite shaykh from the village of Rishmayya in al Shuf, Shaykh Sa'd al Khury, as a guardian for his sons. The exact relationship of Shaykh Sa'd to Amir Mulhim is not made clear in available sources; we do know, however, that the shaykh tutored the Amir's sons.[13]

Amir Yusuf was in the direct line of succession, a fact not lost upon Shaykh Sa'd, a man of great foresight. At the time Sa'd was appointed guardian, his ward, Amir Yusuf, was only about fourteen years old. Shaykh Sa'd kept close watch over political events in the Imarah and tried to prepare his ward to assume power if and when an opportunity presented itself. In 1763 such an opportunity appeared when the Maronites of northern Lebanon, after expelling the Himadah lords from their country, were seeking to have a Shihabi become their ruler. As we saw in the second chapter, the current Shihabi Hakim did not respond very favorably to the Maronites of Jibbat Bsharri, and Sa'd tried to turn this opportunity to the advantage of his ward. He arranged for support and funds from the Maronites and, with the backing of some of the manasib, was able to secure the investiture for Amir Yusuf to be the Hakim over northern Lebanon. This was the first step which seven years later led to the uniting of north and south Lebanon under Amir Yusuf.

[13] Haydar, *Lubnan*, p. 60.

Sa'd was destined to become one of the most important mudabbirs of the Imarah. By virtue of his personal relationship with Amir Yusuf, he enjoyed wide powers and used them very effectively. The Amir relied on Sa'd's advice and leadership almost completely, and it was by his mudabbir's help that he reached the height of power.[14] Amir Yusuf never disagreed with Sa'd on anything, wrote Amir Haydar Shihab, and Shaykh Sa'd made the Amir do whatever he wished.[15] Another contemporary chronicler testified to the same effect:

> ... all the moves and acts of Amir Yusuf were made with the advice and policy decisions of Shaykh Sa'd al Khury, and can only nominally be attributed to the Amir. For the Amir was not skilled in the management of [public] affairs, whereas Shaykh Sa'd was a wise man and enjoyed great insight in [public] matters.[16]

As can be concluded from these comments, Shaykh Sa'd was not a behind-the-scenes man but very much in the public eye. He not only advised the Amir in the privacy of his palace but also handled relations with the manasib in matters of government and settlement of disputes.[17] Moreover, he performed the function of commander of the Amir's forces. For instance, when the Himadahs, former overlords of Jubayl, tried to make a comeback in 1772, the Amir sent Sa'd at the head of a force of Lebanese and of North African mercenaries to repulse them. Shaykh Sa'd led the expedition, rallied the people of Jubayl and Jibbat Bsharri behind him, and defeated the Himadahs. He acted as commander of the Amir's forces in battle on other occasions as well. In the fight in 1785 against the Vali of Sayda, al Jazzar, he led the Amir's forces and defeated the Vali's mercenary army. The war was not fought

---

[14] Yusuf Yazbak (ed.), *Awraq Lubnaniyyah*, 3 vols. (Beirut: n.p., 1956), pp. 325-326 (hereafter cited as Yazbak, *AL*).

[15] Haydar, *Lubnan*, p. 60.

[16] Munayyar, *KTS*, L, 208.

[17] See for example MAA, MS, no. 7450.

to conclusion, though, because some of the manasib conspired with al Jazzar against Amir Yusuf. When Sa'd discovered this, he quarreled with them and returned home with his forces.[18]

In matters of policy, Shaykh Sa'd handled questions concerning the relations of the Amir and the manasib, and the dependent rulers like the Harfush house of Ba'albak and the Shihabi amirs of Wadi al Taym. He was also entrusted with matters of state such as dealing with the Valis and their conflicts with the Amir. Shaykh Sa'd was informally recognized by the Valis, who wrote to him regarding their relations with the Amir.[19]

Sa'd's great influence in the Imarah made the manasib themselves turn to him on several occasions to plead their cases with the Amir. Occasionally such contacts annoyed some others among the manasib. When Shaykh Sa'd pleaded successfully with Amir Yusuf for the Nakad Shaykhs, for instance, the Jumblats became furious because it was done against their will.[20]

The manasib came to feel that Sa'd was concentrating too much power in his hands and they feared that he would encroach on their own. Therefore, during his last years he became the object of their hostility. Their attitude toward him was clearly manifested in 1780 when Amir Yusuf imposed a new tax. The Druze manasib called for a meeting among themselves and rose up

> to expel Amir Yusuf from Dayr al Qamar and kill Shaykh Sa'd because he was [the man] who conducted policy, and everything that Amir Yusuf did was actually his doing and also attributed to him [by the public]. Everybody hated that.[21]

[18] Shidiaq, *Akhbar*, ii, 64-65.
[19] *Ibid.*, ii, 66, and Haydar, *Lubnan*, pp. 138-139.
[20] Munayyar, *KTS*, l, 204.
[21] Haydar, *Lubnan*, p. 127.

The rebels were appeased when the new tax was annulled; but this was not the end of attempted conspiracies against the Amir and his mudabbir.

In 1786, Shaykh Sa'd died and his son Ghandur stepped into his place as the mudabbir of Amir Yusuf. During his short but distinguished career, Shaykh Ghandur enjoyed the same political eminence as his father, whose politics he continued. In particular he advised a tough policy toward al Jazzar, one of fighting rather than placating the tyrant of 'Akka. The outcome of this policy was disastrous for both Shaykh Ghandur and Amir Yusuf, who lost their lives in the Vali's prison in 1791.

During the last years of Amir Yusuf's rule, rivalry among Shihabi contenders for the office of Hakim grew increasingly intense. The manasib were growing more and more assertive in their role of electing the Hakim, a situation which began to challenge the rule of hereditary succession. Thus the hopes of various contenders in the Shihabi house quickened. Amir Bashir II was the main opponent to Amir Yusuf, and led the opposition which, with the help of al Jazzar, eventually defeated the Hakim and his mudabbir. Since Bashir was far removed from the line of succession, it took special effort on the part of the Druze manasib, particularly the Jumblats, to put him in office. Therefore, as we have seen, his heavy reliance on the Druze made him include Druze mudabbirs in his administrative staff during the early years of his rule. It is hard to suppose that his employment of Druze mudabbirs was accidental, because it was by then an established tradition that the mudabbirs were recruited from the Maronite community of Mount Lebanon.[22] But at that time the office had become of obvious political importance and no politically conscious group like the Druze could have missed the point. However, Maronite mudabbirs reasserted themselves again

---

[22] This tradition was explicitly stated by Shidiaq, *Akhbar*, II, 246.

and reached the pinnacle of their power during the following period in the person of Jirjus Baz.

Shaykh Jirjus Baz (1768-1807)

Neither Amir Bashir II nor al Jazzar gained much by getting rid of Amir Yusuf and his mudabbir. The country was fed up with al Jazzar's machinations and was ready to fight both him and the new Amir, whom he favored. Only the Jumblat faction at that time remained loyal to Bashir. The rest of the manasib put forward two Shihabi Amirs, Qa'dan and Haydar, as Hakims. Under the leadership of these two, a campaign was carried on against al Jazzar for two years. Finally, al Jazzar had to concede and the war was terminated. However, the two Amirs soon encountered difficulties caused by the Jumblats and were advised by some of the manasib to turn over the office to the sons of Amir Yusuf.

Amir Yusuf's sons were still children, but they had a capable mudabbir in their service, Jirjus Baz. Jirjus Baz was a Maronite from Dayr al Qamar. His father had been in the service of Amir Yusuf, and his mother was the sister of Shaykh Sa'd al Khury. When Jirjus reached adulthood, his father and Sa'd put him in the service of Amir Yusuf. He was not well known during the critical years when Amir Yusuf was facing serious difficulties. However, after the death of the Amir and his mudabbir Ghandur, Jirjus appeared on the scene as the guardian and mudabbir of the young sons of Amir Yusuf: Husayn, Sa'd al Din, and Salim.

In 1792 when Qa'dan and Haydar became ruling Amirs, Jirjus sought and secured from them the government of Jubayl for his wards. Within a very short time the mudabbir attracted the attention of the whole country to himself and his wards. He became popular with some of the manasib because of his generosity, political skill, and personal charm. From Jubayl he soon started to contact the manasib of Jabal al Shuf and tried to win them over in favor of the sons of Amir

Yusuf. The chronicler Hananiyyah al Munayyar wrote about these events:

> All the Jubayl country and its dependencies came into the hands of Jirjus Baz and into his charge. From there he started to write to the princes and shaykhs trying to win their favors for his lords. He became liberal in spending on gifts and presents. He was blessed with excellent qualities and high spirit. So people became inclined toward him and sought his friendship. . . . When Jirjus Baz started to make the call in favor of the sons of Amir Yusuf, people rallied to them.[23]

With the scheming of Jirjus and the active opposition of the Jumblats, the two Amirs could not continue ruling. At the suggestion of friends of Jirjus, Shaykh Bashir Nakad and Shaykh 'Abdallah al Qadi[24] invited the mudabbir to bring his lords to Dayr al Qamar and rule over the country. It was also hoped that Jirjus would be able to curb the Jumblats.

Thus in 1793 the government of all Mount Lebanon came under the sons of Amir Yusuf, Husayn and Sa'd al Din, who were directed and controlled by Jirjus Baz. Amir Husayn was made ruler of the Shuf and Amir Sa'd al Din of Jubayl, with Jirjus and his brother, 'Abd al Ahad, as their respective mudabbirs.

That was a time of great instability, the country divided between the partisans of Amir Yusuf and later his sons, on the one hand, and on the other, the partisans of Amir Bashir. The Jumblats supported Amir Bashir, whereas the Nakadis and, with some oscillation, the Yazbakis, supported the sons of Amir Yusuf. Since al Jazzar had proved himself a strong party in the Amir's election, the manasib, it was clear, could no longer settle their own differences without interference.

From that time until 1800 the Mountain was to witness a see-saw game with one party gaining, the other losing, with

[23] Munayyar, *KTS*, L, 438-439.   [24] Shidiaq, *Akhbar*, II, 89.

rapid frequency. It was during this struggle between Amir Bashir and the sons of Amir Yusuf that the abilities of Jirjus Baz passed the test. To secure the government for his lords, Jirjus had to prove himself capable of meeting the Ottoman Valis and handling the business of his Amirs directly with them. Previously he had only had to contact the Valis in writing and through special messengers, but with the increasing tempo of the civil strife he had to go and meet them personally.

In 1795 the Vilayet of Damascus was taken away from al Jazzar, and 'Abdallah Pasha al 'Azm was appointed in his place. Taking advantage of this new development, Jirjus went with his lords to meet the new Pasha in 1796. Soon, however, they discovered that the Pasha was weak and not capable of helping them against al Jazzar in their endeavor to regain the government of Lebanon. Thus, in 1797, Jirjus took the risk of going with Amir Yusuf's sons to al Jazzar, the man who had executed their father. It is worth noting that in their company were only Maronite notables, such as the two brothers of Jirjus and Shaykh Sim'an al Bitar.

Jirjus' dangerous mission to al Jazzar eventually bore fruit. In 1799 al Jazzar, angered by Amir Bashir's ambivalent attitude toward Napoleon's siege of 'Akka, sent Jirjus and his lords back to Mount Lebanon supported by a force of 6,000 horsemen and 4,000 footmen.[25] This great force was sufficient to ensure their success, but the fighting proved inconclusive and both sides showed willingness to have a peaceful settlement. Jirjus agreed to negotiate with Amir Bashir; and in December of the year 1800 an agreement was signed by both. The agreement was given additional sanction by Patriarch Yusuf Tiyyan.[26] According to one source, Bashir asked the Patriarch personally to give the oath to the two parties, in

[25] *Ibid.*, p. 101.
[26] Salim Baz, *Al Shaykh Jirjus Baz: Sahifah min Tarikh Lubnan* (Beirut: Matabi' Sadir-Rihani Press, 1953), p. 11.

the Maronite church of Dayr al Qamar, so that Jirjus would be bound by it.[27]

The agreement between Amir Bashir and Jirjus Baz gave Lebanon a seven-year period of tranquility, from 1800 to 1807, and contained the conflict among the Shihabi contenders temporarily. By its terms Bashir was to rule over the original seven muqata'ahs of al Shuf and Kisrwan, while Amir Yusuf's sons would rule northern Lebanon with Jirjus Baz and his brother 'Abd al Ahad as their mudabbirs. Whatever the details of the arrangement were, it is clear that al Jazzar was outdone for the second time by a national consensus among the manasib, and this was to prove his undoing so far as his influence went in Mount Lebanon.

Although by the terms of the agreement Jirjus was to stay in Jubayl with Amir Yusuf's sons, he seems, judging from the events related in the chronicles, to have stayed in both places, Jubayl and Dayr al Qamar, in order to keep close watch over the Hakims of both regions. In 1802 he moved to Dayr al Qamar where he bought a Shihabi amir's palace; and in the chronicles of this period his name begins to appear as the mudabbir of Amir Bashir. One good account of the Baz case, by Mikha'il of Damascus, maintains that Amir Bashir was suspicious of Jirjus and was afraid to let him stay in Jubayl away from his reach.[28] This might have been partly true, but hardly a sufficient explanation, since Jirjus did not simply pass time in Dayr al Qamar—he played a powerful role as a mudabbir to the Amir.

Haydar, who was best informed about Jirjus,[29] wrote the following about his growing influence both in Jubayl and Dayr al Qamar:

[27] Rustum Baz, *Mudhakkirat*, p. 10.

[28] Mikha'il al Dimashqi, *Tarikh Hawadith al Sham wa Lubnan* (*1782-1841*), ed. Lewis Ma'luf (Beirut: al Matba'ah al Kathulikiyyah, 1912), p. 81 (hereafter cited as Dimashqi, *Tarikh*).

[29] Amir Haydar's daughter was engaged to Amir Husayn, the son of Amir Yusuf, before the latter was deposed by Bashir. Haydar, "Nuzhat," p. 271.

They [the Hakims] were under age and lacking also in judgment. Jirjus Baz was their mudabbir, by the capacity of the office as a servant, but only so in name. In actual fact he was the man served, for they were under his orders in all matters which concerned their persons or other people. They never acted without his permission, even in matters that had to do with their dress, sport, slaves, arms, and expenditure. They also had no power to enjoin or absolve; he even kept their rings with him, writing and signing official correspondence of the Diwan in their names as he wished, without their knowledge or permission. Thus he was not accountable for what he did, whereas they were.[30]

In describing his position in Dayr al Qamar, al Dimashqi wrote:

This man enjoyed great prestige and glory such as no one ever had before or after. This made him careless of the misfortunes of time. He made his residence in Dayr al Qamar and decorated the house[31] which he had bought. He became the authority on all matters in the country. Whatever question arose with amirs, shaykhs, or others, it had to be raised with him first, and what he enjoined came into effect. Whatever the Shaykh [Jirjus] wanted done was done, and he became the decision-maker [*bi yadihi al hall wa al rabt*]. The Amir [al Hakim] had of the government its name only.[32]

Thus, the situation in Dayr al Qamar, if not exactly the same as that of Jubayl, was at least comparable with it.

The power which Jirjus Baz enjoyed in the Imarah must have rested on the following grounds. First, it came from the moral force of the agreement which he concluded with Amir

[30] *Ibid.*, p. 266; see also MAE, Tripoli, May 1807.
[31] Jirjus bought the palace of Amir Ahmad Shihab in Dayr al Qamar, where he lived with his family.
[32] Dimashqi, *Tarikh*, pp. 79-80. In the same sense, see Haydar, "Nuzhat," p. 267.

Bashir in the names of Amir Yusuf's sons. The two Amirs ruled Jubayl and had adherents in the Shuf as well. Second, Jirjus himself had successfully built up a considerable following, mainly among the Christians of Dayr al Qamar, Kisrwan, and Jubayl. Third, he established good connections and mutual confidence with the Ottoman Valis.

The Christian following was created by many factors. The Maronites of the north, Jubayl and Jibbat Bsharri, had long been loyal followers of Amir Yusuf and Sa'd al Khury. In the same way they stood for the sons of Amir Yusuf and their Maronite mudabbirs, the Baz brothers. Patriarch Tiyyan, too, enjoyed the confidence of Amir Yusuf and Sa'd from the days when he was still a young priest.[33] He was also on very good terms with Jirjus Baz and keenly understood the importance of these Maronite mudabbirs for the welfare of the community and the political fortunes of the Maronites.

Jirjus himself was active in the Church politics[34] and backed the Church and the orders of monks. He showed a lively religious spirit in his writings to the Congregation of the Propaganda in Rome. In one letter he thanked the Holy See for its love and concern for the Maronite community. He used in that letter the epithet given the Maronite community by the popes, namely "roses among thorns" of persecution, surviving among the other nonorthodox religious communities.[35] In this letter his efforts to advance the cause of the Maronite community, as well as his own self-image, come out very clearly:

> . . . For I have been at the head of this community, indeed of all the Christian communities of Mount Lebanon and its dependencies, by the good grace of their highnesses our princes [Amir Yusuf's sons]. It is my duty, legal and moral,

[33] Ibrahim Harfush, "Mufawwad ibn Sallum al Tiyyan min Bayrut," *al Manarah*, viii (1937), 10-12.

[34] See Mas'ad and Khazin, *UT*, i, 612, 615.

[35] Congressi Maroniti, xv, 333, Archivio Congregazione de Propaganda Fide, Rome.

to approve and act to fulfill your Sacred Council's commands and [uphold] the order of our Maronite Church.[36]

Jirjus also showed definite support and encouragement for the Maronites living under the Druze muqati'jis. For instance, he gave full backing to the priest and Maronite peasants of al Dibbiyyah, a village in southern Lebanon, who were imprisoned by the Amir at the suggestion of Shaykh Bashir Jumblat for a squabble in which a Druze 'aqil was beaten up. Not only did he have the men released from the Hakim's jail but he also quarrelled with Shaykh Bashir on their account, and the whole incident took on a communal character.[37]

As for the attachment of the people of Dayr al Qamar to Jirjus Baz, it could be attributed to more than one cause. First, he had been born in Dayr al Qamar, and was known and accessible to all his fellow townsmen. Also, he was a Maronite, as were the majority of the town's inhabitants. Second, the people of Dayr al Qamar had been deprived of their natural leaders, the Nakadi muqati'jis. This came about in the following way. Although Dayr al Qamar was the major town in Mount Lebanon and the capital of the Imarah, the Hakim who resided there had no direct authority over its inhabitants because they were the subjects of the Abu Nakad muqati'jis. Shaykh Bashir Abu Nakad and his brothers were partisans of Amir Yusuf's sons and Jirjus Baz.[38] In 1796, Amir Bashir became party to a conspiracy among the other chief manasib to assassinate the Abu Nakad muqati'jis of Dayr al Qamar. A few of the young Nakadi sons escaped with their lives, but the blow was almost the *coup de grâce* so far as the political power of the Abu Nakad muqati'jis was concerned.

Although his allies were thereby destroyed, the Nakad affair

---

[36] *Ibid.*, MSS, nos. 332, 333.

[37] Salim Baz, *Al Shaykh Jirjus Baz*, p. 22; also Rustum Baz, *Mudkhakkirat*, pp. 10-11.

[38] Munayyar, *KTS*, L, 440-442.

had the effect of improving Jirjus' position at Dayr al Qamar. The assassination of the Nakads left the people without their leaders; obviously they could not immediately fall in line for the assassins of their former leaders but looked for a new chief with whom they had some kind of natural affinity, and Jirjus was the answer. He was also the ally of their former masters, and a strong mudabbir. Mikha'il Mashaqah, a native of Dayr al Qamar, commented that after the destruction of the Nakads the Christians of that town became increasingly devoted to Jirjus, who gave them protection even from the Hakim himself. He went so far, Mashaqah continues, as to release their prisoners from the Amir's jail, thus exasperating the Amir as well as the Druze manasib.[39] Jirjus was actually performing for the people of Dayr al Qamar what their traditional masters, the Nakad muqati'jis, had done for them, assuming the same functions and prerogatives.

The third source of the power of Jirjus Baz was his good connections with the Ottoman Valis. Al Munayyar makes a brief but emphatic reference to the elements of Jirjus' power, including his relations with the Valis, thus:

> Jirjus reached the epitome of power and state pomp. He was known to the State and its Vezirs. No one among his equals ever reached a fraction of what he had attained. The reigns of the government of Amir Yusuf's sons were in his hands, and he was a friend of Shaykh Bashir [Jumblat]. Thus he had powers of coercion in the land even over Amir Bashir, the Hakim.[40]

We have seen earlier how Jirjus dealt with al Jazzar regarding his lords' investment with the government of the Mountain. After the December 1800 agreement, neither Jirjus nor Amir Bashir dealt directly with the Vali. Not until the latter's

[39] Mashaqah, *al Jawab*, p. 34.
[40] Munayyar, *KTS*, LI, 485. In the same sense see MAE, Correspondance Consulaire, Tripoli, 20 May 1807.

death in 1804 were Jirjus' connections with the State Vezirs in 'Akka resumed, although he kept up his contacts during that period with the Vali of Damascus.

After al Jazzar's death, Ibrahim Pasha was appointed Vali of the Damascus and Sayda vilayets. On his arrival in Damascus he asked Amir Bashir to send him Jirjus Baz. When Jirjus arrived, the Vali gave him a state reception with great honors. The event was described by the chronicler Amir Haydar Shihab:

> Ibrahim Pasha received him with full honors. Before he arrived [in town] Kinj Yusuf and the *dalatiyyah* [delis] went out to meet him. He entered Damascus with great prestige and honors. Ibrahim Pasha would ask his opinion in all matters of policy. . . . The Pasha fixed a large income for him and he had one hundred cavalrymen in his company. When he passed in Damascus [streets] he rode his horse with complete accoutrement. He became close to Ibrahim Pasha and handled [public] affairs [for him] and was immensely liked by the Pasha. Whatever he requested from the Vali was granted and he protected the Christians of Damascus from many losses.[41]

In view of the fact that in Damascus Jirjus Baz was a dhimmi, these honors and the powers which he enjoyed are exceptionally interesting.

When Sulayman Pasha became Vali of Sayda (1804-1818), Jirjus established very good relations with him and his Jewish advisor, Haim Farhi. His visits to Sulayman Pasha were also marked with the honors due a state dignitary.[42] The Imarah's affairs with Sulayman Pasha were left to him to handle.[43] Not only was the Vali of Sayda among his friends but also

---

[41] Haydar, *Lubnan*, p. 415.
[42] See Dimashqi, *Tarikh*, p. 81.
[43] Rustum Baz, *Mudhakkirat*, p. 8; al 'Awrah, *Tarikh Wilayat*, pp. 40-45; MAA, p. 229, no. 6468.

the governor of Tripoli, Mustafa Agha Barbar. Jirjus and Barbar lent each other much political support in their respective relations with other parties.

Jirjus' power and prestige were also enhanced by the successes of his military expeditions. First, he got rid of the Matawilah chief Shaykh Husayn Himadah, who was conspiring to restore Jubayl to Himadah rule. In 1804 he led an expedition against the Sunni Muslim chiefs of 'Akkar and al Dinniyyah, 'Abbud Bey and Shaykh 'Abbas al Ra'd, who had attacked the region of Jubayl during Jirjus' absence in Damascus and 'Akka. He defeated 'Abbud Bey and made him seek a peace settlement, and Shaykh 'Abbas al Ra'd was driven by this example to do the same without actual fighting. Pecuniary punishment was imposed on them and Jirjus returned triumphantly to Dayr al Qamar.

Similarly, in 1806, Mustafa Barbar of Tripoli sought the help of Jirjus Baz and Amir Bashir to subdue the chief of the Nusayris of Safita, Shaykh Saqr al Mahfuz, who officially came under the jurisdiction of the governor of Tripoli. On this occasion too, Jirjus led the expedition and forced Saqr al Mahfuz to seek peace. During all these expeditions Jirjus was acting in the name of the Hakim and had precedence in military and ceremonial matters over the muqati'jis.

The achievements of Shaykh Jirjus Baz were also greatly enhanced by his charm and good personal qualities. Friend and foe testified to the excellence of his character. The chronicler Haydar, who was not particularly friendly toward Jirjus, described his character in the following way:

He was clever, with a generous soul and hand; easy of manners and [gifted] with pleasant talk. His person charmed the people and they followed him. He was also a wasteful person who spent money carelessly on good living and luxury. . . . He liked fun and song. . . . He was forward, dauntless, and heeded no one. Thus he had many friends and

187

many enemies. His brother 'Abd al Ahad came close to him in these qualities, but he did not have his sharp wit.[44]

Poets, not only Maronites but even Sunni Muslims from Beirut, eulogized Jirjus and sang of his success.[45]

Jirjus Baz did not come from a socially ranking family; his house enjoyed no title or power.[46] His father was not a distinguished servant of Amir Yusuf while in the Amir's service; he probably served as a scribe from whom Jirjus learned the calligraphy for which he was famous. The only claim Jirjus had to inherited social prestige came from his being the nephew of Shaykh Sa'd al Khury. By his relations with Sa'd al Khury and Amir Yusuf, he gained his first connections with the ruling class; but the rest should be attributed to his personal qualities, which brought him to the top.

As for the image which Jirjus had of himself, one may have an idea of it from his own writings. As was mentioned above, he considered himself the head of all the Christian communities of Mount Lebanon. He also signed his name in 1804 as "Miqdam Diwan Jabal Lubnan,"[47] a title not previously known, which could be roughly translated as the head of the government council of Mount Lebanon. His delight in the glory he achieved can be observed in a letter he wrote to a friend describing the pomp with which he was received in Sayda, Sur, and 'Akka on his visit to the Vali, Sulayman Pasha, in 1806.[48]

The rise to power of Jirjus Baz contributed to a development which had never before been witnessed in the history of the Imarah and one which laid the foundation for the later

[44] Haydar, "Nuzhat," p. 267. In the same sense see also Mashaqah, *al Jawab*, p. 31.

[45] See poem by Sayyid 'Umar al Bakri, in Salim Baz, *Al Shaykh Jirjus Baz*, p. 16; also al Turk, *Diwan al Turk*, a poem by Ilias Iddi, p. 217.

[46] In a letter written by the Maronite a'yan in 1785 to Shaykh Ghandur al Khury, Jirjus' signature appears next to last. See letter in Daghir, *Lubnan*, p. 538. It must also be borne in mind that he was also young then, only seventeen years of age.

[47] Congressi Maroniti, xv, 332, 333, Propaganda.

[48] See letter in Dimashqi, *Tarikh*, 81.

political realignment in Mount Lebanon along ethnic grounds. During the period of Baz's hegemony, both the Christian and the Druze communities came closer than ever before to a situation in which they enjoyed single leadership, the Christians under Baz and the Druze under Shaykh Bashir Jumblat. We have already surveyed the route Jirjus Baz followed in his rise to power, but not that of Shaykh Bashir. As shown in Chapter III, the Jumblat clan succeeded in keeping their political leadership united, and this factor contributed to their political prominence in comparison with the fragmented authority of other clans. The increase in Jumblati power over the rest of the Druze manasib was enhanced not only by their unified leadership but also by the fact that of the three leading Druze clans in the iqta' system, one, the Nakadi, was removed during the struggle between Amir Yusuf and Amir Bashir, and the other, the 'Imads, were greatly weakened by Jirjus Baz and Bashir Jumblat.

Before 1800, the Yazbaki faction had stood behind Jirjus Baz and against Bashir Jumblat and Amir Bashir II; but the faction, particularly its leading clan, the 'Imads, did not seem quite satisfied with the results of the settlement of 1800. Jirjus, who was the main party to and beneficiary of the settlement, found that his control over the 'Imads was slipping. With the restoration of peace and his secure political position, however, he needed them less. At the same time, the refusal of the 'Imads to accept his leadership and their continuing intrigues against Bashir II were embarrassing to Jirjus in his relations with both the Hakim and the Vali of Sayda. This made him follow a policy of repression toward his former allies, the Yazbakis, and pursue one of cooperation with Shaykh Bashir Jumblat.[49] By 1807, the Yazbakis, much weakened, were becoming extremely angry with Baz.

On the surface, the mudabbir's situation seemed practically

---

[49] Archives of the Maronite Monastery in Rome, letter sent to Rome in August 1803. MAA, MS, pp. 40-41, no. 6469; also Shidiaq, *Akhbar*, II, 124-125.

unshakable. A man like Jirjus Baz, however, should have had the wisdom and foresight to realize the consequences of his power and actions in terms of the basic institutions of the country. But he was naive and too trustful of others, and lacked the caution which a man of great power should never neglect. One of the major defects of his character, which eventually cost him his standing and his life, was his failure to grasp the inconsistency between his powerful position and the institutions of the country. In a system in which authority was acquired by hereditary right, his powers were not considered fully legitimate by the manasib, for they extended beyond the limits of delegated authority. This was the main problem in the Baz case: the principle which justified his political power was never made clear, and consequently he was finally resisted and repudiated by the political system. Since the system had no mechanism in terms of which it could deal with this kind of conflict, violence was the only solution.

Here are some of the instances in which Jirjus gradually came into open conflict with the established order. First, he competed with the ruling Amir in an ostentatious show of power and prestige in the capital. His wealth, the pomp of his public appearance, his encouragement of recourse to him for help and protection, and signs of authority which he displayed could not have passed unnoticed by the Hakim, who only a few years earlier had been at war with him. Still less could they have been overlooked by the manasib. One manifestation of his grandiose ambition was his purchase of the palace of a former Shihabi Hakim at Dayr al Qamar, the entrance to which he then decorated with a lion engraving above the gate.[50] When Amir Hasan Shihab was instigating his brother, Amir Bashir II, against Jirjus Baz, he pointed out these displays as signs of lack of respect for the Amir.

Second, Jirjus trespassed on the traditional political prerogatives of Hakims and muqati'jis. As we have seen earlier,

[50] Baz, *Al Shaykh Jirjus Baz*, p. 19; also MAE, dispatch from Tripoli, 20 May 1807.

he was directly involved in the election of Amir Husayn and Amir Sa'd al Din as Hakims, and his influence in that development was decisive. He went so far as to argue with Amir Bashir that Amir Yusuf's sons were in the right line of succession while he, Bashir, was not.[51] Regardless of the merits of his argument, he was hardly the man to advance it, since according to the political institutions of the Imarah the mudabbirs were the servants of the Hakims, not their makers. There is no reason why, in the light of this, the Hakim and the manasib should not have felt uneasy about Jirjus' position and have tried to rid themselves of him.

Further, he freed people from jail without Bashir's permission, settled public issues, and made his own alliances with the manasib which put the Hakim at a disadvantage. He took a share of the Amir's income and interfered in the order of his business, a state of affairs well described by al Dimashqi:

> But as for Amir Bashir, he was under a state of compulsion with the shaykh [Jirjus], who had shown no reverence toward him; especially since he interfered in what was not his business. For it was [part of the arrangement of 1800] that the Amir ruled the Mountain [i.e., al Shuf] alone, while the government of Jubayl belonged to the mentioned Shaykh. He [Jirjus] started to share with the Amir such extraneous income as might come from gifts and other things,[52] so that not even one quarter of that income reached the Amir. This came about [because Jirjus] judged some cases brought before him, and left some other ones to the Amir. At any rate, whatever the Shaykh wanted done was done. And he [the Amir] was holding his peace, showing him all signs of respect and good will. Most of the time he shared his dinner table with him [the Shaykh]. He always pretended that he was pleased and willing to accept every-

[51] Mashaqah, al Jawab, p. 32.
[52] It should be observed here that part of the legitimate income of the mudabbirs came from this source, though Jirjus seems to have greatly augmented the usual share.

thing [the Shaykh] said. He [Jirjus] felt strong with the Amir's overt signs of love, considering them to be pure.[53]

A serious conflict arose between the Hakim and Jirjus around 1800 over the government of Kisrwan. Jirjus did not like to see Amir Hasan, Bashir's brother, made overseer of Kisrwan, a region adjacent to the domain of his lords, Amir Yusuf's sons. He worked diligently against Hasan, trying to weaken his position and to remove him from the post. The Khazins were Jirjus' allies from an early date[54] and also greatly resented Hasan's presence in their traditional territory. Jirjus supported their cause and strengthened his alliance with them by marrying his brother 'Abd al Ahad to a Khazin girl. Amir Hasan became quite annoyed about this alliance and publicly denounced it.[55]

At every point in his struggle with the Khazins, Amir Hasan found his plans frustrated by Jirjus Baz. When he tried to make a cadastral survey of Kisrwan to reassess the amount of miri, the Khazins sought the help of Jirjus Baz to stop the survey, and the latter managed to produce an order from Amir Bashir canceling the project.[56] Jirjus also helped the Khazins restore the scales for weighing silk to Zuq Mikha'il, where they had been before Hasan moved them to Juniyah under his control.[57] The mudabbir persisted in his hostile policy toward Amir Hasan until in 1807 he succeeded in removing Hasan from his position of responsibility over Kisrwan and returned to the Khazins their free hand over the muqata'ah.[58]

In Church politics Jirjus also opposed Bashir openly. Bashir and the apostolic delegate, Louis Gondolfi, tried to keep the

53 Dimashqi, Tarikh, pp. 79-80.
54 Baz, Al Shaykh Jirjus Baz, p. 20.
55 Rustum Baz, Mudhakkirat, p. 10.
56 Haydar, Lubnan, p. 512.
57 Dimashqi, Tarikh, pp. 82-83.
58 MAE, Correspondance Consulaire, dispatch from Tripoli, 20 May 1807.
Haydar, Lubnan, p. 512; Dimashqi, Tarikh, p. 83.

aged archbishop Bulus Istfan on the diocese of the Batrun, while the Baz brothers stood with Patriarch Tiyyan in appointing Jirmanus Thabit bishop to the diocese.[59]

The Amir was also concerned about the informal alliance between Jirjus Baz and Bashir Jumblat which developed toward the end of Jirjus' career. By collaborating, the two potentates put the Hakim under their power and compelled him to do whatever they wished.[60] Their activities were annoying to the Amir, particularly their intervention on behalf of the Arslan amirs in Shwayfat. Bashir was gradually forced by the two shaykhs to settle the issue with the Arslans.

Shaykh Bashir, though, was more politically astute than Jirjus; he understood the mudabbir's precarious relationship with the Amir and was quite willing to have his powerful ally out of the way. For if Jirjus were to be removed from the scene, Jumblat would become the single force behind Amir Bashir and the Hakim would be forced to be ever more dependent upon him. Thus Shaykh Bashir joined in the intrigues against Jirjus and let the Amir know of his ally's dealings.[61] This was the beginning of the end for Jirjus Baz.

By 1807, therefore, most of the manasib were ready to act against Baz—Amir Hasan, the Yazbakis, Amir Bashir II, and Shaykh Bashir Jumblat. The time set by the plotters for the destruction of Jirjus and his brother 'Abd al Ahad was May 15. This date was dictated by events developing in Mount Lebanon and the surrounding vilayets, for the alliances which Jirjus Baz thought he had under control were in reality cracking. Late in 1806, Sulayman Pasha, the Vali of Sayda, had summoned Jirjus to 'Akka. He sent his advisor, Haim Farhi, to meet Jirjus in Sayda, where the two men discussed matters of policy before they reached 'Akka.[62] The French

---

[59] Tiyyan papers, PAB; also Harfush, "Mufawwad . . . ," *Manarah*, VIII, 94-95.

[60] Munayyar, *KTS*, LI, 485.

[61] Dimashqi, *Tarikh*, p. 83.

[62] MAE, Correspondance Consulaire, dispatch from Sayda, 14 November 1806.

consul in Sayda, calling Jirjus "ministre de la montagne," reported the meeting to his government; he confessed his ignorance as to what was at issue but surmised that it must have been important because of the high positions of the two men.[63] Not all the details about the visit are available to us now, but we know a little more about it than did the French consul.

Besides the Yazbaki affair mentioned earlier, Jirjus and Haim Farhi discussed another case, that of Mustafa Barbar of Tripoli. Mustafa Agha Barbar was a Sunni Muslim soldier of fortune from a Lebanese village, whose adventures brought him to the governorship of Tripoli. He and Jirjus developed a friendly relationship of mutual support. Sulayman Pasha, appointed Vali of Tripoli in 1806 in addition to Sayda, did not have sufficient power to oust Barbar and wanted to enlist the support of the Lebanese against him. The Vali therefore summoned Jirjus to 'Akka to discuss the case of Barbar with him. Refusing to commit himself against Barbar, Jirjus nevertheless promised the Pasha that he would stay neutral in case of an attack against Barbar.[64] This fell short of the Pasha's hopes, and there was some cooling off in the latter's attitude toward Jirjus.

Realizing that the relations of Jirjus with the Pasha were no longer excellent, and that the Yazbaki shaykhs were at their worst with the mudabbir, Amir Bashir II saw that there was no serious obstacle in his way, especially since Bashir Jumblat also approved of destroying Jirjus. The conspiracy was well knit. On the appointed day, Shaykh Bashir brought his men to Dayr al Qamar in case some resistance was made.[65] Amir Bashir sent after Shaykh Jirjus Baz for some urgent business, and in the privacy of their meeting in the serail, he called in his *shurtah* and had them strangle the mudabbir. At the same moment in which Jirjus was being murdered, Amir Hasan and the Yazbaki shaykhs were already in Jubayl

---

[63] *Ibid.*   [64] Dimashqi, *Tarikh*, p. 82.
[65] *Ibid.*, p. 85; Mashaqah, *al Jawab*, p. 35.

under the pretext of seeking the mediation of 'Abd al Ahad Baz with Amir Bashir. There was no attempt to keep them from entering the town, and they proceeded directly to the palace of 'Abd al Ahad Baz and killed him. Meanwhile, Amir Hasan had captured the sons of Amir Yusuf in Jubayl's Crusader castle where they made their residence. The Amirs were cruelly blinded and their property confiscated.

The Baz brothers' following in the country was quite dispersed; and without the Bazes to lead, not much could be done. The people of Dayr al Qamar became agitated and attacked the serail, but when they realized that their leader was already dead, they broke up.[66] The important men in the service of the Baz brothers, such as 'Arab al Shalfun and Ilias Iddi, scribe and poet, were captured immediately. Yusuf al Turk was captured and killed, while Yusuf al Khury al Shalfun escaped. The Christians of Dayr al Qamar in turn were punished in various ways,[67] and also the Khazins.[68] To discredit Jirjus Baz in the eyes of the Francophile Maronites, Amir Bashir spread the rumor that Jirjus was in concert with the British.[69] Then Bashir moved to depose Patriarch Tiyyan, who was a major ally of the Baz brothers and the sons of Amir Yusuf.[70] Similarly he took steps against the Maronite shaykhs of Jubayl and Jibbat Bsharri, intending to remove them from their 'uhad, but failed because they called on the support of Yusuf Pasha of Damascus.[71] As for Sulayman Pasha, the Amir sent him an explanation claiming that the mudabbir had been intriguing against him. He also asked the Vali for an order to the people to keep quiet, a request readily granted

[66] Shidiaq, *Akhbar*, II, 127; Churchill, *Mount Lebanon*, III, 252-253.

[67] Haydar, *Lubnan*, p. 515; MAE, Correspondance Consulaire, dispatch from Tripoli, 22 November 1808.

[68] Shidiaq, *Akhbar*, II, 128.

[69] MAE, Correspondance Consulaire, dispatch from Tripoli, 20 May 1807. Also Dimashqi, *Tarikh*, p. 87.

[70] Congressi Maroniti, xv, 344, 345, 346, 359, 361, Propaganda.

[71] MAE, Correspondance Consulaire, dispatch from Tripoli, 22 November 1808.

by the Pasha,[72] who was already disaffected with Jirjus. Mustafa Barbar, faced with the *fait accompli*, had to keep his peace.

As for the spoils, the first to benefit was Amir Hasan who, as was immediately observed by the French consul in Tripoli, emerged from the "obscurity to which he was condemned by Jirjus Baz."[73] He was appointed by his brother Bashir as ruler of Jubayl in place of the sons of Amir Yusuf.[74] However, Amir Hasan died soon afterwards, and Bashir, instead of appointing his brother's son to the same position, appointed his own son Amir Qasim as Hakim of Jubayl. He sent with him a Druze mudabbir, thus clearly displaying the shift in power in favor of the Druze. However, the Maronite mudabbir of the deceased Amir Hasan struggled against the Druze mudabbir and his master Amir Qasim until he had them both removed.[75]

The second, but more important, beneficiary was Shaykh Bashir Jumblat and the Druze in general.[76] With Jirjus removed, Jumblat remained the sole powerful chief in the Mountain, as he had anticipated. He took the place of Jirjus not only in the Shuf but also in Kisrwan. When, for instance, Amir Hasan attacked the Khazins right after the murder of Jirjus, Shaykh Bashir stepped in and gave the Khazins the support they had previously had from Jirjus. Amir Hasan was therefore prevented from taking the Khazin muqata'ah.[77] As the Khazins, before the intrusion of Jirjus Baz, were of the Jumblati faction, Shaykh Bashir could be considered to have restored his influence where Jirjus had taken it away.

There were other consequences to the downfall of the Baz brothers. The office of mudabbir was reduced in importance

[72] Al 'Awrah, *Tarikh Wilayat*, pp. 324-325.

[73] MAE, Correspondance Consulaire, dispatch from Tripoli, 20 May 1807.

[74] Haydar, *Lubnan*, p. 515.

[75] Jirjus Abi Dibs, "Tarikh Jirjus Abi Dibs," MS, Jafeth Library, American University of Beirut, n.d.

[76] Dimashqi, *Tarikh*, p. 88.   [77] Shidiaq, *Akhbar*, I, 156-157.

and its holder was no longer to have political power or connections; he became simply an administrator.[78] In addition,
Bashir II started to employ his own sons in the major administrative duties instead of strangers. It is true, however, that
after the Baz debacle, Bashir continued to employ Maronites
in his administration until 1828, when he raised the Syrian
stranger Melkite Catholic poet in his court, Butrus Karamah,
to the office of mudabbir. Butrus Karamah was a Syrian from
the town of Hims, and by virtue of being a stranger he had
no personal connections in Lebanon and there was no fear
that his power might grow out of control. The Lebanese
were quite conscious of this change in the office of the mudabbir. As Shayban al Khazin remarked in the 1820's, the mudabbirs in the past were important in the full sense of the word—
they were men of learning and of action, "[unlike] those of
our own days."[79]

To summarize, the impact of the office of mudabbir upon
the Maronite community and the iqta' system was profound.
First, it had an integrative effect upon the system during the
seventeenth century whereby Maronites became part of the
Imarah. The office was the one channel through which Maronite Christians found their way into the ruling class. Maronite peasants were encouraged by the presence of Maronite
lords to migrate in large numbers from northern Lebanon to
the muqata'ahs of the Imarah. The process of Maronite integration into the iqta' political system, starting early in the
seventeenth century, was also furthered by the secular nature
of the political institutions, which made it possible for the
Maronites to be treated equally with the other religious groups
in the system.

The second main conclusion from this study of the mudabbir's role is that delegated authority in the iqta' system proved
to be in conflict with constituted authority. Authority was ex-

[78] See Dimashqi, *Tarikh*, p. 88.
[79] Shayban, *Tarikh*, p. 436.

ercised directly in the iqta' system by the actors without an administrative organization or staff, and the mudabbir held the only administrative office in the Imarah as an aide to the Hakim. The authority held by the mudabbir was delegated to him, in contrast with the authority enjoyed by the muqati'jis who derived their prerogatives by hereditary right. The career histories of mudabbirs which we have just surveyed demonstrate that the delegated authority of the office was expansive. Holders of the post in the second half of the eighteenth century greatly increased their personal power beyond the limits set by the rules of political conduct in the Imarah. They were able to increase their income, to gain personal influence with the Hakim and the muqati'jis by using their position as intermediaries, to establish direct sway over the people, and sometimes to enter into personal alliances with chiefs and Valis outside the boundaries of the Imarah.

The mudabbir's possibilities for augmenting his personal powers, using the prerogatives of the office as a starting point, led to a direct clash with the system, first with the actors whose authority was thereby compromised, and second with the very principle of legitimacy which justified the use of political power. The mudabbirs encroached on the prerogatives of the Hakim as well as those of the muqati'jis, and therefore became involved in a political struggle based on sheer strength. However, they made no effort to justify their actions in terms of the principle of legitimacy, for the simple reason that those actions were in contradiction with the established norms. The mudabbirs in their political roles did not assume a revolutionary character or an innovative one, since they did not enunciate any new principle to justify political action in opposition to the established order. Baz, who might eventually have broken with the system by relying on communal support from the Maronites, went too far in his violation of the rules and brought upon himself the verdict of death by the system.

Finally the conflict between the mudabbirs and the actors

contributed to change in the iqta' system. The prominence of the mudabbir's position and his great influence over political events, particularly in the case of Baz, disturbed the relatively equal distribution of power among the actors, giving rise to a trend toward concentration of strength in the hands of two separate leaders. Baz and Bashir Jumblat emerged at one point as the *de facto* paramount chiefs in the land, a development which proved to be the start of a new political trend. Jirjus Baz was a Maronite and Bashir Jumblat a Druze, and the rise of each as the actual head of his community marked the beginning of consolidation of communal feeling in Lebanon, which eventually replaced the iqta' principle of allegiance.

CHAPTER VIII

Clergymen, Peasants, and Muqati'jis:
The First Phase

BY NOW we have an idea of the position of the Church vis-à-vis the ruling class, and the role of the clergy in forming and spreading Maronite national ideas. Two central points were noted regarding the relations between clergy and manasib. First, that politics was an activity of the ruling class only, revolving in a closed circle from which others were excluded by reason of their birth. Second, that by the end of the eighteenth century the Maronite Church was emerging from its position of subordination to the manasib and assuming greater freedom and responsibility for its own affairs. Thus the stage has been set for the story of how new relations of a revolutionary nature started to develop between the clergy and the iqta' system, and, as a sequel, how clergy and peasants rose to positions of leadership in open defiance of and challenge to the ruling class.

THE MUDABBIR AND THE PATRIARCH

The Maronite clergy's first venture into the political life of the Imarah came about through an informal alliance with the mudabbir, around the last decade of the eighteenth century. The growth in the mudabbir's political importance coincided with the emergence of the Church from the aegis of the muqati'ji class. Organizationally the Church had reached a relatively complex structure by that time and was well provided with material and human resources. Thus it was almost inevitable that a front should develop between the two and that the resources of both Church and mudabbir should be combined in the interest of the Maronite community.

On a simpler level, cooperation between the Church and the Maronite mudabbirs went back to a very early period in the history of the Imarah.[1] As we have already seen, almost all the Maronite muqati'jis started as mudabbirs or servants of the Amir al Hakim. As mudabbirs and as muqati'jis these men extended to the Church the protection and support which they commanded by virtue of their positions of authority. The Church in turn supported them in its own way, by providing the moral support of the people. In the case of those Maronite chiefs the Khazins and Khuris, more-over, the Church helped them acquire the office of French consul in Beirut through its mediation with the French gov-ernment. However, not until the Church and the mudabbirs had reached positions of relative independence did they take discernible steps to support each other's political actions. This development appeared first with the Patriarch Yusuf Tiyyan (1796-1808) and the Baz brothers.

In the history both of the Maronite Church and of Leba-non, Patriarch Tiyyan occupies a special place which has, strangely, remained obscure till now. Very little is written or known about him, even the cause of his resignation from the patriarchate.[2] Yusuf al Tiyyan was born on 5 March 1760, in a humble home. He was chosen by Patriarch Yusuf Istfan to study at the Maronite College in Rome, where he distin-guished himself as an able student. Tiyyan joined the clerical profession at the age of twenty-two, and only three years later was made an archbishop of the diocese of Damascus. Later he resigned this office to become patriarchal secretary until 1796, when he was elected patriarch. Tiyyan became patriarch at the age of thirty-six, the youngest person elected

---

[1] It was these Maronite mudabbirs who made it possible for the clergy to convert the Shihabis. See Hubaysh papers, MS, no. 2794, PAB.

[2] A noted Maronite historian, priest Ibrahim Harfush, writing on the resignation of Tiyyan, surmises that it was for political and religious reasons, "Mufawwad . . . ," *Manarah*, VIII, 93-96. Another Maronite historian, Bishop Pierre Dib, glosses over the issue; see Pierre Dib, *Histoire de l'Église Maronite* (Mélanges et Documents No. 1) (Beirut: Archevêché Maronite de Beyrouth, 1962), I, 218.

to that office in the recorded history of the Maronite Church.[3]

As a young cleric Tiyyan attracted the attention of Amir Yusuf Shihab and his mudabbir Shaykh Sa'd al Khury, and enjoyed their confidence. They chose him as their deputy to Rome to solve the troublesome problem of Patriarch Istfan, who was involved in the famous heresy of the nun Hindiyyah.[4] Tiyyan also held the position of judge and was well informed on the history and law of his community.[5] It was by his efforts and those of Bishop Yusuf Istfan that the famous Maronite College of 'Ayn Waraqah was started.[6] He was a single-minded and very active individual. The French consul in Tripoli described him in 1809 as a man of great talent and excellent education.[7]

The Maronites of Mount Lebanon, as we have seen, supported the cause of Amir Yusuf Shihab and his sons after him, and Patriarch Tiyyan was foremost in his community to stand for them and their Maronite mudabbirs.[8] Tiyyan saw a great opportunity for the political future of the community in the persons of Maronite mudabbirs such as Jirjus Baz. As early as 1793 when he was still a patriarchal secretary, he and the old Patriarch Mikha'il Fadil begged the Curia to send letters of commendation and gifts to Jirjus Baz and the Maronite mudabbirs of Amir Haydar and Amir Qa'dan.[9]

Tiyyan's venture into political leadership in the Imarah was unprecedented in the history of the Maronite Church. This is clear from many of his actions and political decisions. In 1799 he offered the support of the Maronites to Napoleon, who was fighting at the gates of 'Akka in his campaign to

---

[3] By special dispensation from the pope, the requirement that a patriarch must be at least forty years of age was relaxed for Tiyyan.

[4] Ghanim, *Barnamaj*, p. 307.

[5] Ghibra'il, *Tarikh al Kanisah*, II, 710-711, and MAA, MS, no. 7118.

[6] Istfan, *Zubdat al Bayan*, pp. 41-43.

[7] MAE, Correspondance Consulaire, Tripoli, 30 June 1809.

[8] Tiyyan papers, MS, no. 47, PAB; also Harfush, "Mufawwad . . . ," *al Manarah*, VIII, p. 96; also Dahdah, "Al Amir Bashir," *MQ*, XXII, 572-573.

[9] Qirdahi Dossier, MS, no. 84, Archives of the Lebanese Monastery in Rome.

take Syria. As Catholics, the Maronite clergy were not fond of the French Revolution, nor of Napoleon;[10] but the prospects for the Maronites presented by the possibility of a Catholic nation like France becoming dominant in the Levant could not be overlooked by a farsighted patriarch like Tiyyan. In his letter to Napoleon his ambivalent attitude was well expressed. He wrote to the General that he was sending him a delegation for the love of "our brothers the French people, not for you who have persecuted the Catholic Church." Napoleon's answer was intriguing: "I am also Catholic, and you will see that in my person the Church will triumph and spread to distant lands."[11]

However, Napoleon was repulsed at 'Akka and the patriarch did not have to go far in the mobilization of his community; before the French retreat from 'Akka, nonetheless, he sent men with wine and other presents for the European invaders. He also gave orders to some of the Maronite shaykhs to be prepared and have their men ready.[12] The attitude of Jirjus Baz toward Napoleon is not clear; we know very little except that he was accused by Amir Bashir of double-dealing.[13] Jirjus Baz was then seeking from al Jazzar the investiture over the government of the Imarah, and it is unlikely that he would have taken a stand in favor of the French when they had not yet sufficiently demonstrated their power.

In any case, the initiative of the patriarch and the Christians' overt rejoicing at the Europeans' coming aroused the fears of the Druze.[14] For the first time, different attitudes were demonstrated by Maronites and Druze on a clearly communal basis. The Druze manasib made plans to emigrate to the Jabal

[10] See Bulaybil, "Nabdhah Tarikhiyyah," *MQ*, LI, 307.
[11] Ristelhueber, *Traditions Francaises*, pp. 269-270.
[12] Daghir, *Batarikat al Mawarinah*, p. 75, and Butrus Sfayr, *Al Amir Bashir Al Shihabi: Tara'if 'an Hayatihi wa Ahkamihi wa Akhlaqihi* (Beirut: Dar al Tiba'ah wa al Nashr, n.d.), p. 44.
[13] Rustum Baz, *Mudhakkirat*, pp. 8-9.
[14] Haydar, *Lubnan*, p. 192; Munayyar *KTS*, LI, 449; also Shidiaq, *Akhbar*, II, 98-99.

al A'la in northern Syria in the event of a French victory. Some of the Druze shaykhs also attacked the Maronite caravans carrying wine and other supplies to the French troops. The Napoleonic episode was a passing one, but it indicated the growing split between the two communities under new challenges.

What we are mainly concerned with here are the connections which developed between the Church and the ruling establishment, especially the mudabbir and the Hakim. The relationship between Patriarch Tiyyan and the Baz brothers, the mudabbirs of the Shihabi Hakims, was one of mutual support. "He did all that their interest [i.e., the Baz brothers'] suggested to him," wrote Louis Gondolfi, the apostolic delegate to the Congregation of the Propaganda.[15] As already seen, Tiyyan was a party to the reconciliation between Jirjus Baz and Amir Bashir in 1800. The patriarch's political activities, however, did not please Amir Bashir, and the two were at odds not only in matters of politics but also in Church affairs.[16] In his report on the conflict between Tiyyan and the Amir, Gondolfi wrote to the Propaganda that the patriarch created an infinite number of problems and complications for the Hakim by his meddling in affairs of government which were none of his business.

The one overriding cause of the Amir's hostility toward the patriarch was the latter's complete support for his rivals, the sons of Amir Yusuf and their mudabbirs. The patriarch had good reason to support those Amirs against Bashir, though the latter was also a Maronite. Amir Yusuf and his sons always had a special place with the majority of the Maronites of north Lebanon, who served them well, whereas until that time Amir Bashir depended almost entirely on the Druze.[17] The Druze manasib were also opposed to Patriarch Tiyyan.

[15] Congressi Maroniti, xv, 344, Propaganda.

[16] Tiyyan papers; see letter sent by Amir Bashir to Jirjus Baz, and letter from the same Amir to Patriarch Tiyyan, PAB.

[17] See, for instance, KTS, L, 444.

In a judicial verdict affecting Bashir Jumblat which apparently went against the shaykh's interest, he and the patriarch seem to have exchanged uncomplimentary language. Shaykh Bashir raised a complaint with Jirjus Baz against the patriarch's conduct, stating that the language the patriarch had used with him could hardly have come from the ruler of the country to a personage of his stature.[18]

Patriarch Tiyyan's ventures into political leadership were cut short by the assassination of the Baz brothers and the deposition of their lords. In the agreement of 1800 between Jirjus and Amir Bashir, the two men had sworn before Patriarch Tiyyan not to betray each other. Tiyyan was greatly hurt by Bashir's betrayal of this oath, as well as the great loss to himself and to the community in the death of Jirjus and 'Abd al Ahad and the removal of the sons of Amir Yusuf from the government.[19] He apparently wanted to save what was still possible, that is, to keep Kisrwan in the hands of its Maronite muqati'jis[20] and to stop the punishment being dealt the Baz brothers' followers. The Amir refused him audience,[21] which meant in the customs of the country that he had fallen into disgrace.

Having dispensed with the patriarch's main ally, Amir Bashir moved to get rid of the patriarch himself. He wanted to force him to resign, but Gondolfi, the apostolic delegate, realizing the displeasure such a step would create in Rome, advised the Amir to refrain.[22] Gondolfi himself was actually pleased with the turn of events[23] because of his longstanding conflict with the patriarch. Secretly the apostolic delegate was the private chaplain of the Amir and upheld his cause.[24] He promised the Amir to execute his wishes, but with caution.

[18] MAA, MS, no. 7118.
[19] Congressi Maroniti, xv, 359, Propaganda.
[20] Shayban, *Tarikh*, p. 530.
[21] Congressi Maroniti, xv, 344, Propaganda.
[22] *Ibid.*, MSS, nos. 345, 346.
[23] *Ibid.*, MS, no. 344.
[24] MAE, Correspondance Consulaire, Tripoli, 7 June 1807.

Gondolfi then met the patriarch and explained to him that the Hakim was angry with him and that he could not under any circumstances be pardoned.[25] In this way he suggested subtly that Tiyyan should resign, making him understand that such was the will of the Hakim.[26] The patriarch asked for time to think it over and after a few days informed the apostolic delegate of his intentions to resign.[27] On 3 October 1807 he sent his letter of resignation to Rome, asserting that "the violent antagonism toward me of our rulers and the suspicions in the community oblige me to resign my office."[28] He then went into isolation in the monastery of Qannubin awaiting the pope's reply, which came to him on 19 November 1808.

A new patriarch was then elected, Patriarch Yuhanna al Hilu (1809-1823). Though he was described by the French consul in Tripoli as the creation of the Amir,[29] Hilu kept a good measure of independence from the Hakim; and except for some intercession with the Amir for his people, he tried to steer clear of politics. The Amir no doubt supported him because he could not, considering his advanced age, be expected to be as troublesome as Tiyyan. Bashir for his part followed the Latin rite, in order to maintain his freedom from the Maronite clergy,[30] and had his sons do so as well. However, he did return to the Maronite rite after he quarreled with the apostolic delegate, Gondolfi.[31]

The assassination of the Baz brothers and the retirement of Patriarch Tiyyan ended what might have become one of the most interesting developments in the political life of

---

[25] Congressi Maroniti, xv, 345, Propaganda.

[26] *Ibid.*, MSS, nos. 345, 359, 361; see also Daghir, *Batarikat al Mawarinah*, pp. 75-76.

[27] Congressi Maroniti, xv, 345, Propaganda.

[28] See text of letter in 'Anaysi, *Silsilah*, p. 62.

[29] MAE, Correspondances Consulaire Tripoli, 30 June 1809 and 20 October 1809.

[30] *Ibid.*, Tripoli, 7 June 1807; Congressi Maroniti, xv, 362, Propaganda.

[31] Henri Guys, *Beyrouth et le Liban: Relation d'un Séjour de Plusieurs Années dans ce Pays*, 2 vols. (Paris: Imprimerie de W. Remquet et Cie, 1850), II, 303.

Mount Lebanon. However, the diminution of the functions of the mudabbir did not completely break this relationship, and the Church continued to have some rapport with the mudabbirs concerning information and intercession with the palace.[32] The fact that the Church and the mudabbir could reach a working accord even for a short time is indicative of the growing force and purpose of the Maronite Church and community. This new force could not have been stemmed except by violence, and it was soon to reemerge under new forms.

One of the immediate effects of the episode of Tiyyan and the Baz brothers was to bring into the open the undercurrents which were moving the Maronites and the Druze in opposite directions. Henceforth, as the Maronites' challenge to Druze supremacy grew, the two communities moved farther and farther apart. The importance of the Church and its widening activities, as well as the Maronites' growing self-assertion in the affairs of the Imarah, helped to stimulate communal feeling within the two groups. The trend of change, though not always taking overt expression, was nevertheless basically the result of the mutually enforcing factors of religious group feeling and class distinctions. The Maronites were becoming aware that they were both a distinct community and, on the whole, the majority of the peasant class. This trend contributed not only to the separation of the two religious groups but to the undermining of the iqta' political institutions as well. The following analysis of events helps substantiate this generalization.

After the assassination of the Baz brothers, Amir Bashir and Shaykh Bashir Jumblat emerged as the undisputed rulers of Mount Lebanon, as we have seen in the previous chapter. Amir Bashir, whose support came mainly from the Druze manasib, found himself in the unenviable position of leaning heavily on only one chief muqati'ji, Shaykh Bashir Jumblat.

[32] Hubaysh papers, MSS, nos. 158, 8348.

This situation was unprecedented in the history of the Shihabi Imarah, since the Hakim formerly had always been able to count on the support of many important muqati'jis. While the Druze community was in the process of coming under a single man's leadership, the Maronites were finding themselves without an influential figure who could lead them. The Khazin shaykhs had long since ceased to move in the circle of influential manasib, while the Abillama's also were of limited power. Maronite opposition to the Amir, which continued to mount until 1823, was therefore led mainly by clergymen and peasants. Amir Bashir not only was at odds with his religious affiliates, but he had no freedom to choose among the power groups available in the country because of the firm grip of Shaykh Bashir Jumblat.

PEASANT REBELS AND CLERGYMEN

In the following events we can clearly see the manner in which new forces among the commoners—clergy and peasants —started to challenge the political order. The first element to be challenged in the system was the actors' monopoly of political leadership within a closed circle. The first signs of this open opposition came in 1820 when Maronite peasants revolted against the two Bashirs, Shihab and Jumblat. The uprising is known in the annals of Lebanese history as the *'ammiyyah*, that is, the common people's uprising. The circumstances which brought it to a head were the new demands for more revenue made by the Pasha of Sayda. Over the preceding years the Amir had raised the amount of miri several times.[33] By failing to deal effectively with the Pasha and limit his demands, the Amir was forced to collect another tax from the people. He borrowed some of the amount from merchants, and some from the affluent Shaykh Bashir. He could not collect from the Druze muqata'ahs because the Druze

[33] The practice was to collect the original fixed sum more than one time, hence the customary reference to one miri, two miris, etc.

manasib stood in his way.[34] He turned then to the Christians, who he thought had no strong leaders to oppose an additional collection of miri, and made demands on them and their clergy.[35] This sparked the 'ammiyyah revolt, which deserves special attention as a movement reflecting new sentiments as well as introducing political practices which contributed to the undermining of the iqta' system.

There is a consensus among historians that Bishop Yusuf Istfan (1759-1823) was one of the main leaders of the 'ammiyyah rebellion.[36] The bishop's life and career reflect some of the general trends which were gradually developing in the system and the resultant conflicts, and therefore it would be important first to take note of his background and relations with the ruling class. Born Khayrallah Istfan in 1759 in the region of Kisrwan, he lost his father at the age of six; but as a member of a family with an extensive clerical background and connections, he managed to have a good education such as was received by some of the clergy in his times. He had a scholarly bent and, in the absence of adequate higher educational facilities, educated himself.[37] When the Swiss traveler Burckhardt met Istfan, he thought that the bishop had received his education in Rome, commenting that he "had some notions of Europe."[38] Istfan was able, moreover, to acquire a knowledge of law from Bishop Jirmanus Adam[39] and was well versed in Syriac, revising some of the books of prayers.[40] He was also interested in the history of the Maronite com-

---

[34] See letter of Abbot Ighnatius Sarkis in Yazbak, *AL* (1956), p. 390.

[35] Matta Shihwan, "Hayat Matta Shihwan wa ma Jara fi Ayyamihi min al Hawadith fi Lubnan," ed. Basilius Qattan, *Kawkab al Bariyyah* (B'abda, Lebanon, 1911), p. 476; Hattuni, *Nabdhah*, p. 241.

[36] Shidiaq, *Akhbar*, ii, 145; also MAA, MS, p. 48, no. 6468. Also Hattuni, *Nabdhah* (Yusuf Yazbak edn., 1956), pp. 199-200, 206-208. See also 'Isa Iskandar al Ma'luf, "Al Azjal fi al Amir Bashir al Shihabi al Kabir," *al Manarah*, viii (1937), 117-118.

[37] Istfan, *Zubdat al Bayan*, pp. 48-49.

[38] Burckhardt, *Travels*, p. 22.

[39] Yazbak, *AL*, 1956, p. 435.

[40] Bulaybil, *TRLM*, li, 682, n. 1 through to page 683.

munity and is often quoted as an authority on that subject.[41] Abu Khattar al 'Aynturini praises him and acknowledges that he wrote his history with the help, direction, and supervision of Bishop Istfan.[42] In fact, it is interesting to note the similarity in the fates of the two men; both Bishop Istfan and al 'Aynturini were leaders in the 'ammiyyah uprising and lost their lives as a result of it. The intellectual activity and public service which characterized the career of Bishop Istfan were crowned by his role in the most important Maronite cultural achievement, the establishment of the college of 'Ayn Waraqah.

When Istfan was still a priest, he was appointed by Amir Bashir as the Christian judge for north Lebanon.[43] In 1809 the people of the diocese of Jubayl and al Batrun attempted to make him their archbishop, but he accepted instead a titular bishopric and also became patriarchal secretary to Yuhanna al Hilu.[44] He continued, however, in his post as a judge. Although in this capacity he was an official of Amir Bashir, and the Amir respected his judgment, his relations with the Hakim were not very smooth.

There were two issues which created tension between Amir Bashir and Bishop Istfan. The first was caused by Istfan's desire to remain free from the Hakim's interference in his judicial function. In one instance the Amir wanted, curiously enough, to force the bishop to try a case in which one party had a standing suit against the bishop himself. The bishop informed Bashir that he could not in all conscience try a case in which one of the parties had a quarrel with him. When the Amir insisted, the bishop angrily ignored the Amir's request and went home.[45] Another issue which disturbed the relations of Istfan and Bashir was the continually increasing

[41] See Shayban, *Tarikh*, pp. 517-518.
[42] 'Aynturini, *MTL*, XLVI, 175.
[43] Ziadah, *Al Qada' al Maruni*, p. 64, n. 4.
[44] Hilu papers, August 1809, PAB.
[45] Hilu papers, 9 November 1816, and MS, no. 267, PAB.

taxation. The bishop pleaded for the poor people and warned the Amir about his policies, which did not endear him to the Hakim.[46]

The second main reason for tension between the Amir and the bishop had to do with their relationship as two Maronites, one lay and the other clerical. As a member of the Church, the Amir had to heed the princes of the Church on what they thought to be the interests of the community. In 1817 the Amir, together with his chief ally Shaykh Bashir Jumblat, tried to influence affairs in the Church; but they were successfully opposed by Patriarch Hilu and Bishop Istfan. More important was Bishop Istfan's growing displeasure over the Amir's decision to keep the Shihabis' Maronite faith secret while publicly emphasizing adherence to Islam.

The Shihabis' conversion to Maronite faith from Sunni Islam is a long story and as yet little known. Since the subject is outside the scope of this discussion, only a brief account will be given here in order to clarify the question of Istfan's conflict with the Amir. During Patriarch Tiyyan's period, some of the clergy attempted to force into the open the matter of the secrecy of the Shihabis' religious practice. The patriarch did not concur and had to raise the case with Rome for a final decision. He wrote a long letter explaining the whole issue from its beginning, stating that the Shihabs were converted from Sunni Islam at the hands of the clergy,

> but gradually, that is one after the other until they have now all become Christians. [However,] they did not accept the [Christian] faith until they were assured by some of those preceding heads [of the Church] that they [the clergy] would not put them under obligation to declare themselves openly; but they [also] made it a condition upon themselves that if they were asked by those who have the right to ask them about that question, like the Vezirs of the Sub-

[46] Yazbak, *AL* (1957), p. 205; Bulus 'Abbud, *Basa'ir al Zaman fi Tarikh al 'Allamah al Batriyark Yusuf Istfan* (Beirut: Matba'at Sabra, 1911), I, 230-231.

lime State, they would not deny their faith but affirm it. They have continued in this fashion to this day.[47]

Then he went on to explain how they performed their religious duties in secret and how in public they went as Muslims. Gradually they disclosed their faith to their contemporaries to the extent that some of them appeared in church.

In 1818 certain incidents (to be discussed later) took place in Mount Lebanon which upset religious susceptibilities, and Amir Bashir gave an order to his kinsmen, the Shihabis, to show themselves in public as Muslims and to fast during Ramadan. This step was too much for Bishop Istfan and he considered the Amir's action to have broken the original covenant, although actually it had not. The Hakim's order only altered a situation which was by then an open secret, but it constituted a setback to the advance of the Maronite faith. Istfan wrote a letter to Patriarch Hilu urging him to take action against the Amir's order and to have the clergy desist from giving the Amir private religious service. He warned Hilu that if he did not stop the Amir's order then and there, he would find it almost impossible to retrieve the situation in the future.[48] There is no evidence that the patriarch actually brought this issue with the Shihabis to a head. The incident, however, demonstrated the complex relationships developing between church and state during that period.

The conflict between Bishop Istfan and the Amir culminated in the 'ammiyyah protest in 1820 when the bishop stood at the head of the people in resisting Amir Bashir's taxation policy. He was not the only cleric involved in the uprising; there was a general wave of discontent among the lower clergy and some of them took active part in the rebellion.[49] Tannus al Shidiaq,

---

[47] Tiyyan papers, MS, no. 227, see also MS, no. 228, PAB.

[48] Hilu papers, MS, no. C. 118, PAB.

[49] Shihwan, "Hayat Matta Shihwan," *Kawkab al Bariyyah* (1911), pp. 479-480; Shidiaq, *Akhbar*, ii, 159; Ma'luf, "Al Azjal fi al Amir Bashir," *Manarah*, viii, 117; Mashaqah, *al Jawab*, pp. 83-84; Nasim Nawfal, *Batal Lubnan al Shahir al Ta'ir al Sit: Yusuf Karam* (Alexandria: al Matba'ah al Wataniyyah, 1896), p. 92.

who took part in these important events, tells us that Bishop Yusuf Istfan was the organizer of the rebels. He organized the people into village communes in which each village chose one *wakil* (representative), to lead their people and act for them with the rest of the country's wakils and the government.[50]

The institution of wakils established by Bishop Istfan was of long duration in the Mountain and became of great importance in the changing political practices of the Imarah. Fortunately we have a record of the kind of covenant made between the villagers and their wakils which gives an idea of what the wakils stood for. This example is the covenant of the village of Bash'alah written on 15 August 1821. (This was during the second round of the uprising, which is usually referred to as "*'ammiyyat* Lihfid," whereas the first round in 1820 is known as "*'ammiyyat* Intilias.") Following is the text of the covenant made between the people of Bash'alah and their wakil delegating authority to him to represent them with other wakils and the Hakim:

> We the undersigned, all the natives of Bash'alah in general, old and young, have freely accepted and entrusted ourselves and our expenses to our cousin,[51] Tannus al Shidiaq Nasr, and whatever is required of us in general and in detail, with respect to the 'ammiyyah. His word will be final with us in all [matters] of expenses and losses. [Regarding] the call to arms, we shall obey him in the recruitment of men in our interest and that of the common people. We shall not disobey or relent, and whoever disobeys or relents in what we have written here shall incur upon himself our hostility and severe punishment.

> This is what has been agreed upon between us and him [i.e., the wakil], and he shall act according to his conscience,

---

[50] Shidiaq, *Akhbar*, ii, 145; for wakils, see also Haydar, *Lubnan*, p. 685.
[51] The term cousin here is a figure of colloquial Lebanese speech and does not really refer to blood relations.

not favoring anyone over the other nor relenting in the questions of our interests. Whatever he arranges as the tax, we shall accept; and if he relents in pursuing our interests, we shall hold him accountable. Neither we nor he shall go against [what is hereby written] in any way. God be our witness.

If we [suffer a loss], it will be shared by all of us equally. We should all be [united] as one person, [having] one word, and [paying] one tax. . . .[52]

The revolutionary nature of this covenant reflects important new principles in Lebanese politics which deserve special attention. For the first time in the history of the Imarah, commoners and clergy try to assume political leadership roles, with popular support for their endeavor. Second, in the covenants of the village communes a new concept of authority is articulated, substituting popular consensus and interest for status and heredity as the principle defining constituted authority. The third significant development reflected in the covenant is the change in the peasant's political outlook, from the particularistic view bound by personal allegiance to the muqati'ji's house in whose fief he was born to a new outlook based on communal ties and directly relating the affairs of the peasant to the nation as a whole.

The events of the uprising demonstrate how the communal and popular ideas guided the political activities of the people and challenged the iqta' institutions. The rebels from all the Maronite districts, the Matn, Kisrwan, Jubayl, al Batrun, and Jibbat Bsharri, met at Intilias, in the village church of Saint Ilias. The Christians of the Druze-dominated muqata'ahs of Jabal al Shuf and the *iqlims* stayed away.[53] At the meeting the rebels swore that they would stand together, put the public interest first, and refuse to pay more than the basic tax. To

---

[52] Istfan al Bash'alani, *Tarikh Bash'alah wa Salima* (Beirut: Matba'at Fadil wa Jumayyil, 1947), pp. 533-534.

[53] Shidiaq, *Akhbar*, II, 145; Hattuni, *Nabdhah*, p. 242.

this effect they wrote a covenant among themselves, composed by Bishop Yusuf Istfan.[54]

The attitudes shown by the manasib toward the revolutionary stirrings of the people were not uniform. Some of them viewed the event as a threat to their traditional prerogatives, while others showed their willingness to deal with the commoners in defiance of the established rules segregating the ruling class from the common people. The Yazbaki manasib, who were in favor of replacing Amir Bashir, were sharply torn by what was happening. The initiative for political change was obviously taken by the Maronite common people, a step which could only be repugnant to the manasib. Nevertheless, one group under the leadership of Shaykh 'Ali 'Imad decided to work with the 'ammiyyah. The shaykh went secretly and talked with the Maronite leaders who were meeting at the monastery of Mayfuq in al Batrun;[55] he was apparently quite satisfied with his visit upon his return to Dayr al Qamar.[56] Another group of Yazbaki shaykhs showed repugnance toward the idea of acting on equal terms with the commoners. When the Shihabi amirs Silman and Hasan openly espoused the cause of the 'ammiyyah, they sent a messenger, the historian Tannus al Shidiaq, to the Druze Talhuq shaykhs calling upon them to follow the Amirs to the spot where the 'ammiyyah were assembled. The Talhuqs' answer was quite revealing: "We do not get led by the Christian commoners of that country," they replied; "it is held a shame by us."[57]

As the following events clearly show, the willingness of some of the ruling group to join forces with the commoners was the result of the keen competition for office and power among the manasib. Thus, after the meeting of the 'ammiyyah at Intilias, two Shihabi amirs, Silman Sayyid-Ahmad and Hasan, both longstanding candidates for the office of Hakim,

[54] Ibid.; also Yazbak, AL (1955), p. 159; 'Abbud, Basa'ir al Zaman, I, 230-231.

[55] MAE, Correspondance Consulaire, Sayda, 1 May 1821.

[56] Ibid.   [57] Shidiaq, Akhbar, II, 154.

met with the rebels and encouraged them.[58] They also entered into an agreement with the wakils that in return for the people's support, the amirs, once in office, would not charge them more than one basic tax. They gave an oath in confirmation of this pledge.[59] On the other hand, the Hakim, Amir Bashir, tried to appease the 'ammiyyah; but they refused to listen and were determined to force him to give up his orders for collecting the tax.[60]

Amir Hasan and Amir Silman made their pledges to the 'ammiyyah and rallied the Yazbakis to their side. The leader of the Yazbaki faction, Shaykh 'Ali al 'Imad, had long been in exile in Syria and Egypt. Learning of the events in the Mountain, Shaykh 'Ali left his exile in Egypt and went to 'Akka, where he and other Yazbaki leaders were well received by the Vali of Sayda, 'Abdallah Pasha. The 'ammiyyah sent six wakils to the Vali with Shaykh Fadl al Khazin at their head; the latter, being the only Khazin shaykh to join the 'ammiyyah, was elected chief by them. The Pasha promised the 'ammiyyah that he would not exact from them more than the original amount they had paid in the past and made them understand that he was acting against the two Bashirs, Shihab and Jumblat.[61]

At this point Amir Bashir, seeing that the Pasha was changing his attitude toward him and that the 'ammiyyah could not be broken up, decided to retire from the government of Mount Lebanon.[62] Thereupon 'Abdallah Pasha sent an investiture to Amir Silman and Amir Hasan. The two amirs met the deputation of the Pasha near Sayda, where they were invested;

---

[58] Haydar, "Nuzhat," p. 219, and Shidiaq, *Akhbar*, II, 145.

[59] Shihwan, "Hayat Matta Shihwan," *Kawkab al Bariyyah* (1911), pp. 478-479. Also MAE, Correspondance Consulaire, Sayda, 27 March 1821, and MAA, MS, p. 48, no. 6468.

[60] Shihwan, "Hayat Matta Shihwan," *Kawkab al Bariyyah* (1911), pp. 478-479.

[61] *Ibid.*; also MAE, Correspondance Consulaire, Sayda, 27 March 1821.

[62] Shihwan, "Hayat Matta Shihwan," *Kawkab al Bariyyah* (1911), pp. 478-479, and Shidiaq, *Akhbar*, II, 145.

they then marched to Dayr al Qamar and were met on the way by the 'ammiyyah and the Yazbaki followers. Amir Bashir and Shaykh Bashir left Mount Lebanon but kept close watch on the events there. The two amirs proceeded to collect the taxes for the Vali of Sayda, but soon they, too, were faced with the problem of new and increased demands. The Yazbaki shaykhs tried to resist the new impositions but the Pasha did not yield; thereupon the two Hakims sent a message to the shaykhs to accept the Pasha's demands. The amirs Silman and Hasan had no private resources to help them live up to the promise they had given the Pasha, and the resources of the Yazbaki shaykhs were meagre. Meanwhile, the 'ammiyyah sent word through their wakils that if the Hakims changed the terms of their agreement regarding taxes, they would not support them.[63] On top of this, the two Hakims had no real support among the Druze population, who were then mostly inclined toward the Jumblats. The Amirs feared the Jumblats and what they might be preparing for them,[64] but had no choice except to levy a high tax.

At this turn of events, Amir Bashir sought to win the Pasha's favor and asked that he be allowed to return and live in Jazzin, to which the Pasha agreed. Then the people and the manasib started to protest and expelled the Hakims' tax collectors.[65] This paved the way for the return of Amir Bashir, and the Vali grudgingly had to approve. The failure of Silman and Hasan demonstrated the hopelessness of the Yazbaki faction's cause. It also pointed up the need for the two amirs to establish stronger relations with the Maronite 'ammiyyah beyond mere exploitation of their trouble-making potential. However, the amirs failed to establish a positive relationship with the 'ammiyyah which would develop among the latter a real and lasting loyalty to the new Hakims. While the 'ammiyyah problem was not solved, the Yazbakis in their turn

[63] MAE, Correspondance Consulaire, Sayda, 27 March 1821.
[64] Ibid.   [65] Haydar, Lubnan, pp. 675-676.

fell an easy prey to Shaykh Bashir Jumblat by coming to terms with him and giving tacit recognition to his leadership.[66]

After his return to the Mountain, Amir Bashir proceeded systematically and skillfully to execute his new policy. He first settled existing differences among the manasib in Jabal al Shuf, then sent his son to collect the miri from the Maronite north. Again, the people rose up against the Amir's son and sent messengers to all the regions to gather at a place called Lihfid. Having received news from his son about the uprising, Bashir personally moved to settle the issue. He tried to negotiate with the leaders of the uprising, but they insisted on being treated on equal terms with the Druze with respect to taxation and other matters of which there was no explicit mention.[67] The Amir was willing to go along with them on the point regarding the tax, but soon he found something more in the demands of the 'ammiyyah. A very interesting new element appeared during these negotiations which demonstrated the far-reaching effects of the revolutionary spirit among the Maronites at that time.

In the demands which the 'ammiyyah put forward to the Amir, they asked that the governor ruling over them, first, should not be invested by an Ottoman Vali, and second, should be one of them.[68] Haydar wrote of these demands, "they decided on disobedience and sent a copy of their conditions [to the Amir], which were utterly unreasonable. One of these was that whoever is the Hakim, he should not be appointed by the [Ottoman] State."[69]

This independent spirit on the part of the Maronites went

[66] *Ibid.*, p. 677; Shidiaq, *Akhbar*, ii, 157-158.
[67] Haydar, *Lubnan*, p. 659; Hattuni, *Nabdhah*, p. 242. See Yazbak, *AL* (1956), p. 390.
[68] It may be remembered here that the Vali of Tripoli formally invested the Shihabi Amir over the northern part of Lebanon, and when the same Vali held both Tripoli and Sayda, the Amir received two investitures from him.
[69] Haydar, *Lubnan*, p. 685; Shidiaq, *Akhbar*, ii, 155.

too far for the Amir, who categorically refused their demands. There was fighting in Lihfid, Kisrwan, Jibbat Bsharri, and other places. The Amir, who already had some of the Druze manasib with him, sent for Shaykh Bashir Jumblat to come to his aid.[70] In the meantime Amir Silman and Amir Hasan rallied once again behind the 'ammiyyah and joined in the fighting. They also had the help of the Matawilah shaykhs, who had previously made an alliance with the 'ammiyyah to stand with them.[71] But the fighting ended in the defeat of the 'ammiyyah and the two amirs, Silman and Hasan. Bashir then collected the tax as he had originally intended and imposed further penalties for insubordination. Had it not been for the intercession of the elderly Patriarch Hilu, he would also have done much harm to the Maronites of Jibbat Bsharri.[72]

Al 'Aynturini, the writer, was caught, tortured, and then released, to die soon afterward in a Maronite convent in Jubayl. Bishop Yusuf Istfan fled to a place in 'Akkar called Dahr Safra. From his hiding place the bishop wrote to the patriarch not to intercede on his part because he had decided to spend the rest of his life in worship.[73] But the Amir did not leave him in peace, and in 1823, when Bashir had pardoned him and he went to see the Amir, he was poisoned and died after leaving the Hakim's palace.[74]

The demands made by the people underlined certain important ideological aspects of the 'ammiyyah rebellion. First, a sharp breakdown became evident in the political community between Maronite and Druze, based on different group interests and sentiments. Matters reached the stage of open conflict, and fighting broke out in some mixed villages between Christians and Druze over the issues raised by the

[70] Haydar, *Lubnan*, pp. 685, 687, 688, 689; Shidiaq, *Akhbar*, II, 155, 157.
[71] Hilu papers, MS, no. 461, PAB.
[72] Hattuni, *Nabdhah*, p. 247; Yazbak, *AL* (1957), pp. 83-84; Nawfal, *Batal Lubnan*, p. 92.
[73] Hilu papers, MSS, nos. 484, 485, PAB.
[74] Yazbak, *AL* (1955), p. 159; Nawfal, *Batal Lubnan*, pp. 93-94; Hattuni, *Nabdhah*, pp. 206-207; 'Abbud, *Basa'ir al Zaman*, pp. 230-231.

'ammiyyah.[75] The Maronites clearly and explicitly demanded that they should be treated by the Hakim on an equal footing with the Druze. Not only did they stress this point in their demands to the Amir, but the sentiment spread among the people like fire and was expressed in popular poems in colloquial Arabic.

A synopsis of a long poem on the 'ammiyyah uprising, written in 1820, will illustrate the popular feeling. The poet, Yusuf Ma'luf, complains that the new tax was imposed mainly on the Christians and their clergy. But the people were annoyed, the poet goes on, and wondered why the Christians were used only for the payment of taxes while fighting was considered the business of the Druze.[76] The people swore that they would not comply with such a state of affairs and that they were willing to rise against it. Because none of this had ever happened before, the poem continues, and because the Christians and the Druze had not been treated differently since the days of Fakhr al Din, they resolved in a public gathering to resist this new situation.[77] The poem clearly reflects two central ideas. One was historical, namely, a sense of nationhood extending back to earlier centuries, and the second political, i.e. the community desired to impose on the rulers its own sense of what was just.

The new concepts embodied in the 'ammiyyah uprising had serious implications for the principle of legitimacy in the iqta' system. First in importance was the idea of public welfare, *"al salih al 'umumi."* The idea was used by the people to refer to the interest of the subjects as a whole, particularly the Christian public. The distinctions between private interest and that of the public are evident in the covenants written between the villagers and their wakils. The appearance of general concepts of this kind reflected new modes of thought

---

[75] MAE, Correspondance Consulaire Sayda, 6 May 1821.

[76] The same idea occurs in a letter of Abbot Ighnatius Sarkis; see text in Yazbak, *AL* (1956), p. 390.

[77] Ma'luf, "Al Azjal fi al Amir Bashir," *Manarah*, VIII, 120-122.

unfamiliar under the iqta' system, where the mental set had been particularistic. No universal ideas like private versus public welfare had been entertained in the past. The individual then viewed himself as an integral part of the 'uhdah with no sense of political individuality of his own. To start to think in terms of public interest implies an awareness of new relations and an outlook in which the traditional idea of subject and master are no longer acceptable.

There were two aspects to this group consciousness manifested by the 'ammiyyah, which constituted the common condition of existence among them. In the first place, the 'ammiyyah were commoners and of peasant stock, a fact indicated by the name they gave to their movement.[78] The class consciousness is also evident from the fact that peasants participated in the uprising against the wishes of their muqati'jis, particularly the Khazins and the Abillama's, who stood with the Druze manasib and signed their compact.[79] The only Khazin who initially joined the 'ammiyyah was Shaykh Fadl al Khazin,[80] who later in the struggle betrayed the 'ammiyyah and joined the other side.[81] The other feature reflected in the group consciousness of the 'ammiyyah movement was the community feeling. The Christians, mainly Maronites, were looking at the whole event as a struggle of Maronites against Druze domination and privilege.

The second main concept embodied in the whole uprising was that of independence. The independent spirit shown by the Christians in demanding freedom from the Ottomans strikes a familiar note in Maronite ideology. As we have seen

[78] See for instance the ideas expressed in the memoirs of the clergyman Matta Shihwan, of peasant background himself, "Hayat Matta Shihwan," *Kawkab al Bariyyah* (1911), pp. 476-477.

[79] See the text of the pact and signatures of the manasib, Druze and Christians; Yazbak, *AL* (1956), pp. 510-512. The editor mistakenly thinks that the pact was that of the 'ammiyyah; in fact it was that of the manasib referred to in Haydar, *Lubnan*, pp. 676-677; also Hattuni, *Nabdhah*, pp. 246-247; Shidiaq, *Akhbar*, II, 145, 146, 159; Haydar, "Nuzhat," p. 219; Shihwan, "Hayat Matta Shihwan," *Kawkab al Bariyyah* (1911), pp. 479-481.

[80] *Ibid*.   [81] *Ibid*.

earlier, the spirit of independence and the feeling of being a distinct community were major ideas in the clerical view of Maronite ideology. The processes of political life in the Imarah were henceforth to be increasingly shaped by these new ideas and trends, to the detriment of the traditional iqta' institutions.

A strong communal feeling among one group naturally generates the same with their neighbors. The Druze were themselves becoming suspicious and cautious after the unprecedented Maronite demonstrations of communal independence. Unlike the Maronites, the Druze community did not go through internal renovating experiences, and its strong communal feeling against the Maronites is not very easily understood. However, Druze attitudes might be partly explained by the defensive reaction they built against the Maronite challenge and, second, by the course of events over the years immediately preceding the 'ammiyyah uprising, which had given them a single political leadership under Shaykh Bashir Jumblat. After the demise of Jirjus Baz, the Druze came increasingly under the control of Shaykh Bashir Jumblat, as will be seen from the Mukhtarah affair, discussed below. This does not mean that the Druze manasib were removed or replaced by Bashir Jumblat, but simply that they gradually became less powerful and more dependent upon him.

The Mukhtarah Affair

The interesting career of Bashir Jumblat and his changing relations with Bashir II are very important because they served as a catalyst to bring about a new realignment of forces in the Mountain, with far-reaching effects. Therefore, let us go back a bit to follow the course of the political relationship between the two Bashirs, the Maronite Hakim and the most powerful Druze muqati'ji.

There are good indications that Amir Bashir was not happy about Druze leadership falling to a single man. In 1818 he had tried secretly to encourage the Yazbakis and to have them

stage a comeback, but it was already too late. The attempt was
foiled by the vigilance of Bashir Jumblat, who uncovered the
plot and confronted the Amir with it. The Hakim denied
any connections with the Yazbakis; and to make good his
word, he had to have his main conspirator secretly executed.[82]

Amir Bashir had much to fear from the ambitions of
Shaykh Bashir Jumblat. The shaykh's real aspirations were
not clear, but it was known that he was cultivating his relations with the Ottoman Valis and was increasing his forces
at home. For instance, sensing that the Vali of Sayda, 'Abdallah Pasha, was under the influence of the fanatical Muslim
shaykhs of his entourage, Shaykh Bashir started to show public signs of adhering to Islam and built a mosque in his stronghold of al Mukhtarah.[83] An incident that occurred around
1818 also accentuated this trend. Shaykh Bashir encouraged
a rash Shihabi youth to become reconverted to Islam and
aroused in his mind the idea of becoming Hakim.[84] In the
aftermath of an unsuccessful love affair in which this youth
was prevented from marrying a cousin of his, he killed his
uncle and his father and ran away to Damascus, where he
pretended to have killed his kinsmen because they were apos-
tates. In Muslim law, renegades, if not willing to return to
Islam, should be killed; thus the law protected him in Damascus.

However silly was this affair, which had its start with the
conniving of Bashir Jumblat, it left serious impressions on
Amir Bashir and the Christians and was completely distasteful
to both. By that time people already had some notions about
the Shihabis' status as Christians, but they guarded their
mouths in matters affecting other people's susceptibilities,
especially when it concerned the Hakim. It was after the above
incident that Amir Bashir gave orders to the Shihabis to show

[82] See Shidiaq, *Akhbar*, II, 139-141; Haydar, *Lubnan*, pp. 650-651.
[83] Shidiaq, *Akhbar*, II, 139, 197, and Mashaqah, *al Jawab*, pp. 66-67.
[84] *Ibid.*, and MAA, MS, p. 46, no. 6469, and Shidiaq, *Akhbar*, II, 136-139.

public signs of allegiance to Islam[85]—a measure which aroused the ire of Bishop Yusuf Istfan.

No matter how much he wanted to, Amir Bashir was not then in a position to check Shaykh Bashir Jumblat, particularly because of the persisting hostile attitude of the Christians toward him. He therefore grudgingly kept his peace. However, Amir Bashir was a man of great patience and could wait for his moment.

In 1821, after quelling the 'ammiyyah uprising,[86] Amir Bashir became involved in Ottoman politics, allying himself with 'Abdallah Pasha against the Vali of Damascus. The affair ended in the disgrace of the two, the Hakim and 'Abdallah Pasha, although they had military success. The Ottoman government removed both of them. Amir Bashir left for Egypt where he tried to establish relations with the rising star of Egypt, Muhammad 'Ali, while 'Abdallah Pasha defiantly stayed in 'Akka. Muhammad 'Ali, who was cultivating his relations with political chiefs in Syria with an eye to the future, then mediated the dispute and forced the Ottoman government to restore both Amir Bashir and 'Abdallah Pasha to their respective offices.

Bashir Jumblat, who had opposed the alliance between the Hakim and the Vali in the first place,[87] cleverly escaped the Amir's fate. Through his efforts, the new Vali was glad to invest as Hakim the Shihabi candidate of Bashir Jumblat, Amir 'Abbas,[88] instead of the Yazbaki candidate, Amir Silman Shihab. Actually, this step was made with the complicity of Amir Bashir, who regarded it as a makeshift arrangement until he could straighten out his relations with the Ottoman government. Amir 'Abbas proved to be a mere figurehead, as expected, while Bashir Jumblat was the power behind the throne.[89] But the conduct of the two leaders flouted the expectations of Amir Bashir, who had believed they would honor the understanding.

[85] *Ibid*. [86] Dimashqi, *Tarikh*, p. 96. [87] *Ibid*.
[88] Haydar, *Lubnan*, p. 723. [89] Mashaqah, *al Jawab*, p. 91.

When Amir Bashir returned around the end of 1822, however, he had the allied backing of 'Abdallah Pasha and Muhammad 'Ali of Egypt. His hand was stronger than ever for dealing with Bashir Jumblat. Finally, after the Amir had made it clear to the shaykh that he was in disfavor by levying endless demands and imposts on him, Shaykh Bashir decided he had better leave the country.[90]

Impatient with the long period of exile, Shaykh Bashir in 1825 determined to have a decisive confrontation with the Hakim. He sent orders to his lieutenants to mobilize their forces. After gaining the support of Amir Silman Shihab, he won over Shaykh 'Ali al 'Imad by lucrative gifts[91] and ordered his men and supporters to wait for him in his stronghold of the Mukhtarah. Then Shaykh Bashir moved from his exile near Tripoli, without the permission of its Pasha and against the latter's will.[92] Jumblat also sent messages to the shaykhs of Jibbat Bsharri, al Kurah, Jubayl, and Kisrwan to rally behind him and Amir Silman. In these letters he tried to appeal to the recipients' historical antagonism toward Amir Bashir.[93]

However, for the Maronites things had by then changed sufficiently to consider their historical opposition to Bashir II something of the past. In their earlier struggle with Amir Bashir, the Maronites of the north knew very well the decisive role played by Shaykh Bashir Jumblat in quelling their revolts. Besides, a new factor had to be taken into consideration by the Maronite people of the north as well as by those of the mixed areas in the south. Amir Bashir was, after all, a Maronite, while the Shaykh was of the Druze faith, and the main forces he had gathered in al Mukhtarah were Druze with a large number of 'uqqal.[94] The attitude of the Church was another important element. Since the Jumblati shaykh's

---

[90] Haydar, *Lubnan*, pp. 746-747.
[91] *Ibid.*, p. 757.
[92] Hubaysh papers, MSS, nos. 8230, 8232, 8233, PAB.
[93] Hubaysh papers, MSS, nos. 8230, 8232, 8233, PAB.
[94] Hubaysh papers, MS, no. 205, and Haydar, *Lubnan*, pp. 762-766.

fall into disfavor, the Amir's relations with the Church had been improving. The clergy could easily see that the Druze were set against the Amir and were standing behind one leader. Already there were rumors that the meeting at the Mukhtarah had the purpose of subjugating the Christians to the Druze.[95]

The young new patriarch, Yusuf Hubaysh (1823-1845), was on the side of the Amir and sent orders to Maronite shaykhs in Jibbat Bsharri, Jubayl, and Kisrwan to go with their men to his support.[96] He himself kept well informed about Shaykh Bashir's movements through his correspondence with the clergy and Shaykh Butrus Karam of Ihdin. The fact that the patriarch's orders were heeded was clearly demonstrated by the case of a Khazin shaykh who, accused of having supported Shaykh Bashir, went to great pains to clear himself with the patriarch.[97]

In short, partly through the efforts of the patriarch[98] and the Amir, and partly by the intuitive feeling that the battle at the Mukhtarah would affect their welfare as a group, the Maronites decided to support Bashir II. Some even fought for the Amir against the will of their muqati'jis.[99] The war at the Mukhtarah shook southern Lebanon but left the north untouched, except for the effect of the modest support the Maronites of that region gave the Amir. Maronites from the Matn, Qati', Dayr al Qamar, and Jubayl fought for the Amir, whose army was mostly formed of Maronites,[100] with the exception of the soldiers sent to him by 'Abdallah Pasha of Sayda. However, this was not yet a war of Christian versus Druze. A number of Druze shaykhs allied themselves with

---

[95] Shidiaq, *Akhbar*, II, 191.

[96] Hubaysh papers, MSS, nos. 261, 8230, 8232, 8233.

[97] *Ibid.*, MS, no. 8245.

[98] On the attitude of the clergy, see Mashaqah, *al Jawab*, p. 94.

[99] See letter from Bashir II to Amir Haydar Abillama' reproduced in Sfayr, *Al Amir Bashir*, p. 152.

[100] Hubaysh papers, MS, no. 205, PAB; also Abu Shaqra, *Al Harakat fi Lubnan*, p. 13.

Amir Bashir—for instance some Talhuq and 'Abd al Malik shaykhs[101]—while, on the other hand, a small number of Abillama' amirs and Maronite shaykhs from Kisrwan joined forces with the Jumblati faction.

The war resulted in victory for the Amir; Shaykh Bashir Jumblat and Shaykh 'Ali al 'Imad escaped and their forces were dispersed. Shaykh 'Ali was captured in Damascus and killed, while Shaykh Bashir Jumblat was later sent to 'Akka by the Vali of Damascus, where he was strangled by the Pasha's orders. Most of the Druze and, strangely enough, some of the Melkite Orthodox Christians were punished by the Amir for siding with Shaykh Bashir.[102]

The Mukhtarah affair in 1825 marked a turning point in the politics of Mount Lebanon. It resulted in reorganization of political forces and alliances. The Amir's complete dependence upon Druze support shifted for the first time, and he started to rely on the Maronites. A new bridge was also built between him and the Maronite clergy; but before we get to that stage, we should summarize the changes seriously affecting the political institutions of the iqta' system which have taken place thus far.

We have seen first that the clergy tried to establish a favorable political position with the government through the mudabbir, an effort which, after a good measure of success, was curbed violently. But the venture itself served as a portent of the growing strength and assertion of the churchmen.

In the second place, we have observed how, under the guidance of some of the clergy, the people organized into new units for political action at the local and national level. The assumption of leadership by wakils chosen by the people, in matters of taxation and war and in relations with the higher authorities, was a direct threat if not an outright repudiation of the established system of iqta' institutions.

---

[101] Haydar, *Lubnan*, pp. 757-761; Yazbak, *AL* (1956), p. 31.
[102] Hubaysh papers, MS, no. 205, PAB.

Third, the principle of political allegiance, ismiyyah, to the house of iqta' under which the subject lived was threatened by a new principle of communal solidarity based on interest and consensus. Moreover, the social cohesion reflected in the village communes was based not only on interest but also on ethno-religious identification.

Fourth, the 'ammiyyah movement demonstrated that commoners in the system could assume a place of leadership along with the hereditary actors. The fact that they were able to affect the election and deposition of Hakims, and the way Shihabi candidates and manasib resorted to the peasants for support, clearly shows that the common people had made a dent in the old system and had come to occupy a place in the affairs of the Imarah.

Another very evident aspect of change was the weakening of the political power of the manasib. Partly by Amir Bashir's own design and in part by developments beyond his control, gradually the major Druze manasib were crushed. First, the Nakads were destroyed by the other manasib as the result of rivalry among faction leaders, with Bashir's complicity. Second, the Yazbakis lost their power and effective leadership after the alliance between the mudabbir, Jirjus Baz, and Shaykh Bashir Jumblat. Although Amir Bashir went along with this Jumblati policy, he did not intend to carry it as far as it actually went. He wished but was unable to save the Yazbaki faction, for its leaders, the 'Imads, were greatly weakened by almost two decades of oppression and exile.

Finally, the Jumblats' growing power menaced the Amir, who took a decisive stand to destroy the foremost muqati'ji of the Imarah, Shaykh Bashir Jumblat. The destruction of the Jumblat power was the only overt and deliberate action taken by Amir Bashir II to overcome the muqati'jis. With the removal of the Jumblats, the last powerful muqati'ji house in Lebanon was deprived of political power, and Bashir set out to build a new policy which would suit his ends.

CHAPTER IX

Clergymen, Peasants, and Muqati'jis:
The Second Phase

THE MAJOR TRENDS which we observed in the preceding chapter continued and came to a climax during the following two decades. The clergy assumed a greater political role, the Maronite peasants continued to be restive under the iqta' system, and the Hakim, in a dramatic change of policy, turned to the Maronites for support. The paramount Druze manasib were isolated and remained under political constraint until the downfall of Bashir II and the collapse of Egyptian power in Syria.

The Mukhtarah affair, at which Shaykh Bashir Jumblat and his followers were crushed, signaled a definite change in political conditions under the Imarah. Both ruling class and political institutions were effected. The muqati'jis in general were put under firmer control by Amir Bashir, and many of them lost their muqata'ahs because of their roles at the Mukhtarah. Bashir thereafter employed commoners, mostly Christians, as his officials and appointed members of his family to run the 'uhdahs taken from their former legitimate holders.[1]

For support Bashir relied more on the backing which the Church could muster for him, as well as his direct influence with the people.[2] The clergy's venture into politics thus received an additional and significant push forward. The consequences were very important for the configuration of political alignments and roles. All the new tendencies and changes in the system pointed out earlier took a stronger expression. Though the new alliance between Bashir and the Christians did not replace completely the older iqta' alignments, its ap-

---

[1] Dahdah, "Al Amir Bashir," *MQ*, xxii, 574-575; also Abu Shaqra, *Al Harakat fi Lubnan*, pp. 15-16, 26.

[2] See for instance Ma'luf, *TZ*, pp. 154, 156, 157-159.

pearance seriously challenged the continuation of the manasib's undisputed leadership.

The basic change in the relations of Amir Bashir with the Maronites and their clergy came at just about the time Patriarch Yusuf Hubaysh (1823-1845) was elected as head of the Church. The new patriarch was well educated, the first graduate of the 'Ayn Waraqah College to rise to that dignity. He was young and had not yet attained the legal requirement of forty years of age when elected; the Holy See had to give him a special dispensation to waive the age requirement. Patriarch Hubaysh belonged to a family of small shaykhs in Kisrwan which, though not powerful, was still one of the oldest Maronite houses of the a'yan.

The Amir's collaboration with Patriarch Hubaysh was in marked contrast with the guarded and cool relations he had maintained with Patriarch Yuhanna al Hilu, Hubaysh's predecessor. This difference becomes particularly clear from examination of the archives of the two patriarchs kept at Bkirki in Lebanon; the papers of Hilu indicate few connections with the Amir al Hakim, whereas those of Patriarch Hubaysh are rich in such references. An analysis of these records gives an idea of the nature of the Church's political relations with Bashir II, as well as the political roles which the clergy came to play at that time.

THE NEW BASIS OF POLITICAL SUPPORT

Amir Bashir's conflict with the leading Druze manasib and his determination to weaken the hold of the manasib over him made it necessary that he seek new bases of support in the country and promote new political forces. The Maronite Church, as an agency free from the muqati'jis' control, was the only alternative for Bashir to advance his political ambitions. Thus less than two decades after the initial and abortive bid made by the Church under Patriarch Tiyyan for a top political role in the Imarah, the Church reemerged as a strong leading organization. In entering the political arena, the Church represented a new political element, reinforcing the Amir's power and giving him the support which he could no longer receive from the muqati'jis.

The clergy, it is important to remember, did not replace the muqati'jis; they simply entered the hitherto closed circle of actors as competitors. While the muqati'jis, Druze and Maronite, were weakened, many of them were still in control of their 'uhdahs, though in a precarious manner unlike the past. Their main weakness now lay in the fact that their traditional involvement in national politics (that is, their influence over the Hakim) was almost completely terminated. Without influence in national politics, a muqati'ji's role amounted simply to administration of his 'uhdah. The patriarch, on the other hand, was gaining the upper hand in political influence over the Hakim, and his community-wide appeal gave him a national character in contrast to the narrow local character of muqati'jis.

At this stage of the relationship between patriarch and Hakim, the patriarch's leadership depended upon the extent of confidence and support given him by the Amir. Likewise, the Amir's delegation of power to the patriarch depended on the extent to which he needed the patriarch and the extent to which the latter was willing to support his policies. To judge from the Hubaysh papers, the Amir backed the patriarch both by giving him power to make decisions and by satisfying his demands.

This relationship of mutual support can be observed in the role the patriarch played vis-à-vis the muqati'jis and the people. In the first place, the Amir honored the patriarch's decisions and encouraged him to settle disputes and problems among Maronite muqati'jis and among various other classes of people.[3] For instance, in cases where Maronite muqati'jis had some differences among themselves over land, 'uhdahs,

---

[3] See Rustum, *UATS*, iii-iv, 228; Hubaysh papers, MS, no. 2281, PAB.

or personal matters, they raised these problems with the patriarch.[4] The patriarch's authority to settle these questions was informally delegated to him by the Amir. Such matters were also sometimes raised with him because, as a man of influence, he could have them settled in the Amir's court. Thus the patriarch became a man of much political influence, but not a holder of political office.

For his part the Amir encouraged the muqati'jis to look to the patriarch as a man of prestige to whom they should turn for problem-solving, and actively supported the patriarch's decisions and views.[5] The case of a certain dispute which arose between two Khazin shaykhs will illustrate this process. The two shaykhs went to the Amir with their quarrel, but instead of taking action himself, Bashir made them go and seek a settlement from the patriarch. Then the Amir sent a briefing to the patriarch through Archbishop 'Abdallah al Bustani as to the most desirable way of handling the problem. Bustani wrote to the patriarch:

> Your Holiness should order this restoration [of land] . . . and should enjoin on both parties to end all disputation and quarrels. His highness's purpose in making this peace is to put an end to trouble, and it is his intention to have this take place under your orders and with your efforts. . . .[6]

As is clear from this account, the Amir's policy seems to have been definitely aimed at strengthening the power of the patriarch in his community. The muqati'jis and the common people, as a result, turned more and more toward him, and increasingly demands were mediated by the intercession of the patriarch. He handled such problems as disputes among the muqati'jis and between the latter and the common people.[7] The people, usually proceeding through their bishops or

[4] *Ibid.*, MSS, nos. 151, 260, 752, 2281, 3529, 6162, 7383, 7562, 8056, 8127, 8581.
[5] *Ibid.*, MSS, nos. 260, 7464, 7465, 8122.
[6] *Ibid.*, MS, no. 3238.
[7] *Ibid.*, MSS, nos. 151, 752, 768, 3128, 3129, 3489, 3529, 5301, 8059, 8122.

priests, also used the good offices of the patriarch to solve their own problems, including disputes with their muqati'jis, both Christian and Druze, over land, taxes, and personal matters.[8] Even administrators in the Amir's service were anxious to win the patriarch's good will and favors.[9]

The muqati'jis' need for the patriarch lay not only in connection with general disputes, but went much further to include questions over 'uhdahs. Sometimes muqati'jis found it necessary to seek the help of the patriarch in order to be reconfirmed on their 'uhdahs or to have a sequestrated muqata'ah returned to them.[10] Requests for help came not only from Christians but also from Muslims, particularly from the region of Tripoli and al Dinniyyah,[11] which during the Egyptian period became a dependency of the Amir's government. One letter from a Muslim notable of Tripoli puts the reason behind the patriarch's power quite plainly: ". . . your requests are well received by his highness [the Amir] and thus we hope that you will fulfill what we have mentioned above."[12] However, the Amir was not at ease about the patriarch's interceding on behalf of the Muslims and once wrote to him that he was not happy about the consequences of such efforts.[13] Also, it seems, the patriarch received requests from Druze shaykhs for mediation with the Hakim.[14] On the whole, the patriarch assisted those who sought his support with good effect, and did successfully reinstitute some shaykhs over their muqata'ahs.[15]

Some of the clergy who enjoyed power as the Hakim's judges were also able to help the Maronites considerably. Thus

---

[8] *Ibid.*, MSS, nos. 2305, 3217, 3242, 3522, 3526, 3541, 3542, 3535, 3541, 5812, 6382, 8215.

[9] *Ibid.*, MSS, nos. 3763, 6188, 8581.

[10] *Ibid.*, MSS, nos. 3764, 6188, 8581.

[11] *Ibid.*, MSS, nos. 2493, 2958, 3746, 4608, 5893, 7320, 7324; see also Rustum, *UATS*, ii, 59-60.

[12] Hubaysh papers, MS, no. 7320.

[13] *Ibid.*, MS, no. 8122.

[14] *Ibid.*, MSS, nos. 7320, 7452, 7482.

[15] *Ibid.*, MSS, nos. 3764, 3863? (number not clear), see year 1835.

on two important occasions, after the Baz affair and after the 'ammiyyah movement of 1820, Maronite clerical judges in northern Lebanon helped the Maronite village shaykhs to return to their former positions and to regain their property confiscated by the Amir.[16] They also were able to uphold the Maronite people's rights against claims made by the former Matawilah lords to land then held by Maronites.[17]

The patriarch attended to all this business and solved independently those problems that he could, and the rest which had to be handled directly by the Amir he sent to Bayt al Din, the Hakim's palace. The increase in the volume of daily work was managed by the clergy, particularly the two patriarchal secretaries.

These activities and involvements all pointed to the growing power of the Church and the dependence on it of the manasib as well as the common people. Naturally, to the extent that the people looked to the patriarch as their patron they also placed themselves under his leadership. The Church's attempts at political leadership which had earlier ended in failure were now becoming fruitful. The short-lived link between the Church and the Maronite mudabbir was successfully replaced, a little more than a decade later, by an alliance between the Church and the Maronite Amir al Hakim.

As we have seen, the relationship between the Amir and the patriarch was built on mutual service and support. On the patriarch's side, he needed the Amir for the continued progress of the Church, its activities, liberties, and welfare. The Amir readily granted this, since it was traditional under the Imarah to respect religious liberty and to offer the Church protection.[18] The patriarch also needed the Amir for protection and favors for the Maronite people. The Maronites were then becoming more assertive and had visions of in-

---

[16] Hilu papers, 13 September 1811, also 21 August 1823, PAB.

[17] *Ibid.*, see papers of 1811.

[18] For the Amir's pecuniary awards to the Church, see Hubaysh papers, MSS. nos. 7344, 7382, 7387.

creasing their political power in the Mountain. The Amir could enhance that cause immensely. The patriarch and other prelates repeatedly used the good offices of the Amir in the service of the Maronites.[19]

The Amir's support was also sought by the patriarch against the Druze. The patriarch did not hesitate, for instance, in 1832, to request the Amir's help on behalf of Maronites who were subjected to some oppressions by the Druze. The Amir granted the patriarch's request, letting him know that "his highness was well disposed, though in secret, toward the Christian's welfare. . . ."[20] Further, the Amir firmly supported the patriarch's efforts to keep the Protestant missionaries out of the Mountain, obliging them to remain in the coastal cities.[21]

THE DYNAMICS OF THE NEW POLITICS

In supporting the Amir, the Maronite clergy were assisting a Maronite Hakim who was friendly toward the Maronites and faced a problem with his Druze subjects. This policy was in line with the interests and aspirations of the Maronite community. It was in this spirit that the Church and the Maronite people readily came to the help of Amir Bashir in his war with the Jumblati faction in 1825.

The Amir's need to mobilize popular support among the Maronites became urgent after the Mukhtarah affair and during the development of the conflict between Muhammad 'Ali of Egypt and the Pasha of Sayda, 'Abdallah. As soon as news started to reach the Amir that Muhammad 'Ali was preparing for the occupation of Syria, he took his usual stance of wait-and-see,[22] at the same time, however, secretly assuring Muhammad 'Ali of his support. Taking advantage of the

[19] *Ibid.*, MSS, nos. 2288, 2305, 3217, 3242, 3526, 3535.
[20] *Ibid.*, MS, no. 2490. For this alliance with the Christians against the interest of the Druze, see also Ma'luf, *TZ*, 139, 156-159.
[21] Hubaysh papers, MSS, nos. 1095, 2288, 2305, 3217, 3242, 3535, 6223.
[22] See, for instance, Rustum *UATS*, I, 103-104.

fluid situation created by the Egyptian preparations against
'Akka, Amir Bashir postponed the payment of tribute to
'Abdallah Pasha under the pretext that he was short of money.
Although the Vali accepted this answer, it was clear that the
Amir was no longer going to put up with the Pasha's demands for more tribute and was preparing for resistance if
the latter wanted to press them. The Maronite clergy backed
the Amir on this stand, promising Maronite support, for
which he was grateful.[23] Similarly, when Amir Bashir made
up his mind to stand with Muhammad 'Ali and his son
Ibrahim Pasha, the Maronite clergy threw their full weight
behind him, with moral backing as well as mobilization of
the Maronites for war.[24] The Church's hierarchical organization with its clergymen in every community in the Mountain
proved to be a great help in that effort.[25] The patriarch sent
orders through the archbishops and bishops to have the parish-
ioners made ready to support the Amir and his allies the
Egyptians.[26]

The disaffection of the Druze with the Amir and their
early resistance to his allies, the Egyptians, no doubt had a
weakening effect on Bashir's position with Ibrahim Pasha.
Thus the Maronite community's support was all the more
valuable to the Amir to maintain his standing with his senior
ally. The Amir's reliance on Maronite backing continued
throughout the Egyptian period, and as the events of 1840
demonstrated, his position became vulnerable as soon as he
lost Maronite support.

To cope with the situation, the Amir thus arranged with
the Church prelates to bring the Maronites together and form
a united body. This effort included the writing of a covenant
among the Maronite people pledging unity and loyalty to

[23] Hubaysh papers, MS, no. 2357.
[24] *Ibid.*, MSS, nos. 5217, 6680, 6685, 7262, 8073, 8628; also Rustum,
UATS, I, 124-125.
[25] Hubaysh papers, MSS, nos. 3217, 3242, 6347, 6381, 7262.
[26] *Ibid.*, MSS, nos. 2399, 2448, 2490, 2492, 2504, 2515, 5781.

the Amir.[27] The prelates carried out the plan and tried to make it known to the whole community by means of the Church organization. Letters were sent to the outlying districts stressing the importance of being on guard and maintaining unity.[28] The Amir and his son Amin took certain additional steps to encourage Maronite group solidarity, thus further benefiting the clergy and giving them more power and satisfaction.

In an effort to mobilize Maronite support behind his father, Amir Amin wrote to the patriarch in 1838 regarding the latter's efforts to unite the Maronites and ward off the Druze danger against them. The letter read:

> The movement of the Druze in the Mountain is not unknown [to you], and that the Christians, in order to guard against the evil consequences of this movement, have become one solidary group [*ta'assabu*] in this country and are united in the bond of religion. They have become like one man under the command of his highness [Amir Bashir]. They came to his highness and received arms to protect themselves and [to enter] the service. . . . We beg your beatitude to summon the shaykhs and notables of Jibbat Bsharri and to form a unity among them, then to choose . . . three hundred young men . . . [and send them here] so that as soon as they arrive we can give them arms.[29]

The first sentence in this letter refers to the conflict which had arisen between the Druze of Hawran in southern Syria and the Egyptian forces. The impact of the Druze revolt in Hawran upon Lebanon was marked and served to revive the hostile sentiments of the Lebanese Druze against Bashir. A good number of them went to the support of their coreligionists in Syria. The failure of the Egyptian soldiers to subdue

[27] *Ibid.*, MS, no. 5217. Also Rustum, *UATS*, I, 124-125, and III-IV, 228.
[28] Hubaysh papers, MSS, nos. 5294, 22 April 1838; 5293, 20 June 1838.
[29] *Ibid.*, in 1838 (1254 A.H.)—number illegible.

the Druze of Hawran made Ibrahim Pasha request the help of Amir Bashir. Having to depend entirely on Christian forces in this campaign, the Amir's policy of cultivating relations with the Church and of building up the strength of the Maronites began to pay off. The Maronites gave the Amir full backing in his campaign against the Druze.

In short, we can see that in most of his relations with the Maronite community, the Amir needed the clergy in executing his policies as well as in mobilizing support.[30] The clergy helped amply, even in supplying fighting men and organizing them for war.[31]

The clergy were also able to assist the Amir by collecting political and military intelligence. By virtue of the large number of Maronite clergymen scattered throughout Lebanon, Syria, Egypt, and Europe, the patriarch had an excellent network providing him with information from near and far.[32] For example, during the beginning of the Egyptian-Ottoman war, the Amir asked the patriarch to have his clergymen in Aleppo write to him about the movements of troops and their commanders. This correspondence was carried on in the unfamiliar Karshuni script and in Syriac.

Up to this point we have been concerned with the relations between the ruling Hakim and the clergy. Now the discussion will focus on how the clergy used their influence and advantage to shape the course of events, which to a considerable extent contributed to the downfall of the iqta' system.

First, how did the patriarch put his policies into effect? Patriarch Hubaysh stayed almost all the time in his patriarchal residences at Qannubin and Bkirki. We know of only one public visit he made to the Amir in Bayt al Din, on which he was received ceremoniously by the Amir and with

---

[30] *Ibid.*, MSS, nos. 2272, 3996, 4032, 6347, 7441, 7444.

[31] *Ibid.*, MS, no. 7262.

[32] *Ibid.*, MSS, nos. 2242, 2257, 2416, 3278, 3583, 5298, 5299, 6392, 6663, 8356, 8357.

acclaim by the Maronite people in the area. Therefore, in the conduct of public affairs and the administration of his policies, the patriarch used the facilities of the Church organization. With him at his residence he had two bishops as secretaries who not only helped him in the day-to-day business but were also his advisors; particularly influential was his secretary, the later patriarch Bulus Mas'ad. The archbishops in their dioceses and the priests in their villages were the agents of the patriarch in carrying out Church policies. For instance, Archbishop 'Abdallah al Bustani of the diocese of Sayda, whose See was near the Amir's capital, handled some of the patriarch's affairs with the Amir. The Archbishop of Beirut, Butrus Karam and later his successor Tubiyya 'Awn, dealt mainly with the European consuls in Beirut and with representatives of the Ottoman government. Bishop Niqula Murad was a patriarchal emissary in Istanbul and Europe. Other figures in the Church each performed the role within the scope of his office and connections, such as the priests Arsanius al Fakhury, Yuhanna al Islambuly, and others.[33] And in 1840 the patriarch appointed as a personal representative to the Porte in Istanbul a Maronite merchant, Ilias Hawwa.[34]

With this idea of the patriarch's ability to communicate his wishes and policies, we can continue with the account of the clergy's role in influencing political events in the Mountain. During the period between the affair at the Mukhtarah in 1825 and the Egyptian occupation in 1832, the government of Amir Bashir was not faced with any major problem. The destruction of Bashir Jumblat left the Druze community with weak leadership and depressed hopes, while the Maronites improved their relations with the Amir's government and benefited politically and economically from the weakening of the Jumblati faction. The muqata'ah of Bashir Jumblat and his land came under the direct control of the

---

[33] *Ibid.*, MSS, nos. 3242, 3996, 3997, 5217, 6240, 6347, 6373, 6381, 6382.
[34] Bulus Qar'ali, *Al Bayraq*, 31 October 1949.

Amir, who governed it by appointed officials chosen from among his supporters.

However, the Egyptian occupation of Syria required the Amir, the Church, the Maronite people, and the Druze to make serious decisions. By taking sides with the manifestly superior power, the Amir saved his country—at least temporarily—from the effects of conquest and from drastic changes in its traditional institutions. As a result, the Egyptian reorganization of governmental affairs in Syria had minimal effects in Mount Lebanon. Although the political institutions of the Imarah were not directly disturbed, the challenges of the Egyptian power nonetheless affected the newly forming group alliances in the Mountain and had corresponding effects on the institutions themselves, as we shall soon see.

The Maronites, motivated by the liberal reputation of the Egyptian government and their own united front with the Amir, threw their full weight behind the Amir's senior ally, Ibrahim Pasha. The Maronites' decision to follow the Amir in this instance, however, was not entirely free from problems. A certain archbishop, for example, wrote to the patriarch about the Maronites' disappointment over the Egyptian taxation policy. The prelate explained how the promise to reduce imposts, which he had conveyed to the people earlier, had not been realized. He described how disappointing this was for the people and how he was having a hard time explaining the situation to them.[35] Nevertheless, while the higher clergy could try to appeal for relief and better treatment for the people, they could not let specific unpleasant measures prejudice the Amir's policy of alliance with the Egyptians. Thus they had to bear patiently the inconveniences created for them by the new situation.

Meanwhile, the Druze on the whole remained loyal to the Ottoman government and resisted the alliance between the Amir and the Egyptians. Seeing a possibility of perma-

[35] Hubaysh papers, MS, no. 2515, PAB.

nently weakening the political hold of the Druze on Mount Lebanon, the Church and the Amir employed the advantages that fell to them from the hostile attitude of the Druze toward the Egyptians to build up stronger feelings of solidarity among the Maronites. The effort to consolidate a community distinct from that of the Druze, and the breaking of the iqta' ties binding the Maronites to Druze muqati'jis, took a sharper turn during the 1830's.

An incident which took place in 1832 will illustrate this point and the way the Church acted to achieve its objective. The incident concerned a certain Maronite, Lutfallah, from the village of Falugha in the Matn region, who was a subject of Amir Haydar Abillama'. The population of the Matn region was composed of Maronites and Druze, while their muqati'jis, the Abillama' amirs, were mostly Christians converted from the Druze faith. This Lutfallah became the subject of a multiple complaint: that he had been acting in complicity with the heads of the Druze clans; that he was friendly with a certain Druze in the village and was not cooperating with Hanna 'Asi, apparently an influential Maronite villager who had the backing of the clergy; and third, that he had joined hands with still another Druze in beating a Christian. All this was reported by Amir Haydar to Abbot 'Ammanu'il. The archbishop of Beirut, Butrus Karam, instructed the abbot to summon Lutfallah to the monastery of Saint Rukuz and tell him to redress the situation and stand with the Christians.

Lutfallah went to the monastery for the hearing and cleared himself with the abbot and the archbishop, who then reported the affair to the patriarch. In effect, Lutfallah claimed that he was not acting in a way prejudicial to the interest of his fellow Maronites; on the contrary, he was behaving in line with the general policy and orders of Amir Amin Shihab and his father the Hakim. Second, he explained that the Druze with whom he was friends were those who declared themselves obedient to the Abillama' amirs, not to the rest

of the Druze community in the country; third, that the mis-
understanding with the mentioned Hanna 'Asi was caused
by ill-founded suspicions; and finally, that so far as the rest
of the Druze were concerned he was always alert, and that
he was consistently encouraging the Christians and acting in
their interest.[36]

Some generalizations about the changing political process
can be drawn from this particular incident. First, the Church
and even the Maronite muqati'jis were acting together to
build up the solidarity of the Maronite people as a community.
Second, the clergy clearly were active in trying to sever political and social relations between the Maronites and the Druze.
This meant, in effect, not only the separation of the two communities but also the rejection of the iqta' tie of ismiyyah
between the Maronite subject and his Druze lord, or between the Druze subject and his Maronite lord. The implications of such an effort for the position of the Druze muqati'jis
in southern Lebanon and the institutions of the Imarah obviously were quite serious. The Druze manasib had no doubt
as to the threat to their authority coming from the Maronite
clergy. By 1841 the Druze muqati'jis were convinced that
the patriarch's purpose was to dislodge them from their position of authority and power in Lebanon.[37]

The process of building up the group solidarity of the
Maronites and of marking their separateness from the Druze
continued throughout the 1830's. We have already seen how
the Amir's policy in 1838 was to emphasize this solidarity
so that he could rely more heavily on Maronite support. He
needed men not only to fight but also to demonstrate to
Ibrahim Pasha that he was still strong in Lebanon and thus
to dispel any ideas the latter might have had about interfering directly in the affairs of the Mountain. The Maronites
were firmly behind him in all this.

Meanwhile the political goal of the Church was taking

[36] *Ibid.*, MS, no. 2255.   [37] *Ibid.*, MSS, nos. 6656, 6657.

distinct form: it was to have a Maronite Imarah in which power would be concentrated in the hands of a Maronite Amir supported by the Maronite people. The government of Amir Bashir II and his policies after the battle at the Mukhtarah represented to the Maronites the ideal they were seeking. To ensure the firm establishment of that regime and prevent its collapse was therefore a paramount concern of the Church. Thus the Church hoped for the weakening of the predominant Druze manasib and actively tried to draw away the loyalty of their Maronite subjects.

The Maronite prelates' dream of perpetuating the situation which in effect had obtained since 1825, that is, the existence of a Maronite Imarah, was to pass through serious tests and upheavals. Indications that something was going amiss started to appear around 1840. The situation in Mount Lebanon at that point was becoming very complicated, beyond the ability of any single party to solve it. At the same time, the Egyptians' relations with the Amir were getting tense; after the major wars were fought, they ceased to show the Amir the same warmth they had earlier.[38] There were signs that Ibrahim Pasha was contemplating far-reaching changes in the Mountain which would include the deposing of the Hakim. The clergy became so upset about these matters that, on their own initiative, they asked the French consul in Beirut to use his government's offices to prevent any such interference on the part of the Egyptians.[39] Another complicating issue was the fact that the Amir was forced by Ibrahim Pasha to let some of his Druze subjects be drafted into the regular Egyptian army, which further deteriorated the Amir's relations with the Druze community. Added to this, the new tax imposed by the Egyptians was unusually high.

The Church for its part was willing to put up with anything short of compromising its major aim, a Christian Imarah. This meant going along as far as possible with Amir

[38] *Ibid.*, MS. no. 8122.   [39] *Ibid.*, MS, no. 2767.

Bashir's policy of alliance with the Egyptians. The Maronites, it should be noted, in contrast with the Druze showed no concern over the fact that the Egyptian conquest had severed the centuries-old relations with the Ottoman State. Patriarch Hubaysh told the French consul clearly that the high taxes they paid to the Egyptian government were at least compensated for, to a certain extent, by the security and order under the new rule, whereas he found no purpose in the tax paid to the Ottoman government.[40] Thus utilitarian considerations were replacing the established norms of Ottoman sovereignty.

So far as the people were concerned, the last year of the Egyptian occupation was marked by increasing restlessness. The impact of the corvée, the high taxes, and the fear of conscription brought popular feeling to a head. At the beginning of 1840 the people of Dayr al Qamar wrote to the patriarch, sounding him on the problem and expressing their fears of conscription.[41] The patriarch and his prelates, however, were in no way willing to go along with premature adventures, although they were unhappy about many of the Egyptians' policies.[42] The Maronite muqati'jis, too, were unhappy about Amir Bashir and the Egyptian administration, but they were reluctant to take action themselves; and with unusual lack of spirit, they hid behind their subjects and let them take the initiative and bear the responsibility. Not much could be expected from the Druze muqati'jis in 1840, since most of them were in exile. The Druze population, without their traditional leaders, were not in a position to show much vigor. The spirit of revolution among the Christian common people, on the other hand, was by that time well ignited and

[40] Ismail, *Histoire du Liban*, IV, 171, n. 1.

[41] Hubaysh papers, MS, no. 5845, PAB.

[42] Patriarch Bulus Mas'ad, "Tarikh Suriyyah wa Lubnan fi 'Ahd al Dawlah al Misriyyah," MS (Jafeth Library, American University of Beirut, n.d.), p. 2. Also Arsanius al Fakhury, "Tarikh wa Tawaqqa'a fi Jabal Lubnan min Shahr Ayyar Sanat 1840 wa Sa'idan," MS (Jafeth Library, American University of Beirut), pp. 1-2. See also Qar'ali, "Al Batriyark Yusuf Hubaysh," *al Bayraq*, 31 October, 1949.

threatened with its flames not only the Egyptians but also the muqati'jis of Mount Lebanon.

REVOLUTION AND CIVIL STRIFE

In May of 1840, revolt against the Egyptians broke out among the Maronite people and some of the Druze[43] in a fashion reminiscent of the Intilias 'ammiyyah uprising. The similarity between the two movements was in fact readily perceived by Amir Haydar Abillama' who made the point in a letter to the patriarch.[44] A meeting and covenant were made at Intilias in the same church where the covenant of the 1820 rebellion was formed.

The parties, the organization, and the slogans of the rebellion, though shaped by different circumstances, were also similar to those of 1820. With respect to the participants, the rebels were mainly Maronite peasants from north and south Lebanon. Some of the Maronite a'yan rallied behind them, but others were reluctant to commit themselves and willing to let the responsibility fall entirely upon the peasant subjects. Only a few of the peasant leaders of the rebellion are known to us and they were almost all Maronite, like Habib 'Aql, Abu Samra, and al Shantiri; and one Shi'i, Ahmad Daghir. There is no question that the lead was taken by the peasants themselves. The truth of this statement is not altered by the fact that in certain cases the rebels chose a member of the a'yan to be their leader, because such arrangements proved to be only formal. The accounts of the revolution given by the chroniclers show beyond doubt that in the course of events the leaders were of the 'ammiyyah. In an interesting reversal of roles, the a'yan, amirs, and shaykhs followed behind the peasant leaders both in deciding on the conduct of the war and in action.[45]

[43] For a detailed account of this revolt, see Laurent, *Relation Historique*, I.
[44] See report of Amir Haydar Abillama' to Patriarch Hubaysh, in Rustum, *UATS*, v, 92.
[45] See for instance Shidiaq, *Akhbar*, II, 226, 228, 229. Also Bulus Mas'ad, "Tarikh Suriyyah wa Lubnan," MS, p. 6.

As for the Druze, they again dropped out of the picture early in the struggle and agreed to accept Bashir's promises—some of which, if true, are fine examples of the cynicism of that old Hakim. We are told, for example, that Bashir promised to make the Druze masters of the Maronite heartland of Kisrwan.[46] At any rate, the peasants carried on with the rebellion after the Druze left off, with only some of the Christians from the mixed areas turning back in fear of the Amir and the Druze.[47]

The higher clergy were at first greatly disturbed by what the Maronite peasants had done. Partly on their own initiative and partly at the request and exhortation of the Amir, the clergy attempted to calm down the people and to mediate their complaints with the Amir.[48] This was not successful, and the peasants wrote to the patriarch begging his understanding.[49] By the middle of July, some two months after the revolt had broken out, the patriarch reversed his position and came out openly in support of the rebellion, urging all the Maronites to rise in arms.[50] The clergy then took an active part in encouraging the people.[51]

The reasons behind the patriarch's move to support the rebels are not very clear, especially since at stake was the whole dream of a Christian Imarah at last made possible by Bashir II. However, one can detect some good reasons for the patriarch's decision. In the first place, his enthusiasm for the Egyptians had slackened off after the latter had demon-

---

[46] Ismail, *Histoire du Liban*, IV, 67; also Ferdinand Perrier, *La Syrie sous le Gouvernement de Mehemet-Ali Jusqu'en 1840* (Paris: Arthus, Bertrand, Librairie, 1842), p. 381.

[47] Fakhury, "Tarikh ma Tawaqqa'a," p. 5.

[48] Hubaysh papers, MSS, nos. 5783, 5784, 5845, 8071; also Rustum, *UATS*, V, 80-81, 85-92, 117-118.

[49] Hubaysh papers, MS, no. 5844.

[50] Ismail, *Histoire du Liban*, IV, 71, n. 1. See also Poujade, *Le Liban*, pp. 119-120. Great Britain, Parliamentary Papers, IX (Accounts and Papers, 1841) *Correspondence Relative to the Affairs of the Levant*, Part II (London: T. R. Harrison, 1841), 192.

[51] *Ibid.*, p. 289; also Perrier, *La Syrie*, p. 379.

strated their high-handed ways in dealing with the Amir and the affairs of the country.[52] Second, the rebels were his people. Third, the harshness with which the Amir suppressed the rebels in Kisrwan and other Maronite regions could not have failed to arouse the patriarch's antipathy toward the Hakim. Fourth, in mid-July the European powers had just concluded the Treaty of London aimed at ousting Muhammad 'Ali from Syria—which helps explain the patriarch's timing of his open commitment in favor of the rebellion.

Whatever the reasons behind the patriarch's position, the effect of his stand with the rebels was quite salutary. For one thing, it prevented the development of a gap between the people and the clergy with their newly acquired community leadership. Furthermore, in terms of relations with the Ottoman government and the European powers, the patriarch's standing improved greatly.[53] When the revolt succeeded and the European and Ottoman presence in Syria became dominant, the victorious powers recognized the patriarch as the leader of his people and settled down to deal with him.[54] Amir Bashir was the first to foresee this eventuality as he was leaving his palace. He ordered his treasurer to send a large sum of money to the patriarch, declaring that he needed the patriarch then more than anyone else in the world[55]—he had his eye on the future, of course, hoping for a comeback.

As for the organization of the rebellion, to a large extent it followed a pattern similar to that of 1820. Elected wakils were summoned by the leaders of the movement, five from each village, to form a central committee, the *diwan*, and take charge of the rebellion.[56] For the purposes of fighting, the

[52] Qar'ali, "Al Batriyark Yusuf Hubaysh," 31 October 1949.

[53] The patriarch's political influence was attested to by Mr. Wood in a letter to Viscount Ponsonby; see Great Britain, Parliamentary Papers, ix, *Correspondence*, Part ii, 192.

[54] See Rustum, *UATS*, v, 112-120, 188; also Hubaysh papers, MS, no. 6702.

[55] Mashaqah, *al Jawab*, p. 146.

[56] Rustum, *UATS*, v, 102-103. This call to revolution is also given by

Mountain was divided into four camps (*kashat*): one in al Shuf, the second in Jazzin, a third near Beirut, and a fourth in Jubayl.[57] Each of these camps had its own chosen leaders. During the second phase of the rebellion, 1841-1845, when the Maronites fought against Druze supremacy, the patriarch organized the people by dividing the country into six muqata'ahs, with one wakil from each.[58]

Similarly, the slogans used by the people reflected the same ideological bearings of the 1820 uprising. First, the rebellion had Christian overtones clearly expressed by its leaders in a letter to the patriarch: "We have come together in a real Christian unity free from [personal] purposes and from spite, made rather for the welfare of the common folk [*jumhur*] of the community."[59] The initial agreement of some of the Druze to rise with the Maronites, it will be remembered, was broken off, and the Christians accused them of bad faith. The ideological note stressing the Maronites' separateness from and contrast with the Druze took a stronger expression after 1840.

Both religious and class consciousness were distinctly expressed in a letter from the people of Zahlah to the French consul, Poujade, in 1843(?). In this document the Christians explained that the Druze were forced by their muqati'jis to fight against the Maronites, and had they been free they would not have taken to arms; that no peace was possible in Lebanon so long as the Druze chiefs continued to have special privileges and immunities; nor would there be peace

---

Baron I. de Testa, *Recueil des Traités de la Porte Ottomane avec les Puissances Étrangères depuis le Premier Traité Conclu en 1536 Entre Suleyman I et François Jusqu'à nos Jours* (Paris: Amyot, Bibliothèque Diplomatique, 1868), III, 75.

[57] Fakhury, "Tarikh ma Tawaqqa'a," p. 2.

[58] Hubaysh papers, MS, no. 7487. See also the patriarch's order to the Maronite peasants in Druze muqata'ahs regarding the election of wakils and preparation for the eventuality of conflict; MS, no. 6288(?), 28 April 1841. Regarding the office of wakil, see further Poujade, *Le Liban*, p. 35; Testa, *Recueil*, III, 139-162, 169, 173.

[59] Rustum, *UATS*, v, 94.

if they continued to rule "our brethren," the Christians in the Druze-dominated areas, for such a situation was entirely unacceptable. Then, offering their theory on the origin of the Druze muqati'jis' privileges, the people from Zahlah maintained that these prerogatives had been given by Amir Bashir and could be taken away at his will. Finally they asserted:

> Lebanon is not the property of the Druze, it is ours. The Druze are refugees whom we received among us when they escaped from Egypt after the murder of the imposter the Hakim bi Amrihi. Thus they are by no means the proprietors of the country, but strangers here.[60]

Another feature of the ideological aspect of the rebellion was the resistance to the foreign ruler and the spirit of independence. The rebels made it clear that they were not acting against the Amir himself nor against the Shihabi dynasty and its prerogatives, but against the foreign power, the Egyptians, who were tyrannizing over both the Amir and the people.[61] In a remarkably sophisticated revolutionary tract, the leaders of the rebellion dwelt on the subject of how the Egyptians had deprived them of their freedom and how they had defiled whatever the Lebanese held sacred. In recapitulating the lessons which, they said, the Egyptian experience had taught them, they summed up the whole situation in one sentence: namely, their aim was to rise against this "slavery whose end is death." They took as their example the Maccabeans, and also recent Greek revolutionary experiences:

> The cause of justice is invincible and will succeed with God's help. . . . Let no one fear the might of this state [i.e., the Egyptian] because the end of injustice is perdition; the Greeks have risen before you and have attained absolute freedom.[62]

[60] Poujade, *Le Liban*, pp. 245-246.
[61] Fakhury, "Tarikh ma Tawaqqa'a," p. 4; also Laurent, *Relation Historique*, I, 35, 57.
[62] Rustum, *UATS*, v, 102-103; also Testa, *Recueil*, III, 74-76. In Rustum

Other rebel demands concerned taxes and plans for governmental reorganization. A long list of grievances was presented to the Amir regarding taxation, the corvée, and suggestions for the future reorganization of the people's affairs. Specifically, first the leaders of the rebellion repeated the demands made in 1820 that they should pay only the original basic tax, annulling all the additions which had been made over the succeeding years. They insisted, second, that the corvée in the iron mines of al Matn should be ended, and third, that their arms not be confiscated as instructed by Ibrahim Pasha. The fourth and most interesting demand was for reorganization of the administration. It will be remembered from the discussion of the mudabbir's role and history that, after reducing the Maronite mudabbirs to simple administrators for a number of years, Bashir next employed as his mudabbir, in 1828, the Syrian Melkite Catholic, Butrus Karamah. It is quite likely that the Amir took this step to protect himself from too much influence on the part of the Maronites. As a result, Butrus Karamah became the object of Maronite hostility. Demonstrating their broad view of the issues, the rebels requested that the Amir should expel Butrus Karamah from his diwan (administrative council) and form a diwan of new composition.[63]

Reorganization of the Hakim's administration was a major aim of the Maronites for the political future of Lebanon. The Church and the Maronite people[64] wanted a council representing the various communities to help the Amir in the administration of public affairs. The Druze at first approved the scheme,[65] thinking it would give them the advantage of

---

the revolutionary experience of the French, not the Maccabeans, is mentioned, *UATS*, v, 102; whereas in Testa the Maccabean experience is given as the rebels' example, *Recueil*, p. 75. On the Greek revolt, cf. Albert Hourani, *A Vision of History: Near Eastern and Other Essays* (Beirut: Khayats, 1961), p. 81.

[63] Hubaysh papers, MS, nos. 8206 seq.; Shidiaq, *Akhbar*, ii, 227.
[64] Hubaysh papers, MSS, nos. 5805, 8217, 8218; Shidiaq, *Akhbar*, ii, 227.
[65] *Ibid.*, p. 275.

being represented in the administration of the Amir's business whereas previously they had had no members of their community in administrative posts. Apparently the Druze had no idea of the far-reaching consequences of the plan as it was conceived by the patriarch, although they were particularly apprehensive of a Maronite majority in the council.[66] The Maronites envisaged an administrative council which would conduct the business of government directly and whose jurisdiction would cover the muqata'ahs.[67] This meant encroachment upon the independent prerogatives of the Druze muqati'jis. In any case, the Druze soon dropped their support for the plan and attacked it violently once it was instituted.[68]

The Ottoman government, meanwhile, approved the Maronites' demand since reorganization of the country's administration was in line with the Sultan's reform.[69] Thus the Ottomans instructed the new Hakim, Bashir III, to convene an administrative council of ten men to settle disputes and conflicts according to the law.[70] This council was to be formed of three Maronites, three Druze, one Sunni Muslim, one Melkite Orthodox, one Melkite Catholic, and one of the Matawilah.[71] These were to receive a fixed salary and be elected by the people; however, as it turned out, the Christian members on the council were chosen by their respective clergies. The Amir was to preside over the council in person or by deputy. The Christians sent deputies to the council, but the Druze refused to do so in defiance of the Amir and in anger over the threat it posed to their prerogatives.

Thus the participants, the organization, and the slogans of the first phase of the revolt showed a clear and persistent pattern. The revolt was popular in formation, communal in

---

[66] Laurent, *Relation Historique*, I, 269.

[67] Shidiaq, *Akhbar*, II, 249; and Hubaysh papers, MS, no. 5779.

[68] Shidiaq, *Akhbar*, II, 249; and Hubaysh papers, MS, no. 5779.

[69] This question will be discussed later on in the chapter.

[70] Testa, *Recueil*, p. 90. In Shidiaq, council members are said to have been twelve; *Akhbar*, II, 253.

[71] Testa, *Recueil*, III, 91.

ideology, and representative in organization—free from iqta'
ties.

In its course of action, the anti-Egyptian phase of the rebellion went through two stages. The first lasted from mid-
May to around the end of July 1840. This ended in failure,
with the people put down and dispersed by the forces of Amir
Bashir and the Egyptians. Some of the leaders of the rebellion, a'yan as well as commoners, were captured and exiled.
Although exile was not a punishment inflicted normally on
the common people, the majority of those exiled were commoners: there were twelve members of the a'yan among the
exiles and forty-five commoners.[72] However, the uprising
was resumed successfully in the first part of September when
a small contingent of Ottoman, English, and Austrian forces
disembarked at the Bay of Juniyah on the coastal strip of
Kisrwan. Encouragement and supplies of ammunition from
the allied forces revived the spirit of popular revolt. The fighting again rested on the shoulders of the Maronites, while the
Druze remained aloof; some of the Druze, in fact, were fighting in the army of Ibrahim Pasha, since they formed part
of his troops.[73] The Maronites distinguished themselves in
the field and harassed the Egyptian forces effectively. The
gratitude of the Ottoman Empire was expressed by a promise
to exempt the Maronites from taxes for three years, and the
Sultan sent the patriarch a diamond-framed medal.[74]

In the meantime, the Ottomans with the support of their
European allies, mainly Britain, invested with authority Amir
Bashir Qasim Mulhim, known as Bashir the Third, making
him the Hakim of Mount Lebanon. Bashir II had tied his
fortunes with those of the Egyptians down to the last moment
and was sent into exile.

The rebellion in the country, however, did not end with the

---

[72] Shidiaq, *Akhbar*, II, 236.

[73] Hattuni, *Nabdhah* (Yazbak edn.), pp. 234-237; Laurent, *Relation Historique*, I, 97, 108.

[74] Hubaysh papers, MSS, nos. 5810, 6142, 6184, 6360.

defeat of the Egyptians, but continued to smolder until 1845. The whole country, in fact, was in revolt, the Druze manasib no less than the Maronite peasants. With the downfall of Bashir II and the defeat of the Egyptians, the country was again open for the Druze manasib, who returned home and took over their former muqata'ahs.[75] But by then a new kind of alliance had been formed in the political forces of the Mountain. The old established system of alliances between the Hakim and the factions of the manasib was largely replaced by the alliance between the Amir and the Maronite Church and people. The return of the Druze muqati'jis meant that they would challenge this new situation, as well as the recently acquired powers of the Church and its people. The Maronites readily saw this. As the priest Arsanius al Fakhury wrote, the Druze insistence on rejecting the Shihabis was motivated by their desire to continue their dominion in the Mountain (*al taghallub fi al Jabal*), which was no longer possible.[76] In so doing, the Druze manasib were caught between their superiors, the Shihabi dynasty, and their subjects, some of the Maronites living in their muqata'ahs. Thus they had to fight on two fronts.

The Druze manasib were soon made to feel unwelcome by the Maronites.[77] When the people of Dayr al Qamar refused to receive their former muqati'jis, the remaining Abu Nakad shaykhs,[78] Amir Bashir III appointed a Maronite shaykh as an overseer for the village, and the Nakads had to take up new homes in the village of 'Baiy.[79] The Maronite subjects of the Jumblat muqati'jis were quite displeased by the return of their former lords, the sons of Shaykh Bashir Jumblat, and sent complaints to the patriarch. One of the villages, Jun, complained to the patriarch about the harsh treatment they were receiving from their lords; they specifically

[75] Mas'ad, "Tarikh Suriyyah wa Lubnan," p. 11.
[76] Fakhury, "Tarikh ma Tawaqqa'a," p. 25.
[77] Poujade, *Le Liban*, p. 30.   [78] Shidiaq, *Akhbar*, II, 255.
[79] *Ibid.*, p. 249; and Rustum, *UATS*, v, 195.

sought the patriarch's help in persuading the Jumblats to withdraw the Druze officer who had been appointed to keep the villages under control, because he was obnoxious to them and it was too costly for them to pay for his upkeep.[80]

The direct relations which the people had earlier enjoyed with the Shihabi rulers made it difficult for them to accept their former lords. They became ever more attached to the idea of a Shihabi Hakim who would protect them against the muqati'jis.[81]

TOWARD A NEW COMMUNAL SYSTEM

By 1840 the ideas of Maronite nationalism had become a political platform of the community for the future. The Maronite patriarch took the lead in working toward a new Imarah in which the Maronites would be the dominant group, with the Shihabis at their head as the ruling dynasty.

Patriarch Hubaysh's efforts to establish a Maronite Imarah came into the open in 1840 and continued vigorously until his death in 1845. On 29 October 1840, he forwarded to the Ottoman government a petition on behalf of the Church and the Maronite community. This petition discussed the freedom of the Church, the freedom of religious practice, and the regulation of taxes. But the most important point the patriarch made in that document was to stress the Maronite insistence that the prerogatives of the Shihabi government should be guaranteed, unchanged, in Mount Lebanon. This was emphasized to prevent any possible schemes, either on the part of the Druze or the Ottoman government. Thus the petition read:

That the Hakim of Mount Lebanon and Anti-Lebanon should always remain, in accordance with the ancient custom, a Maronite of the noble Shihabi family; [also] because

---

[80] Hubaysh papers, MS, no. 5812; for the complaint against the Arslans by the people of 'Aramun of the Gharb, see *ibid.*, MS, no. 8215. Others, see *ibid.*, MS, no. 3522.

[81] Poujade, *Le Liban*, p. 30.

the Maronite inhabitants of Lebanon . . . are larger [in number] than all the rest. That the investment of this Hakim should be made by edict from the Sublime Porte only, not from anyone else. That an Advisory Council [*Diwan Shawra*] should be instituted in Lebanon for the administration of the affairs of the Mountain and all its interests, as will be reckoned by us later.[82]

The patriarch received a promise from the Ottoman government on this point,[83] which he later used skillfully to influence the European powers in favor of the Shihabis.

During the same period, without wasting any time after the dispatch of his petition, the patriarch proceeded to strengthen the solidarity of the Maronite community, with its different classes, so as to be prepared for a possible later showdown with the Druze and to demonstrate public support for the Shihabi Amir.[84] On 29 March 1841, he brought the Maronite leaders together and had them sign a covenant pledging unity.[85] The existing document for this pact is lengthy and agrees in substance with the one published in Shidiaq's account, except that Shidiaq failed to mention the major Maronite demand, namely that the Hakim should be a Maronite of the Shihabi family.[86] The main points of the pact were as follows: that the Hakim should always be a Maronite of the Shihabi family; that the Maronites should stand together in Christian love; that all should be obedient to the Sultan; that the public interest should be carefully guarded; that the ranks and titles of each person should remain respected as in the past; that wakils should be instituted in all the muqata'ahs to "reform the people," and pacts should be written by the

---

[82] Hubaysh papers, MSS, nos. 5805, 6157.

[83] *Ibid.*, MSS, nos. 6335, 6381.

[84] See his orders to the Maronites in the mixed areas, *ibid.*, MS, no. 6288(?), 28 April 1841.

[85] *Ibid.*, MS, no. 6198.

[86] Cf. *ibid.*, MSS, nos. 6157, 6690; and Shidiaq, *Akhbar*, II, 250-251; also Rustum, *UATS*, V, 208-211.

people and their wakils; and finally, that all the Maronites should be united in respecting this agreement and whoever should break his oath would incur the hostility of them all, and that if other Christian sects should wish to join them they would be welcome.[87]

This covenant was signed by all the Maronite a'yan and circulated by the patriarch's orders to the various villages north and south.[88] The clergy were also active in keeping the Maronites aware of what was going on so that they would not give in to the attempts of the Druze to induce their Maronite subjects to sign new agreements with them.[89]

There were a number of elements in the policy of the Church up to 1841 which this pact illustrates and which should be carefully noted. The Church wanted to effect changes in the Imarah without alienating any more than necessary the Ottoman government, the Maronite manasib, and the Druze manasib. The pact carefully stressed the loyalty of the Maronites to the Sultan and adroitly asked that the appointment of the Shihabi Amir should be made by the Sublime Porte. The effect of this second point was to preclude the Druze manasib from their traditional role of election, and at the same time to contribute toward a possible later clash between the Druze and the Ottoman government over the prerogative the Druze manasib had long held in choosing the Hakim. The Maronite plan also would protect the Hakim from the vacillations of the Ottoman Valis nearer home. Further advantage to the Maronites lay in the fact that as the Shihabi Amir would be appointed for life, the Ottoman government could not have strong control over him.

In the second place, the pact included a stipulation regarding respect for the ranks and governmental privileges of the Maronite manasib. Thus the Church was put on record as supporting the traditional rights of the nobility. As the Church

[87] Hubaysh papers, MSS, nos. 6157, 6198, 6690.
[88] *Ibid.*, MS, no. 6288(?), 28 April 1841.
[89] *Ibid.*, MS, no. 5779.

had to maintain unity among the socially divided Maronites, it therefore tried to steer a middle course between the peasants and the Maronite nobility by recognizing the social ranks of the latter and their prerogatives, on the one hand, and on the other, by conceding some rights to the peasants. Therefore, another requisite was made which satisfied the Maronite common people, who had proved their political importance over the preceding few decades. This was the point about wakils being appointed in the muqata'ahs to reform the people. Although this statement about reforming the people was vague, in actual practice the wakils were to share the powers of the muqati'jis, as we can tell from the events of 1841. Thus the Church sought to maintain unity among the opposing interests of its community by making guarantees to the muqati'jis while conceding to the people a measure of leadership. The effect of this was to strip away some of the functions and powers of the muqati'jis without abolishing their office.

In the same way, the patriarch aimed at initiating all these changes without unduly arousing the hostility of the Druze manasib. He therefore maintained some rapport with a number of the Druze manasib and tried to settle differences through mediation.[90] He was partially successful in mediating their dispute with Bashir III when the latter tried to take away some of their estates in the Biqa' valley.[91] Yet simultaneously he was trying to divest the manasib of some of their functions by sponsoring the Diwan al Shawra and by establishing wakils in their muqata'ahs.

If these gradual political changes at which the patriarch was aiming could not be realized peacefully and without bloodshed, the explanation was to be found in the increasing complexity of the situation and the impossibility of con-

[90] *Ibid.*, MSS, nos. 6399, 7174, 7452, 7482; see letter of 11 June 1841. Also Shidiaq, *Akhbar*, II, 253.

[91] Hubaysh papers, MS, no. 6451, 28 August 1841; Shidiaq, *Akhbar*, II, 253.

trolling all the pieces in the game, in the right time and the right way. Persisting divisions in the community and accidents also accounted for the difficulties, as will be seen from the following.

The most troubling complication came from the Hakim, Bashir III, who was in many ways a problem for the patriarch and the other prelates. The Church was determined to support him because he was a Maronite Shihabi Hakim and the appointee of the Ottoman government and its European allies. Yet he was an incompetent person, lacking in tact, foresight, and the art of politics. The Amir rarely listened to the patriarch's advice and warnings,[92] and he took a very hostile attitude toward the Druze manasib,[93] exasperating almost everybody. The uneasiness which he created among his supporters as well as his enemies is illustrated by a report sent the patriarch by a cleric who frequently represented the patriarch with the Amir, complaining that because of the Amir's instability, nothing could be certain.[94] This situation created several complications for the Church and seriously hindered the success of its policy as we have seen it develop, for the Amir did not even impress the Maronite people themselves. The Church had to go to great trouble in trying to unite behind him the Christians with all their prevailing differences.

Nevertheless, it should be clearly understood here that the Church supported Bashir III during his rule, even though many Christians were trying to have Bashir II or one of his sons return to Lebanon. The patriarch's instructions to his representative in Istanbul leave no doubt that the Church took the reasonable risk of supporting the ruling Amir rather than advocating the return of Bashir II.[95] The reason behind this stand was that any opposition to the Ottoman-supported rul-

---

[92] Hubaysh papers, MS, no. 7444.
[93] See Ismail, *Histoire du Liban*, IV, 110-111.
[94] Hubaysh papers, MS, no. 7570(?).
[95] *Ibid.*, MSS, nos. 6182, 6381, 6423, 6483, 6487, 8206.

ing Amir would threaten the Maronite Shihabi dynasty's ability to maintain its rights to the government of Lebanon and would thus play into the hands of the Druze and the Ottomans.[96] Furthermore, a hostile attitude toward the Hakim would divide the Maronite community.

Bashir III, however, continued to embroil his relations with the Church, particularly mishandling the question of taxation.[97] His unfriendly attitude toward the Church which was supporting him and the crudity of his methods were clearly demonstrated in his encounter with Archbishop Tubiyya 'Awn, the patriarch's right-hand man in dealing with the European consuls in Beirut and the representatives of the Ottoman government.[98] Angry at the patriarch's opposition to the taxation policy and his independent course in general, the Amir summoned clerical and lay Christian leaders to his palace, including Archbishop 'Awn. In the meeting he "started preaching," as 'Awn put it, about the evils of listening to the clergy, drawing examples of their fate in Spain and France. These ideas, 'Awn noted, had been put in his head by his advisor, Francis Misk, who was a British agent. Undaunted, Archbishop 'Awn retorted to the Amir's charges. Reporting later to the patriarch, he said that the Amir did not scare him, "for the people are in our hands, not in his."[99]

Regardless of the numerous quarrels which Bashir III picked with the patriarch and his clergy, during his sixteen months in office the Church remained steadfast in its support, not for his person but for what he represented.[100] Finally, realizing how greatly he depended on the cooperation of the Church,

[96] *Ibid.*, MSS, nos. 5776, 6381, 6427, 6488; see also year 1841, drawers 17 and 18.

[97] *Ibid.*, MS, n.d. and no number, see year 1841; also MSS, nos. 5776, 6488.

[98] *Ibid.*, see for instance MS, no. 6382.

[99] *Ibid.*, MS, no. 6425.

[100] *Ibid.*, MS, no. 6427; see also year 1841, drawer 17; also MSS, nos. 6182, 6423.

the Amir had to bow down in humiliation to the patriarch, demonstrating that the people really were with their clergy and not with him. In a dramatic encounter with the patriarch's representative, he succumbed to the patriarch's demands and agreed to his conditions for cooperation. He wrote and signed a statement that he would do whatever the head of the Church bade and act upon his advice as to whom he should employ in his service.[101]

Unfortunately, the Amir's willingness to let himself be directed by the patriarch came too late and nothing could be done to stem the growing feeling against him. His ineptitude forced the Church and the Maronite people to settle their differences with the Druze by force. Infuriated by the Amir's hostility toward them and suspicious of the patriarch's policies which aimed at curbing their powers, the Druze manasib decided to take up arms against the Amir and his Maronite supporters.

In general the attitude of the Druze toward the Shihabis had changed after Bashir Shihab II, and their lack of enthusiasm, if not disaffection, toward the Shihabis could be traced back to the fight at al Mukhtarah in 1825 and the Hakim's policies of allying with the Maronites against them. With the downfall of Bashir II and the return of the Druze manasib to the Mountain, the whole question of Shihabi legitimacy became subject to debate. Bashir III proved to be insensitive to this delicate situation and, instead of trying to pacify their discontent, aroused their enmity and fears further by continuing his predecessor's policies of withholding from them the muqata'ahs which they had earlier governed. They prepared to resist him and also petitioned the Ottoman government to remove the Shihabis from the government of the Mountain. In this petition the Druze argued that the Shihabis were Christian and therefore, being Muslim themselves, the Druze could not accept their authority. They requested in-

101 *Ibid.*, MS, no. 6449.

stead a Druze or Sunni Muslim Hakim and let the Ottoman government understand that they would be willing to accept an Ottoman governor.[102]

The breakdown in the legitimacy of the system was demonstrated in action when the Druze rose up in arms against Bashir III. In their assault on the Amir, the Druze did not, as their former traditions had prescribed, raise the banner of revolt in the name of another Shihabi amir. This showed that they were acting against the whole dynasty and not just against the particular ruling Hakim.

In the meantime the Maronites were becoming quite offended by the Druze attitude toward the Shihabis, and for their part declared their intention not to submit to an Ottoman or any other governor except one of the Shihabi house and the Maronite faith.[103] Thus once during the vital years of struggle, 1840-1845, when the Druze attempted to put up as Hakim a Shihabi who had earlier reconverted to Islam, Amir Silman, the Church adamantly refused to accept him and insisted on a Maronite Hakim.[104] Generally speaking, though, the chances of reunion between the two groups and agreement by some of the Druze to accept a Shihabi Amir were not yet completely destroyed. What attempts were made, however, were weak and inadequate for real cooperation to develop toward such a difficult goal.[105]

In October 1841 the Druze attacked the Amir al Hakim in the predominantly Christian town of Dayr al Qamar, where he was staying in the traditional palace of the Shihabi rulers. The people of Dayr al Qamar defended their Amir and town courageously and were able to keep the Druze out for some time, although they were isolated in the midst of Druze territory.

---

[102] Hubaysh papers, MSS, nos. 5779, 6421, 6898. Also letter from Arsanius al Fakhury to Patriarch Hubaysh, 14 July 1841.

[103] *Ibid.*, MSS, nos. 6335, 6381.

[104] Ismail, *Histoire du Liban*, IV, 112-115.

[105] Some of these attempts are discussed in Dib, *L'Église Maronite*, II, 377, 379. Also Poujade, *Le Liban*, pp. 57, 77-78.

The preparations which the patriarch had made were imme-diately activated. He mobilized the whole Maronite com-munity, directed them, and provided for most of their expenses from the funds of the Church and orders of monks.[106] As a result a sizable Christian army congregated at the town of B'abda, midway between north and south Lebanon.

Before we follow the actual outbreak of hostilities, it is im-portant to note the stand which the Shihabis took in the con-flict. They all turned to the Christian side and fought at the head of the Christian forces.[107] Leadership was given to Amir Mulhim Shihab,[108] but as we shall soon see, his leadership was not effective. Some of the Shihabis still would have liked to keep some link with the Druze manasib; but when a certain Shihabi was known to have established contact with the Druze, he was unanimously denounced as a traitor by the Christians at B'abda and had to be rushed off to a distant place away from the wrath of the people.[109]

The purpose of the gathering at B'abda was to go to the rescue of the Amir and of Dayr al Qamar. But the Christian army stayed too long in B'abda without acting, regardless of the urgings of the patriarch, the Amir, and the people of Dayr al Qamar.[110] The reason was not that the leaders of the Christians did not realize the urgency of the situation, but rather that they could not act. There was no real leader-ship among them. In a letter by one of the clergymen repre-senting the patriarch, the condition of the Christian army was described as hopeless because every person there con-sidered himself a leader; conflicting opinions were legion and no one seemed to take any action.[111] How did this degree of confusion develop, especially in view of what we know of

[106] Hubaysh papers, MS, no. 6481; also Laurent, *Relation Historique*, I, 286, 325, 353-354.

[107] Hubaysh papers, MS, no. 7174; also Laurent, *Relation Historique*, I, 302; Shidiaq, *Akhbar*, II, 259-264.

[108] Ismail, *Histoire du Liban*, IV, 120.

[109] Shidiaq, *Akhbar*, II, 266.

[110] Hubaysh papers, MS, no. 6424.   [111] *Ibid.*

the painstaking efforts by the patriarch and his prelates to unite their community for action in the eventuality of war?

The fundamental cause was the rivalry between the old leaders, the Maronite muqati'jis, and the new leaders, the clergymen and the commoners. It should be remembered that the political breakdown on the basis of religious alignment had destroyed the old iqta' ties between the muqati'jis and the subjects. This disintegration of the iqta' bond had affected Christian muqati'jis as well as Druze. Thus Maronite muqati'jis, feeling the blow to their privileges, were reluctant to fight.[112] Many of them were on the point of defecting, were it not for the patriarch, who threatened them with excommunication.[113] Even with that threat there were secret dealings and compacts with the Druze manasib. When such clandestine agreements became known to the people, they accused their a'yan families of bad faith. For instance, Shidiaq, who was by no means a fanatic, nor a careless writer, keeps repeating the term "traitors" in referring to these Christian shaykhs.[114]

Whether the Maronite muqati'jis were traitors or not is debatable, but one thing is certain: their established political prerogatives were being jeopardized by the actions of their own community. They could see that what was happening to the Druze muqati'jis in that war was also happening to them. Like the Druze muqati'jis, their power and privileges were contravened by the institution of wakils.[115] Nor were they pleased by the alliance between the Church and the

[112] Hubaysh papers (no number), 31 October 1841(?), a letter from Shaykh Kisrwan al Khazin to the patriarch justifying and defending himself against the charge that no men of his 'uhdah went to fight. See also *ibid.*, MS, no. 7174.

[113] Cyrille Charon, *Histoire des Patriarchats Melkites (Alexandrie, Antioche, Jérusalem), depuis le Schisme Monophysite du Sixième Siècle Jusqu'à nos Jours,* ii, fasc. 1: *La Période Moderne (1833-1902),* (Leipzig: Otto Harrasowitz, 1910), 89.

[114] Shidiaq, *Akhbar,* ii, 258-261, 265-267.

[115] Testa, *Recueil,* iii, 159-161, 173; Ismail, *Histoire du Liban,* pp. 235-236, 244.

Shihabi Amir, to say nothing of the Church's plan to strengthen the Amir against the muqati'jis.[116]

An open conflict which developed between some shaykhs and a wakil in Kisrwan illustrates these issues very clearly. Angered by the wakil's encroachments on their rights, the shaykhs tried to reassert their powers in a traditional iqta'i manner, namely by having their men camp on the wakil's property. The patriarch sent instructions to some clergymen in Kisrwan to remedy the situation. In his report to the patriarch, the wakil wrote:

> The next day they [the local clergymen] wrote a letter to the shaykhs who are quartering with their men [on our property, ordering them] to return to their places. But Shaykh Kisrwan [al Khazin] demanded [that we offer him] service; after many appeals he insisted on five hundred piasters.

No intercession helped in any way, he explained, and the shaykhs acted against the patriarch's orders: "They did not agree to go, and things rather worsened by their declaration, 'We do not receive orders from anyone.'" Then the crux of the matter was made clear as the wakil continued his case:

> . . . When his Holiness issued the orders to us to go to the Dog River and in compliance with these orders we went there, the common people chose us with the consent of the archbishops and the shaykhs to be their wakil. Then as we were carrying out our functions, we talked with them [the shaykhs], in matter of fact, regarding some arrangements [to be made]. At that point, ideas started to roll in their minds that no peasant should become illustrious or know how things are run. . . . We became sensitively aware of that and realized that [their] purpose is not what we had hoped. . . . Regarding what they say, that we in-

116 *Ibid.*, pp. 257-259.

terfered with them by drafting their men, that could be investigated by impartial persons.[117]

Then, after referring to some of the points of conflict between him and the shaykhs concerning the assertion of his authority as wakil over their men, the writer concluded his letter with an interesting remark about the similarity of his position and that of the Christians living under Druze muqati'jis.[118]

The Church policy of promoting wakils who would take over a part of the functions of the muqati'jis without entirely displacing them would probably have worked under less critical conditions. Had the scheme to appease the Druze muqati'jis been successful and armed conflict with them avoided, the policy of the Church would have been conducive to the development of the political system and the peaceful breakdown of the iqta' institutions without the disastrous course of events which actually followed. The intensity of the conflict between the two groups, Druze and Maronite, however, was aggravated by the combination of religious as well as class differences.

The friction resulting among the Maronites from the existence side-by-side of these two offices, muqati'ji and wakil, prevented effective action in the war. Particularly because of the war, the Church had to try to submerge these class differences within its community. Thus the fact that the Church was unable to declare itself decisively and quickly enough for one side or the other, the wakils or the muqati'jis, the commoners or the a'yan, left the Christian front in B'abda torn with indecision and lack of leadership.

Later, however, after the Christian manasib had shown themselves ineffective, divided, and wayward in their loyalty, the Church expressed its populistic sentiment more forcefully. This attitude was reflected in a petition presented to the Ottoman government through the French consuls. This docu-

---

[117] Hubaysh papers, MS, no. 6233.
[118] *Ibid.*

ment should be considered as the first major political program put in writing in the political history of Mount Lebanon, and because of its importance it will be included in full in the Appendix. Suffice it here to say that it embodied the principles of a Christian Imarah, headed by a Shihabi Christian Amir over a rationalized system of administration consisting of a central council with the Hakim and provincial administrators, all bound by law.[119] There is, significantly, no reference to the muqati'jis, whose jurisdiction the program abolished, both Christian and Druze.

BREAKDOWN AND REORGANIZATION

The inconclusive armed clash between the Druze and the Maronites in 1841 left the political situation unsettled. The Shihabi Hakim was disgraced, and the Lebanese found themselves without a consensus on a future government. From this early date in the protracted civil war, it was clear that the Lebanese were no longer capable of settling their political differences by themselves. Three major outside parties now entered the conflict: the Ottoman government, the British, and the French. Other European governments were involved but were of minor importance and need not be mentioned here.

England's involvement in the Levant grew rapidly following her active role in driving Ibrahim Pasha back to Egypt. Political and commercial British interests in the Eastern Mediterranean, too, made British presence greatly felt in Lebanon after 1840. As for the French, their influence was weakened after the defeat of Ibrahim Pasha; but their traditional cultural interests among the Maronites in Lebanon and other Catholic communities continued to be strong.

It was the Ottoman government, however, which had the major role to play, since Lebanon was officially a province of the Empire. By 1840 there were major developments taking

[119] *Ibid.*, MS, no. 5817.

place in the Ottoman capital which had direct bearing on Lebanese affairs. First in importance was the reform movement known in Ottoman history as the *Tanzimat*, and second, the trend toward greater centralization in provincial administration. While reform and centralization went together, they were not inseparable, as can be seen from the fact that centralization of administration continued to be the policy of the Ottoman government even when the reformers were out of office.

In November of 1839 the Noble Rescript of the Rose Chamber was promulgated by the Sultan, introducing radical changes in law and administration. This was followed a few months later by an Imperial Rescript which *inter alia* specified the terms of the new centralized provincial administration, modeled on the French system by the great Ottoman statesman and reformer, Rashid Pasha. However, the liberal reform period was short-lived and Rashid Pasha fell from power in March 1841, to be replaced by a government of reactionary tendency. Thus the reform movement was almost completely suspended from 1841 to August of 1845, at the end of which period the reformists again gained control. It was during this short interval, 1841-1845, that the Lebanese conflict was at its height.

Policy changes in the Ottoman capital had repercussions in the Lebanese situation. While the reformists were out of office, Ottoman policy was running against the interests of all parties concerned in Lebanon. The conservative government in Istanbul sought greater control over the country by trying to put it directly under Ottoman administration like the rest of the provinces, but without the reforms which were declared in the Imperial Rescript of 1840. The first step in this direction was the Ottoman government's withdrawal of support from Amir Bashir III. Exploiting the situation of civil war in the Mountain, they permitted the Hakim's Druze subjects to disgrace him in public, then shipped him off to

Istanbul, declaring at the same time the end of the Shihabi dynastic rule over Lebanon. An Ottoman officer, 'Umar Pasha, was then appointed as governor of Lebanon in January of 1842.

This policy of direct control over Lebanese affairs was disagreeable to both parties in the conflict, Maronites as well as Druze. The Druze manasib were outraged over the loss of their traditional prerogatives under the autocratic rule of 'Umar Pasha, while the Maronites were appalled by the downfall of the Shihabi dynasty, which frustrated their hopes for an autonomous Christian Imarah, and by the failure of the Ottoman government to satisfy their demands for equality and freedom from Druze domination. The opposition of both Druze and Maronites to the appointment of 'Umar Pasha finally forced the Ottoman government to dismiss him before he had completed a year in office. This step signified the failure of the opponents of reform in Istanbul to solve the Lebanese question.

Britain and France both played a part in preventing the Ottoman government from imposing direct administration over Lebanon, but failed to reconcile the Maronites and Druze.[120] Consequently, in 1843, they approved a plan (which will be discussed shortly) to divide Lebanon into two separate provinces, one Druze and the other Maronite. They then pressed for guarantee of Maronite rights to equitable treatment under Druze muqati'jis. However, the most significant development was the return to power, in August 1845, of the Ottoman reformists, who were more receptive to European demands for reform in the provinces. This event coincided with the second major clash between Maronites and Druze for domination in the Mountain, which prompted the reform government to try to settle the situation. The reorganization of the Lebanese polity which resulted, and which we shall

---

[120] See Harold Temperley, *England and the Near East: The Crimea* (n.p.: Archon Books, 1964), pp. 157-198. Also Poujade, *Le Liban*; and Testa, *Recueil*, III and V.

return to presently, had the distinguishing characteristic of
having combined some of the Ottoman reform principles
with Maronite demands for abolishing the Druze muqati'jis'
authority over their Christian subjects.

We can now return to our analysis of the consequences of
the armed conflict of 1841 between Druze and Maronites.
The result of the Christian army's inaction was, naturally,
defeat. The Amir was rescued by Ottoman officials from the
Druze assault and was taken to Beirut, from where he was
sent on board an Ottoman ship to Istanbul; and no one
bothered to protest except himself.

Behind him, Bashir III left a tangled problem made much
worse by the Christians' failure. The situation was something
like this: the Druze, now isolated from the Maronites, appeared to be quite a small minority but a determined one. The
fact that they took up arms against their Maronite subjects
and neighbors, nevertheless, served to publicize the Maronite
claim that the Druze muqati'jis were oppressors and not
qualified to remain rulers. This greatly hurt the Druze cause
with the European powers,[121] whose presence in Lebanon
after the Egyptian withdrawal was a major determining factor
in the settlement of the Lebanese question. The Druze problem was still the more intractable because of the Druze manasib's adamant insistence that they would have nothing more
to do with the Shihabi dynasty. This attitude, whether the
Druze realized it or not, was a serious blow to the whole iqta'
system of political organization in Mount Lebanon, and therefore affected them more than it did the other groups. As they
could not create a new ruling house overnight, the Druze
played into the hands of the Ottoman government by asking
for a Muslim governor. The newly installed Ottoman ruler,
'Umar Pasha, was, as they were themselves to see soon after,
by no means inclined to tolerate the autonomy of the
muqati'jis.

[121] Ismail, *Histoire du Liban*, IV, 228.

The Maronites' inability to reach a military victory complicated the question enormously. While the Druze victory did not solve anything, a military victory for the Maronites would have been politically more decisive for the following reasons: the Maronites were a majority in the country; they had the ruling dynasty, the Shihabis, on their side; they were also legally less vulnerable than the Druze since they were fighting on the side of the Hakim sanctioned by the Ottoman government. The uprising of the Druze against the Shihabi Hakim was technically against the Ottoman government. If the Maronites had been able to demonstrate by forceful action that they could protect the Amir and keep him in power, the Druze muqati'jis would have been subdued and forced to compromise, exactly as they were under the able Amir Bashir II.

After the debacle at Dayr al Qamar the Maronites continued to struggle, hopelessly, to reinstate the Shihabis at the head of the government. This attempt absorbed most of the diplomatic efforts made by the Maronite Church. In vain they invoked the arguments of legitimacy and tradition with the Ottoman government. The Ottomans were indisposed toward the Shihabis after seeing the effectiveness with which the Lebanese Hakim could play the game of foreign policy independently of the Porte. They made it clear to the Maronite prelates negotiating with them, Archbishop Tubiyya 'Awn and the priest Yuhanna al Islambuly, that although the Shihabis had a legitimate claim to the government of Lebanon, they had proved themselves incompetent and therefore no longer merited that dignity. The Ottoman authorities further argued that the Shihabis could not rule because the Druze had ceased to recognize their dynastic claims. The prelates insisted that the Ottoman government had promised, through the patriarch and the European consuls, to maintain the Shihabi dynasty,[122]

[122] Hubaysh papers, MSS, nos. 6335, 6381. Also Qar'ali, "Al Batriyark Yusuf Hubaysh," *al Bayraq*, 31 October 1949.

and that the Druze were rebels and it was the duty of the government to suppress them. But all this went unheeded by the Ottoman authorities.[123]

With the demise of the Shihabi dynasty in Mount Lebanon and the failure of direct Ottoman rule under 'Umar Pasha, the Ottoman government approved a plan for the division of Lebanon into two provinces. Thus at the beginning of 1843, Lebanon was divided into two provinces, Qa'immaqamiyyah, each having a chief executive. For the northern part of Lebanon a Maronite governor, Amir Haydar Abillama', was appointed, at the suggestion of the patriarch. Southern Lebanon was given a governor from the Druze community, Amir Ahmad Arslan. This plan of dividing the country into two governments had the approval of the European powers, particularly Britain. But the indecision of the Ottoman government and the European powers, and at the same time the opposition of the Maronites and Druze, prevented a solution to the problem of how to treat those who belonged to one community but happened to be living under the government of the other.

Thus the division plan was not a satisfactory solution. The Christians continued to clamor for the restoration of the Shihabis, without success.[124] A major grievance, as just suggested, was the status of the Maronites living under the Druze governor and their subjection to Druze rulers. Attempts were made by the Church to remove these Maronites from the jurisdiction of the Druze governor and to attach them directly to the Christian governor.[125] In a petition to the Ottoman government, the patriarch and the prelates asserted that it was easier for Christians to die than to consent to live under Druze rule.[126] Meanwhile, the patriarch's emissary in Europe, Bishop Niqula Murad, sent reports to the

[123] Hubaysh papers, MS, no. 6453, 30 December 1841, and no. 6381.
[124] Hubaysh papers, MS, no. 6898.
[125] *Ibid.*, MS, no. 6676.
[126] *Ibid.*, 7 November 1844; MAA, MS, no. 803.

Christian governor not to submit to the Ottoman authorities regarding the Christians of the mixed areas, since he had received favorable promises from the European powers.[127] However, nothing definite was done on this question until after hostilities had broken out again between Druze and Maronite, first in 1843 and again in 1845.

After the last major armed encounter in 1845, the Maronites again failed to impose themselves upon the Druze by military force. The resumed fighting, though, did have the result of pointing out the inadequacies of the plan by which the country was divided in two. However, instead of embarking on a thorough reorganization of Lebanon, the Ottoman government, with the approval of the European powers, modified the existing plan of division, which did ameliorate the condition of the Maronites living under the Druze Qa'immaqamiyyah by giving the subjects a power of representation. The new plan is known in Lebanese history as the Shakib Afandi Regulations, after the Ottoman official who was responsible for its promulgation.

The new constitution established under the Regulations consisted of six articles and thirteen sections pertaining to the government and administration of each of the two provinces. The governor, who was to be appointed by the Vali of Sayda in consultation with the a'yan and prelates, was to be selected from the princely families of the Abillama's for the Maronites, and the Arslans for the Druze. The most significant reform measure in this connection pertained to the establishment of an elected council to assist and advise the governor. The council in each of the two provinces consisted of twelve members, two for each sect living in Mount Lebanon: Maronites, Melkite Orthodox, Melkite Catholics, Druze, Sunni Muslims, and Shi'ites. Thus each community was represented by a councilor and a judge, with the excep-

[127] Lebanese Monastery in Rome, Dossier Abbot Qirdahi, MS, no. 71, 20 April 1843.

tion of the Shi'ites, who were to elect a councilor only, while their judicial affairs were handled by the Sunni Muslim judge. Thus the total number of the council members was eleven, and the twelfth was a deputy governor chosen from the sect of the governor, a Maronite in the north and a Druze in the south.

The functions of the council struck at the root of the muqati'jis' authority. The councils were to apportion taxes in their respective provinces, and in the case of the Druze province the tax was to be collected by a new agent, the wakil. Second, the council, with the governor, had the highest judicial function, or power of appeal. Those cases which were raised to the governor were referred to the judge, or judges, of the sects to which the parties involved belonged. Third, the councilors acted as advisors to the governor in matters of policy and administration.

The twelve council members were selected at large from the people without any restrictions as to birth or status. Among the Christians the clergy had the strongest voice in determining the election, while Muslim members were appointed by the Vali of Sayda. The council members received fixed salaries as full-time officials.

With respect to local administration in each province, the regulations differed between south and north. In the south, the stronghold of Druze muqati'jis houses, five muqati'jis were appointed, each to be in charge of the whole muqata'ah which traditionally belonged to his clan. Thus the major clans were represented as follows: one Jumblati muqati'ji, one 'Imad, one Talhuq, and two Nakad muqati'jis.[128] No particular functions of any significance were stipulated for these five muqati'jis, since the judicial and taxation functions were already taken away by the high council and the wakils.

[128] Caesar E. Farah, "The Problem of the Ottoman Administration in the Lebanon: 1840-1861," unpublished Ph.D. dissertation, Department of Oriental Studies, Princeton University, 1957, p. 206.

In each muqata'ah a wakil was elected from each of the Druze and Maronite communities. The wakil had judicial authority of first instance over his coreligionists as well as the power to collect the taxes apportioned by the council. Again, the wakils were not selected from the nobility but from the common people; their election was something of a co-optation by the governor, the clergy, and other influential persons in the community.

While the five muqati'jis serving as administrators of their clans' muqata'ahs had no official function, they were still the real holders of power in their domains. Their appointment was a concession to the powerful clans, an acknowledgement of the Druze nobility's leadership among their people, who continued to be loyal to them. Nevertheless, the fact that they were deprived of authority over their Christian subjects, plus the introduction of legal arrangement as the new principle of legitimate authority, damaged their positions irreparably.

With respect to the northern provinces, Maronite muqati'jis suffered from the new Regulations in a similar way, but not to the same extent as the Druze. The Shakib Afandi Regulations did not stipulate similar measures as in the south for the establishment of wakils on the local level to collect taxes and administer justice. This was mainly because the Ottoman government continued to regard the Lebanese conflict as sectarian only, without fully appreciating its popular and social aspects. In addition to this, the European representatives, particularly the French, who fought hard for instituting Maronite wakils in the Druze muqata'ahs,[129] did not push for the same in the north, since their argument was based on the communal difference between subjects and rulers. This fact is all the more peculiar since Maronite peasants in the north had already shown their ability to organize themselves into small units led by village wakils in times of crisis, first in the

[129] See Poujade, *Le Liban*, p. 114.

'ammiyyah movement of 1820, and later in 1840. Moreover, the 'uhdahs of the northern muqata'ahs were not reorganized as in the south, and the old abusive practice in which several muqati'jis in one clan exercised authority over the same subjects of an 'uhdah continued to plague the life of the peasant subjects.

The failure to institute wakils in the Maronite province, and the maladministration by the muqati'jis, led to a revolt by the Maronite peasants in Kisrwan against their lords a little over a decade after the Shakib Afandi Regulations were promulgated. Again, the Maronite peasants organized themselves in village communes, each under a wakil, and then selected one leader to head the whole movement. Ideas similar to those that had appeared earlier were repeated, perhaps with a little more clarity and sharpness, dominant among which were demands for freedom, equality, and the right to have a voice in determining their own affairs.[130] This Maronite revolt against the muqati'jis broke out in 1858. Two years later hostilities between Druze and Maronites were resumed, culminating in the complete official abolishment of the iqta' institutions in 1861 and the reunification of Lebanon.

The outbreak of fighting in 1860 was instigated by the leading Druze manasib, who continued to enjoy power among their Druze subjects and to command the latter's loyalty. Since they still had military power, they were not willing to put up with the loss of their prestige and traditional prerogatives under the new Regulations. The Druze muqati'jis' constant violation of the Regulations and interference with their Maronite subjects, and the domination of the council by the Druze governor, who did not respect the new law, added fuel to the problem. At the same time, the defensive-

---

[130] For details regarding the events and ideas expressed during the peasant revolt in Kisrwan see documents translated and edited by Malcolm Kerr, in *Lebanon in the Last Years of Feudalism, 1840-1868: A Contemporary Account by Antun Dahir al 'Aqiqi and Other Documents* (Beirut: Catholic Press, 1959).

ness and insecurity of the Maronite muqati'jis in the north was reflected in their increasingly arbitrary attitude toward their subjects. All these factors contributed to the restlessness of the Maronite peasants both north and south, and eventually to the hostilities of 1858-1861. Though the whole conflict was strongly sectarian in 1860, it continued to have the dimension of class division.

At the conclusion of the struggle in 1861, the European powers, with the especially active participation of France, intervened to reorganize the system of government. The Mountain was reunited under a new arrangement known as the *Mutasarrifiyyah* which lasted until World War I. Under the Mutasarrifiyyah a new constitution was given to Lebanon, and the last iqta' prerogatives were officially abolished. The administrative system was made hierarchical, from the local base of elected village officials to the Administrative Council of twelve on top, presided over by a Christian Ottoman governor appointed for five years by the Porte with the approval of the European powers.

The goals which the Christians could not achieve through armed conflict were mostly compensated for by the achievements of the Maronite Church in the diplomatic line. The compromise reached in the establishment of the Mutasarrifiyyah could have been much worse for the Maronites, considering their repeated military failures. Their position was further strengthened by the convergence of the Ottoman reform movement with British and French interests in Lebanese autonomy.

To summarize the developments in this chapter, the alliance established between the Amir al Hakim and the Maronite Church and people affected the class of ruling lords unfavorably. This alliance not only tied the Shihabis to one community, but also affected the whole sense of legitimacy upon which the political institutions of the Imarah rested. The Maronites with their new outlook viewed as the only legitimate ruler a Maronite Amir of the Shihabi house, while the Druze finally rebelled against the Shihabi dynasty, refusing to accord them any ruling rights or respect.

In the second place, newly awakened communal consciousness conflicted with traditional loyalties and eventually supplanted them. The iqta' bond of ismiyyah, which had tied the subject to his muqati'ji and to the muqati'ji's faction, was shattered by the efforts of the Church to arouse national and religious feeling among the Maronites. New institutions conforming with ethno-religious ideology replaced the personal tie to the muqati'ji and the secular institutions which had regulated the political relations. Elected representatives of the common people—wakils—were established, challenging the authority of the muqati'jis and sharing their power. The right of the muqati'jis to choose their Amir al Hakim also gradually slipped out of their hands until at last it was lost completely in 1843.

In the muqati'jis' place the Church took up political leadership. It mobilized the people for political and military action, articulated their views and interests, settled their disputes, and defended them. In addition, the Church filled the new need for diplomatic relations with the European powers and also handled the community's relations with the Ottoman government.

Armed conflict between the two main groups, Maronite and Druze, during the years between 1840 and 1845, led to the reorganization of the whole political system on a communal basis. The new political ideas, group consciousness, and interest constituted the main forces moving and shaping events in the Mountain. The result was the disintegration of an old established order of political life and the introduction of a new system and mode of thought based on communal relationships.

CONCLUSION

In this study we have been concerned with political change

in Mount Lebanon from the mid-eighteenth to the mid-nine-teenth century. As our starting point we assumed a relation-ship of interdependence between the three main constituent parts of the system: the principle of legitimacy, the institu-tions, and the actors. Underlying this statement is the assump-tion that political change may be the outcome of institu-tional conflict and/or conflict between the constituent parts of the system. The forces activated by conflict are such that their effect will be to reduce imbalance in the systemic forces either by stemming the sources of change, in this case returning to the status quo ante, or by reaching a new state of balance.

The book has presented as accurate a picture as possible in the hope that such a description would facilitate drawing theoretical conclusions. Now, therefore, we may devote this brief résumé mainly to theoretical considerations. The observa-tions that this study has yielded are two: one is related to the nature of conflict, and the second to the conditions under which political change took place in Mount Lebanon.

The first observation is this: a communal concept of legitimate authority was inconsistent with the iqta' system in which the concept of authority rested on status and kinship. This was the source of unrest in Lebanese society in the first half of the nineteenth century. With the division of society into two groups with incompatible views, expectations, and in-terests, steps were taken by each side to reduce the dangers of the threat coming from the other side. The fact that the conflicting groups could no longer resort to a common frame of reference to resolve their differences led them on a course in which force and violence became the arbiter.

The second observation is that political change in Lebanon was directly related to the distribution of power in the sys-tem. The power arrangement prevalent in the iqta' system facilitated the growth of new forces in the population, who eventually challenged the very order under which they had flourished. The coexistence of two principles—fragmentation of authority among various chiefs, and central coordination by the Hakim—limited the freedom and power of each actor and created conditions of relative stability necessary for social and political growth.

In order to understand the proposition that the distribution of power among relatively equal chiefs facilitated change in Lebanon, it is important to remember that change was not introduced by the ruling chiefs but started among the subjects. For the subjects to introduce new ways and to alter the conditions of their existence indicates that sufficient freedom was given them to develop certain aspects of their lives. This was made possible by the system of fragmentation and coordination of power under the Shihabi Imarah. The Shihabi overlord, who occupied the highest political office, represented unity in the land and enjoyed sufficient authority to deter the chiefs from irresponsible or despotic action against the subjects or against one another. At the same time, although he provided for relative stability in the system by reducing the possibility of political chaos, he himself did not enjoy power to impose strong central control. His authority over the subjects was one step removed by the interposition of the muqati'jis. In short, then, deference to the manasib according to deep-rooted traditions of the land and the lack of an independent source of power for the Hakim prevented the centralization of authority.

As we have seen, freedom and protection were extended by the feudal lords to their subjects, particularly in matters of personal safety, property, and the exercise of religious activities. Toleration and respect for private property encouraged religious groups to expand their activities, increase their wealth, and gain political influence.

The Maronite Church in particular started to grow and flourish under the auspices of the feudal lords, who welcomed the religious services among their subjects as well as the Church's economic enterprises. Maronite peasant workers were attracted to domains where the lords encouraged the building of monasteries. The monks and their orders were themselves economically enterprising; they cultivated the land of the feudal lords, reclaimed other properties, and bought land of their own where they could. Thus, while lay peasants were also able to acquire land, the main economic force to emerge at the close of the eighteenth century was the Church, and particularly the orders of monks. In Chapters IV and V, the manner in which the clerical organizations became enriched was discussed. Here we are only concerned with their effects on the feudal order and with the political role of the Church. In the early stages of economic relations between the Church and feudal lords, the interests of the two parties converged. The Church at this point in the alliance was the weaker and more dependent partner. The complicated relationships by which some monasteries essential to the administration of Church business were held jointly by feudal families and the Church put the latter under the control of temporal authorities. In both clerical policy and appointment to higher Church offices, the Church followed the guidance of the powerful lords. But with the growing economic independence of the Church by the end of the eighteenth century, the alliance started to crack. The Church began to show a strong spirit of independence from the aegis of the ruling class. Eventually, as a result of its growing economic strength, the Church could bear the costs of its own administration without the help of the feudal lords. Thus it became possible for the Church to pay its own officers, build its own monasteries, and establish sees for its archbishops. The trend toward independence from the ruling class was further strengthened by the internal reorganization and reform of the Church.

The reform movement in the Maronite Church, though it goes back to earlier periods, took a strong course only around the middle of the eighteenth century and continued through the middle of the nineteenth century. The purposes of reform included both religious matters and the organization of the Church, but what we are primarily concerned with here is the effect of reform upon Church administration. The objective of the reformers was autonomy for the Church in the administration of its own business through the control of the material means and regulation of both recruitment and election to offices on the bases of law and merit. The major Church Council of 1736 laid down the legal foundation for a reformed Church.

Another remarkable development associated with reform was the increasing cultural activities of the Church. The achievement of autonomy in Church administration permitted its leaders to pursue their own policy course, culturally and politically. The ability to carry out its various activities freely, and the adequate economic base to support these activities, made the Church the most influential cultural agent in the land. No other organization or group was as well prepared to assume the task of cultural leadership as the Maronite Church with its cadre of educated clergymen— virtually the sole group of educated elite in the country. These clerical literati played two major and related cultural roles: as creators of new political symbols and as disseminators of ideas. The Maronite clergy not only preserved the history, religion, and ideological myth of the Maronite people but also contributed to the development of Maronite ideology to meet the needs of the community at that time. In the second place, the Church and its clergy established and ran the only schools in the country. Their effectiveness in propagating their ideas was facilitated by their widespread organization, schools, societies, and printing facilities.

The rise of the clergy to positions of cultural and economic leadership could not long be separated from political affairs. Early in the first decade of the nineteenth century, the Church's influence in politics became visible and its political involvement rapidly became deeper. The political role of the Church in the affairs of the Imarah was quite dramatic from its very beginning. Soon after the Church's connections with the mudabbir, Jirjus Baz, came to a frustrating conclusion, its clergy became involved in revolutionary activities visible in the peasant risings of 1820-1821.

An important fact about the nature of political change in Lebanon was its grass-roots character. The political revolution was generated and resolved in terms directly relevant to the people of the country and their problems. The new ideas were developed by Lebanese thinkers inspired by their own culture and history; political demands were of a practical sort related to the daily problems of the people; and leadership came from the people themselves. Though the revolution was influenced by outside events and developments in the Ottoman world, it was not the making of outside forces.

In turning to the proposition on conflict and change, we shall focus on the principles which explain dissension and revolution. There were two sources of conflict observed in the iqta' system: institutional and systemic conflict, as defined in the introductory chapter. The first refers to incompatibility between various injunctions governing political relationships, whereas systemic conflict refers to incompatibility between the constituent parts of the system, namely legitimacy, institutions, and actors. In Chapters III and VII we discussed two types of institutional conflict: kinship and authority on the one hand, and delegated versus constituted authority on the other. The distribution and transference of authority in the iqta' houses were regulated in terms of kinship. Authority passed from father to son, with each son being treated more or less equally in the inheritance. The law of inheritance and succession led to endless fragmentation, not only in the property of the individual muqati'ji, but also in his authority. Yet the political strength of each iqta' house depended upon the unity of the whole clan. The demand for unity in the patrilineal kinship group and, at the same time, the independent authority of each muqati'ji created friction and conflict among members of the same house.

There was another political conflict generated by the fact that while the office of Hakim was hereditary in the line of the Shihabi house, the choice of the particular Hakim lay with the manasib. This gave rise to intense rivalry and politicking among various chiefs to impose the Hakim of their choice; and this situation became all the more chronic because the political rules of the iqta' system allowed one Hakim to be removed and replaced by another. The resultant rivalry generally weakened the position of the ruling class and forced them to accept support from outside sources, regardless of the fact that such tactics might eventually impinge upon the very political institutions by which they ruled.

The second kind of institutional conflict observed in this study lay in the relationship between the delegated authority of mudabbirs and the constituted authority of the muqati'jis. The mudabbir was the appointed official and servant of the Hakim. Upon taking office the mudabbir was raised to the rank of nobility. His status, however, did not put him on an equal footing with the established feudal aristocracy. The functions of the mudabbir were not clearly circumscribed, and his power depended to a great extent upon his skill in exploiting the political opportunities provided by the office. Mudabbirs under the Shihabi dynasty were able to build a tradition of political leadership, a role resented and resisted by the muqati'jis and sometimes even by members of the Shihabi dynasty. The line between delegated and constituted authority proved to be very thin, and it was difficult to keep mudabbirs and muqati'jis from clashing. It can be clearly seen from this case that delegated authority is expansive, and the best examples of this rule were the mudabbirs Sa'd al Khury, his son Ghandur, and Jirjus Baz. Shaykh Jirjus Baz encroached on the traditional rights of both muqati'jis and Shihabi Hakims. The intensity of the conflict led to a serious struggle for domination in which Baz was the loser, though only as a result of assassination by conspiracy rather than by direct confrontation. Thereafter, the office of mudabbir was considerably diminished in importance and political power. However, by resorting to violence to remove the source of institutional conflict in this case, the traditional political actors did not succeed in doing away with its effects. The influence of mudabbirs on the feudal institutions of Mount Lebanon and on the fortunes of the Maronite community had by that time become profound, and they left their mark upon future developments.

We may turn now to the second main problem, namely systemic conflict. The political ideas and activities we observed on the part of Maronite peasants and clergymen leave no doubt that the whole social and political order was in question. The adverse effects of contradictory rules which we have already considered, as, for instance, between kinship and authority, remained within the framework of general consensus, not leading to new ideas which challenged the basic legitimacy of these institutions. In contrast we see that ideas of Maronite nationalism and the political activities of commoners rejected the established beliefs and practices of the iqta' system. Social cohesiveness and political solidarity were no longer defined by the traditional personal allegiance of subject to lord, but in terms of membership in the national community and active sharing in its ideals. Similarly, the venture of peasants into politics and their assumption of leadership independent from their lords clearly shows that legitimacy of the iqta' rules which invested political rights of governing exclusively in the hands of the aristocratic houses was no longer a generally accepted principle. It was the struggle of common people to break up the closed circle of the ruling class and to become members of the political community that characterized the revolution throughout.

We have discussed in the preceding pages how these forces

came into being. Here we shall briefly refer to the revolution and then give typologies of the iqta' system and the communal system which was inconsistent with it. The purpose of the typology, of course, will be to draw the lines of conflict plainly rather than to represent reality in its details.

The challenge to the feudal order by Maronite clergy and peasants started to take the form of violence early with the rise and fall of Jirjus Baz. Then from 1820 to 1821, the peasants revolted against the Hakim and his main supporters among the muqati'jis. They scored a minor success at the beginning of the revolt, then in 1821 were defeated with relatively little loss of lives and property. Another attempt to check the power of the feudal chiefs was manifested in the Maronite Church's political support for the Hakim, Bashir II, after the latter's feud with the major Druze muqati'jis. By crushing the Jumblat muqati'jis, the Hakim lost his main support among the Druze, and he was therefore willing to enter into a political relationship with a new force to make up for his lost power. Revolution broke out again in 1840 between the Maronite people, supported by the Shihabi dynasty, and the major muqati'jis in the land. This was the beginning of a protracted civil war which passed through critical periods in 1843, 1845, 1858, and finally culminated in the massacre of a large number of Maronite peasants in 1860. Yet the muqati'jis were not able to hold on to their old positions, and the whole system was undermined, to be reconstructed with the aid of the Ottoman government and the major European powers who became involved in the civil war in its last stages.

A summary of the main features of the iqta' system and the communal system of the Maronite people will serve to emphasize the incompatibility between the two orders.

The iqta' system of Mount Lebanon differed from the communal system which succeeded it consistently along the lines of the three primary variables which defined the system typology in this study. The principle of political legitimacy in the iqta' system was derived from age-old established practices and beliefs based on kinship ties and inequality in status. The rules which governed political relationships and the definition of actors as an exclusive group were consistent with the principle of traditional legitimacy. Thus deference was given each actor in accordance with his status in the community. The power base was land, and the system of its exploitation reinforced the political privileges of the chiefs. However, the pattern of authority relationships was one in which autonomy and interdependence obtained among the political actors. The pluralistic arrangement of authority affected the relations between the actors and the subjects. The latter, though lacking political character of their own and merely following the bidding of their lord, nevertheless enjoyed social, economic, and religious rights.

The system which emerged from the disintegrating traditional order is referred to here as communal to emphasize membership in a community as the basis of political solidarity, rather than kinship and status. The source of legitimate authority in the communal system was the nation—the symbol of solidarity, collective identity, and sentiment of an ethnic group. In the traditional system, the sense of legitimacy was maintained by transmitting social values from one generation to the next by imitation. In the communal system, in contrast, the sense of legitimacy was stimulated actively by direct appeal to the individual for emotional commitment to the national group and by rational efforts to see that his behavior conformed with the imperatives of this commitment.

Likewise, political institutions in the communal system of Mount Lebanon were more inclusive in that they regulated authority relationships within the community as a whole, and according to criteria unrestricted by ascriptive considerations. The new values expressed in Maronite ideology were communal and egalitarian, and consequently the rules regulating authority relationships in the community were universal, not particular to kinship or status groups.

Consistent with the new communal values and institutions, membership in the leadership group was open. However, while everyone who belonged to the community was by virtue of that fact entitled to hold a position of authority, it was primarily those who were able to impress their compatriots with their leadership qualities and their ability to embody the national values who were actually recognized as actors. Thus the leaders' claim to authority rested on their active sharing in the group's national sentiment and values. The actors in a communal system are not anonymous and impersonal, they are fully individualistic personalities.

It is important to remember here that the preceding is a typology which serves analytic purposes, highlighting the main features of the political development of Lebanon during the nineteenth century. Thus it does not correspond completely and descriptively with the Lebanese polity under the iqtaʻ system or thereafter. The nobility continued to play a role in Lebanese politics, of course, and attitudes carried over from the past continued to manifest themselves in the communal system.

A problem which requires further consideration here is the strong resistance to political innovation and the relatively slow process of change manifested in Mount Lebanon. The time span between the beginnings of change in the iqtaʻ order and that order's transformation into the communal system was both long and characterized by violent struggle. The most visible cause of this was the incongruent processes of social change which complicated the nature of the conflict. For the period of a century covered in this study, radical changes were affecting the internal structure and cultural makeup of the Maronite community, with no corresponding developments or changes in the Druze community. My basic assumption regarding systemic change suggests that political transformation will develop along horizontal lines across the whole population of which the system is composed. Instead, we witnessed here a more complicated course in which change divided the whole population vertically along ethnic lines, while another split, this a horizontal one, pitted Maronite commoners against the nobility of both communities. Nothing similar was going on in the Druze community to line up the common people against their nobility, and the communal character of the Maronite movement prevented any dialogue between the commoners of the two communities. Therefore the Druze muqati'jis were able to muster considerable strength against the Maronite rebels, who had to fight alone against both the Druze people and their own ruling class.

Another factor which slowed down the process of change and intensified its violent character was the difficulty of mobilizing political forces in a system which was pluralistic both in its social membership and in its political structure. Centrifugal forces pushed people away from the center of authority in the system in diverse directions, toward their ethnic groups and/or their traditionally autonomous chiefs. This is perhaps the reason why political change originated among the people, not with the Hakim or the ruling class. When the Hakim, Bashir II, tried to assume greater power and extend the limits of his authority by combining forces with the popular movement, he faced fierce opposition from the manasib, who not only attacked his person but became alienated from the Shihabi dynasty itself. This was the main reason for the downfall of the Shihabis during the civil war.

The decline and final disintegration of the iqta' system, and the popular revolution against it, should not obscure the fact that it was this same iqta' order which had given the Lebanese people security, relative freedom, and unity for many generations. One of the most interesting and significant features of the iqta' system in this respect was the close association of the chiefs with the people, and the involvement of the people themselves in the political problems of their leaders. The muqati'jis of Mount Lebanon lived in the villages among their subjects and attended to their business in person, something quite unusual in the provinces of the Ottoman Empire. Reflection upon these facts and these developments during the history of Lebanon may be quite relevant to present realities.

The Maronite Imarah: The Church Plan for the Political Reorganization of Lebanon[1]

REQUESTS made to the Sublime State with respect to the Maronite community and the inhabitants of Mount Lebanon through the French government, the defendant of the above-mentioned community.

First, the Hakim of Mount Lebanon must be of the Maronite Shihabi house, in accordance with the existing tradition. He should always be designated by the Sublime Porte itself, not subject to the authority of any of the Pashas (Valis). The Hakim's kakhya [mudabbir] should also be Maronite. The Hakim must maintain and act in accordance with the laws handed down by the Sublime State. As for the rest of the amirs, shaykhs, muqaddams, etc., they should not have any authority or power over the people at all. Everyone without distinction should be subject to the current Hakim and to the Sultan's laws.

Second, a definite sum, not subject to increases, should be fixed as a tax on land. It should be charged on all lands including those of amirs, shaykhs, and muqaddams, etc., even on the land of the Hakim himself, without special favors or exemptions to anyone whatsoever. A known and supportable amount of this money is to be paid annually to the Sublime State in conformity with ancient custom. This sum should not be increased at all. Also, out of this tax plus the *faridah*[2] and the government land or *bakalik*[3] in Mount Lebanon, an amount should be fixed as the Hakim's salary and the salaries of one hundred retainers only, for his service.

If any money is still left from this sum, then it should be turned over to the treasury for such expenditure as is

---

[1] Hubaysh papers, MS, no. 5817, n.d. [1840-1845].

[2] *Faridah* was a head tax imposed on all adult males.

[3] *Bakalik* (pl.) was special land owned by the Ottoman government but which came under the governmental control of the Lebanese Hakim and was cultivated by Lebanese peasants.

necessary for the welfare of the public. The mentioned *faridah*, which is imposed on every male from the age of twenty to sixty, excluding the poor and the infirm, should not exceed three to ten piasters. As for tradesmen, shopkeepers, and craftsmen who own no land but live in Mount Lebanon, whether strangers or native, they should pay a *faridah* of twenty to one hundred piasters per head.

Third, twelve councilors, elected by the votes of the people from different muqata'ahs, should serve with the Hakim. These are to advise and discuss the matters of state with the Hakim. They will have no power at all over the people, nor will the people be compelled to offer them anything. These councilors will be either replaced or reconfirmed every three years by the will of the people. In case any one of them [councilors] behaves improperly or commits what he has no right to, the Hakim will dismiss him from his duties and call for the election of another in his place.

Fourth, the Hakim will have no power to punish any wrong-doer (*mudhnib*) arbitrarily, but according to the law after a necessary investigation has been carried out with precision and in writing. The examination should also be repeated several times. Moreover, no confession should be extracted from the detained by torture. The Hakim may not subject the culprit to extortions (*bals*) nor charge him more than what is defined by law. Prisoners should not be beaten or tortured, regardless of what wrong they have committed. Also, something should be given them for necessary sustenance while in jail, like bread and some cooked food, twice a day. If a person is convicted or condemned by law to death, the execution of the verdict should be carried out without torture.

Fifth, one officer only should be installed in every muqata'ah[4] to keep peace and order among the people, and to detain the wrongdoer, examine his case in the manner discussed above, and present a report to the Hakim. The

---

[4] The term muqata'ah must have been used in the sense of an administrative unit or region, not in the sense it had in the iqta' system. To this day in Lebanon the same term is used to refer to a region.

Hakim will give the report to the judges and councilors to make a judgment according to the law. The officer should have an assistant with him to register the miri, the imposts, and the incomes from the *bakalik* in the muqata'ah. No huwalis should be sent out for the collection of the miri. [Collection should be carried out by means of] records [related to the amount of miri] including the names of the villagers. Then the date for paying the miri should be fixed for the people, and he who fails to pay his miri on the fixed date should suffer a penalty of paying five piasters per hundred the first ten days. If he again fails to pay, then the amount should be doubled and so on. If after all this he does not pay, the crops of his land should be confiscated as payment of his debt. The accounts should be presented every year by the mentioned [?] finance officer (*sarraf*), through the twelve councilors previously mentioned, to the chief of treasurers.

Those who are in debt to private individuals and have failed to pay their debt, should be sent a written warning from the Hakim or the officers fixing a time for payment. If again they fail to pay on the fixed date, their properties should be confiscated until they pay or they should be sent to jail, as may seem advisable.

Sixth, all corvée (*sukhrah*), that imposed by the Hakim or by others, should be terminated and prohibited among the people of Lebanon; especially in the cities they [the Lebanese] should be free in their persons and animals, and no *kharaj* [dhimmi tax] should be collected from them in any of the Sultan's cities. This is because it [the *kharaj*] would have been paid by them as part of the imposts arranged [*al matalib al muratabah*] by the Sublime State. If the Hakim needs men for works, like masons and workers from the people, he may have them on condition that he pay their salary in amount equal to what they were earning elsewhere. Their service should be requested kindly and with their willing approval; their employment should not be by force.

Seventh, all the Maronites, wherever they happen to be in Mount Lebanon or any other place, should be under the protection of the French government as they were in the past. That is, if any Maronite should be insulted or treated badly by someone in the cities, he may claim the protection of the French consul, who will see that he receives justice.

Eighth, neither the Hakim nor the mentioned officers have authority or power to punish the Maronite clergy, bishops, priests, monks, nuns, etc. If any one of these should do wrong, his case should be raised with the patriarch, who resides in Mount Lebanon, who will examine the suit and punish the wrongdoer in accordance with the clerical laws and the principles of his religion.

Ninth, let there be permission granted to the Hakim and the Maronite patriarch to have a special representative [for both of them] with the Sublime State in Istanbul to deal with the State regarding the affairs of the Mountain. None of the three patriarchs who reside in Istanbul, i.e., the Greek Orthodox, the Armenian, and the Catholic patriarchs, has any powers, claims, or rights of objection concerning the Maronite community in any possible way.

Tenth, Amir Haydar Qayyidbay [Abillamaʻ], the Maronite who is known for his good qualities and good name and who is well received by all the Lebanese people, should be the head of his community and observe its affairs and look after its interests and the interests of all the people of Lebanon. He should also see that the conditions written above remain in order. If any of these conditions should be changed, he should defend them. He should be on good terms with the Hakim for the good of all the people.

While waiting for confirmation of these written conditions by the Royal authority, the inhabitants of Mount Lebanon promise to offer themselves even to the point of shedding their blood to win the favor and pleasure of the Sublime State.

A Covenant Between the Hakim, Amir Mansur Shihab, and Shaykh Kin'an Nakad
(1177 H., 1761 A.D.)[1]

THE REASON for writing this is that we have made a promise and a confirmation to our brother Shaykh Kin'an Nakad that [in return] for his service to us, [he will receive] our favor; and his status, influence and intercession [with us] will be first among his equals. As for his recompense, we shall assign to his interest from the *bakalik* one thousand piasters, two hundred piasters in addition [will he receive] from our person, and two hundred piasters from our house. His wife, Um 'Ali, will receive annually a set of assorted things. The miri of his villages will be 470 piasters including costs. The *khafar* [custom house of al Na'imah], three hundred piasters. [The miri for the following villages]: sixty piasters for Dfun; M'alaqah and al Salhiyyah, seventy; and the Miyyah-w-Miyyah, one hundred. [All the above-mentioned miri] will be discounted from his recompense, and what remains due him we will provide personally. With respect to Baq'un, we shall consider it on equal footing with the villages of his cousins. If we charge miri [on these villages, the Baq'un share] will be discounted from his original recompense. As for the *jawali*[2] in the Shuf that are in his charge and the charge of his family, we shall not collect from him in the years of exemption, in accordance with the usual practice. For the *jawali* of al Shihhar, during exemption years he will be exempted, and when there is no exemption we shall request of him only half a *jaliyah*. . . .

After this covenant which we have given him, we shall not grant precedence to any of the shaykhs in the land over him,

---

[1] Text in Nakad, "Tarikh al Nakadiyyin."
[2] Head tax on Christian and Jewish subjects.

nor conspire against him, nor transgress over his cultivated land[3] with *deli*[4] or with *imarah* [soldiers], nor with shaykhs or [my] relatives anywhere in the country. In matters of interest to him he will be given preference with us over Shaykh 'Ali [Jumblat] and Shaykh 'Abd al Salam [al 'Imad],[5] because he will be acting in our interest better than they.

As for the people of Dayr al Qamar[6] and the Abu Nakad family, we shall never take any action with regard to them except with his knowledge. . . . We shall not keep any secrets from him but will let him know of them, since it is proven that he will keep our secret. We shall not conceal from him things which take place in the country and among the circle of the prominent. He will be first to be consulted.

We shall not retreat a word from what we have promised him here so long as he continues to be faithful in our service, and [to remain] better than the rest of the shaykhs of the land, both of his own family and of others. He will put our interest above all other interests, including his own. He will serve us well according to the writ which we have in our possession from an earlier date. If he changes any of these conditions which he has accepted, it will be known by his deeds and words.

For all this we have proclaimed our will in his favor. By God and his Messenger Muhammad and Shu'ayb his Prophet, we will not change any of these conditions. . . . Dhu al Qi'dah in the year of the Hegira 1177.

Mansur Shihab

---

[3] The word used is "terraces."

[4] Mercenary soldiers.

[5] These were the two leading manasib at that time.

[6] Dayr al Qamar was the Hakim's capital, but its people were the subjects of the Nakad muqati'jis.

Dioceses of the Maronite Church

I. Aleppo—the city of Aleppo.

II. Tripoli—the city of Tripoli, the district of al Zawiyah, 'Arqa (extinct), Banias, the Island of Arwad and Jablah (where there were no Maronites), and Latakia (where there was only one church).

III. Jubayl and al Batrun—Jibbat Bsharri, Bilad Jubayl, Bilad al Batrun, and Jibbat al Munaytara.

IV. Ba'albak—the town of Ba'albak (hardly any Maronites) and the district of al Futuh in Kisrwan.

V. Damascus—the city of Damascus (a very small community), Kisrwan including Baskinta, Zabbugha, half the district of Ghazir and Zuq al Kharab.

VI. Cyprus—the Island of Cyprus (a small community existed here) and al Qati' to the bridge of the Beirut river.

VII. Beirut—the city of Beirut, al Matn, al Gharb, al Shihhar to al Damur.

VIII. Sur and Sayda—the towns of Sur and Sayda, al Shuf, al Biqa', Wadi al Taym and south to Jerusalem.

NOTE: With the exception of the diocese of Aleppo, all the areas outside Mount Lebanon, or present-day Lebanon, can be ignored because of the negligible Maronite communities living there.

Selective Bibliography

BOOKS

'Abbud, Bulus. *Basa'ir al Zaman fi Tarikh al 'Allamah al Batriyark Yusuf Istfan.* Vol. 1. Beirut: Matba'at Sabra, 1911.

Abu 'Iz al Din, Sulayman. *Ibrahim Basha fi Suriyyah.* Beirut: al Matba'ah al 'Ilmiyyah, 1929.

Abu Shaqra, Yusuf Khattar. *Al Harakat fi Lubnan ila 'Ahd al Mutasarifiyyah.* Ed. 'Arif Abu Shaqra. Beirut: Matba'at al Ittihad, n.d.

Anaissi, Tobia. *Bullarum Maronitarum.* Rome: n.p., 1911.

'Anaysi, Tubiyya. *Silsilah Tarikhiyyah li al Batarikah al Intakiyyin al Mawarinah.* Rome: Matba'at al Sinato, 1927.

Aouad, Ibrahim. *Le Droit Privé des Maronites au Temps des Émirs Chihab (1607-1841).* Paris: Librairie Orientaliste, Paul Geuthner, 1933.

Asaf, Butrus. *Al Irth al Maruni wa Masadiruhu al Shar'iyyah al Qadimah wa al Hadithah.* Juniyah, Lebanon: n.p., 1954.

Aucapitaine, Henri. *Étude sur les Druzes.* Paris: A. Bertrand, 1862.

Al 'Awrah, Ibrahim. *Tarikh Wilayat Sulayman Basha al 'Adil.* Ed. Qustantin al Basha. Sayda, Lebanon: Matba'at Dayr al Mukhallis, 1936.

'Awwad, Ibrahim. *Tarikh Abrashiyyat Qubrus al Maruniyyah.* Beirut: Matba'at Fadil wa Jumayyil, 1950.

Al 'Aynturini, Antonius Abi Khattar. *Kitab Mukhtasar Tarikh Jabal Lubnan*, ed. Ighnatius al Khury, in *MQ*, XLVI-XLVII (1952-1953).

Al Bash'alani, Istfan. *Tarikh Bash'alah wa Salima.* Beirut: Matba'at Fadil wa Jumayyil, 1947.

———. *Lubnan wa Yusuf Bayk Karam.* Beirut: Matba'at Sadir, 1925.

Al Basha, Qustantin. *Tarikh Duma.* Sayda: n.p., 1938.

Al Basha, Qustantin (ed.). *Mudhakkirat Tarikhiyyah.* Harisa, Lebanon: Matba'at Al Qiddis Bulus, 1933.

Baz, Rustum. *Mudhakkirat Rustum Baz.* Ed. Fu'ad Afram al Bustani. Beirut: Manshurat al Jami'ah al Lubnaniyyah, 1955.

[Baz, Salim]. *Al Shaykh Jirjus Baz: Sahifah min Tarikh Lubnan.* Beirut: Matabi' Sadir-Rihani Press, 1953.

Besson, Joseph. *La Syrie Sainte ou la Mission de Jésus et des Pères de la Compagnie de Jésus en Syrie.* Paris: n.p., 1860.

Binder, Leonard (ed.). *Politics in Lebanon.* New York: John Wiley & Sons, 1966.

Bouron, Narcisse. *Les Druzes: Histoire du Liban et de la Montagne Houranaise.* Paris: Berger-Levrault, 1930.

Bowring, John. *Report on the Commercial Statistics of Syria.* Presented to both Houses of Parliament by Command of Her Majesty. Printed by William Clowes and Sons, for Her Majesty's Stationery Office, London: 1840.

———. *The Syrian Question.* London: T. R. Harrison, 1841.

Brayk, Mikha'il. *Tarikh al Sham: 1720-1782.* Ed. Qustantin al Basha. Harisa, Lebanon: Matba'at al Qiddis Bulus, 1930.

Bulaybil, Lewis. *Tarikh al Rahbaniyyah al Lubnaniyyah al Maruniyyah.* 3 vols. Egypt: Matba'at Yusuf Kawwa, 1924. Vol. III is published in *MQ,* LI-LIII (1957-1959).

Burckhardt, John Lewis. *Travels in Syria and the Holy Land.* London: J. Murray, 1822.

Al Bustani, Butrus. *Qissat As'ad al Shidiaq.* Beirut: n.p., 1878.

Al Bustani, Fu'ad Afram. *'Ala 'Ahd al Amir.* 3rd edn., Lebanese University publication. Beirut: n.p., 1961.

Chasseaud, George Washington. *The Druzes of the Lebanon: Their Manners, Customs, and History.* London: Richard Bentley, 1855.

Chebli, Michel. *Une Histoire du Liban à l'Époque des Émirs (1635-1841).* Beirut: Imprimerie Catholique, 1955.

Churchill, Colonel [Charles Henry]. *The Druzes and the*

Maronites under the Turkish Rule from 1840 to 1860.
London: Bernard Quaritch, 1862.

———. *Mount Lebanon: A Ten Years' Residence from 1842 to 1852.* 3 vols. London: Saunders and Otley, 1853.

Coulborn, Rushton (ed.). *Feudalism in History.* Princeton: Princeton University Press, 1956.

Daghir, Yusuf As'ad. *Batarikat al Mawarinah.* Beirut: n.p., 1958.

———. *Lubnan: Lamhah fi Tarikhihi wa Atharihi wa Usarihi.* Juniyah: Matba'at al Mursalin al Lubnaniyyin, 1938.

Dandini, Jerom. *Voyage to Mount Libanus.* Published in John Pinkerton, ed., *General Collection of Voyages and Travels* Vol. x, London: Longman, Hurst, Rees, and Orme, 1811.

Dib, Pierre. *Quelques Documents pour Servir à l'Histoire des Maronites.* Paris: G.-P. Maissonneuve, 1945.

———. *L'Église Maronite.* Vol. ii: *Les Maronites sous les Ottomans, Histoire Civile.* Beirut: Imprimerie Catholique, 1962.

———. *Histoire de l'Église Maronite* (Mélanges et Documents No. 1). Beirut: Archevêché Maronite de Beyrouth, 1962.

Al Dibs, Yusuf. *Al Jami' al Muhassal fi Tarikh al Mawarinah al Mufassal.* Beirut: n.p., 1905.

——— (ed.). *Kitab Qawanin Akhawiyyat al Habal Bila Danas.* Ihdin, Lebanon: al Matba'ah al Lubnaniyyah, 1865.

———. *Tarikh Suriyyah.* Vol. viii. Beirut: al Matba'ah al 'Ummiyyah, 1905.

———. *Tarikh al Ta'ifah al Maruniyyah.* [Beirut: 1893].

Al Dimashqi, Mikha'il. *Tarikh Hawadith al Sham wa Lubnan (1782-1841).* Ed. Lewis Ma'luf. Beirut: al Matba'ah al Kathulikiyyah, 1912.

Dirian, Yusuf. *Asl al Ta'ifah al Maruniyyah wa Istiqlaluha bi Jabal Lubnan.* Beirut: n.p., 1919.

Dirian, Yusuf. *Lubab al Barahin al Jaliyyah 'an Haqiqat al Ta'ifah al Maruniyyah.* n.p., 1911.

Al Duwayhi, Istfan. *Tarikh al Ta'ifah al Maruniyyah.* Ed. Rashid al Khury al Shartuni. Beirut: n.p., 1890.

———. *Tarikh al Azminah: 1095-1699.* Ed. Ferdinan Tawtal, in *MQ*, XLIV (1950). Beirut: al Matba'ah al Kathulikiyyah, 1951.

Fahd, Butrus. *Hawl Kitab al Huda wa Tarikh al Ta'ifah al Maruniyyah.* Juniyah: Matba'at al Mursalin al Lubnaniyin, 1954.

Fa'iz, Khalil Hammam [pseud.]. *Abu Samra Ghanim aw al Batal al Lubnani.* Cairo: n.p., 1905.

Ghalib, Butrus. *Sadiqah wa Muhamiyah.* Beirut: al Matba'ah al Kathulikiyyah, 1923.

Ghanim, Yusuf Khattar. *Barnamaj Akhawiyyat al Qiddis Marun.* Vol. II. Beirut: al Matba'ah al Kathulikiyyah, 1903.

Ghibra'il, 'Abdallah. *Tarikh al Kanisah al Intakiyyah al Siriyaniyyah al Maruniyyah.* 2 vols. B'abda, Lebanon: al Matba'ah al Lubnaniyyah, 1900-1904.

Gibb, Hamilton, and Harold Bowen. *Islamic Society and the West: A Study of the Impact of Western Civilization on Moslem Cultures in the Near East.* 2 vols. London: Oxford University Press, 1957.

Great Britain. *Parliamentary Papers.* Vol. IX (Accounts and Papers, 1841): *Correspondence Relative to the Affairs of the Levant,* Parts II and III. London: T. R. Harrison, 1841.

———. *Correspondence Relative to the Affairs of Syria.* Part I: *With Her Embassy in Constantinople, 1841, 1842.* London: T. R. Harrison, 1845.

Guys, Henri. *La Nation Druze: Son Histoire, sa Religion, ses Moeurs, et son État Politique.* Paris: Chez France, 1863.

———. *Beyrouth et le Liban: Relation d'un Séjour de Plusieurs Années dans ce Pays.* 2 vols. Paris: Imprimerie de W. Remquet et Cie, 1850.

Al Hakim, Yusuf. *Bayrut wa Lubnan fi 'Ahd Al 'Uthman.* Beirut: al Matba'ah al Kathulikiyyah, 1964.

———. *Suriyyah wa al 'Ahd al 'Uthmani.* Beirut: al Matba'ah al Kathulikiyyah, 1966.

Haqqi, Isma'il (ed.). *Lubnan.* Beirut: al Matba'ah al Adabiyah, 1334 H [1918].

Harfush, Ibrahim. *Dala'il al 'Inayah al Samadaniyyah.* Juniyah: n.p., 1935.

Al Hattuni, Mansur. *Nabdhah Tarikhiyyah fi al Muqata'ah al Kisrwaniyyah.* Beirut: n.p., 1884.

Heyd, Uriel. *Ottoman Documents on Palestine 1552-1615: A Study of the Firmans According to the Mulhimme Defteri.* Oxford: The Clarendon Press, 1960.

Al Hilu, Yusuf Khattar. *Al 'Ammiyyat al Sha'biyyah fi Lubnan.* n.p., 1955.

Hitti, Philip K. *Lebanon in History: From the Earliest Times to the Present.* London: Macmillan & Co., Ltd., 1957.

Holt, P. M. *Egypt and the Fertile Crescent, 1516-1922.* London: Longman's, Green, and Co., 1966.

Hourani, Albert. *Arabic Thought in the Liberal Age: 1798-1939.* London: Royal Institute of International Affairs, Oxford University Press, 1962.

———. *Minorities in the Arab World.* London: Royal Institute of International Affairs, Oxford University Press, 1947.

———. *A Vision of History: Near Eastern and Other Essays.* Beirut: Khayats, 1961.

Hubayqah, Butrus. *Tarjamat al Batriyark al Hwayyik.* Beirut: al Matba'ah al Kathulikiyyah, 1926.

Hurewitz, J. C. (comp. and ed.). *Diplomacy in the Near and Middle East: A Documentary Record: 1535-1914.* Vol. 1. Princeton: D. Van Nostrand Co., 1956.

Ismail, Adel. *Histoire du Liban du XVIIe Siècle à nos Jours.* Vol. 1: *Le Liban au Temps de Fakhr-ed-Din II (1590-1633).* Paris: Librairie Orientale et Américaine, G.-P. Maissonneuve–M. Besson. Succ., 1955.

Ismail, Adel. *Histoire du Liban du XVIIe Siècle à nos Jours.* Vol. IV: *Redressement et Déclin du Féodalisme Libanais (1840-1861).* Beirut: Matba'at Harb Bijjani, 1958.

Isma'il, 'Adil, and Emile Khury. *Al Siyasah al Dawliyyah fi al Sharq al 'Arabi min Sanat 1789 ila 1958.* Beirut: Dar al Nashr li al Siyasah wa al Tarikh, 1960-1961.

Istfan, Khayrallah. *Zubdat al Bayan aw Khulasat Tarikh umm Madaris Suriyyah wa Lubnan: 'Ayn Waraqah.* New York: Syrian-American Press, 1923.

Jessup, Henry Harris. *Fifty-Three Years in Syria.* 2 vols. New York: Fleming H. Revell Co., n.d.

Jouplain [Paul Njaym]. *La Question du Liban: Étude d'Histoire Diplomatique et de Droit International.* Paris: A. Rousseau, 1908.

Karam, Butrus. *Qala'id al Murjan fi Tarikh Shamali Lubnan.* Vol. I, Beirut: Matba'at al Huda al Lubnaniyyah, 1929. Vol. II, Beirut: Matab'at al Ittihad, 1937.

Karam, Joseph. *Réponses à des Attaques Contre l'Auteur et Contre d'Autres Chrétiens du Liban.* Paris: n.p., 1863.

———. *Aux Gouvernements et Nations de l'Europe: Situation du Liban.* Rome: n.p., 1877.

Karamah, Rufa'il. *Nuzhat al Zaman fi Hawadith Jabal Lubnan, aw Tarikh bani Shihab 1730-1800.* Ed. Basilius Qattan. Beirut: al Matba'ah al Kathulikiyyah, 1919.

Kerr, Malcolm H. (ed. and trans.). *Lebanon in the Last Years of Feudalism, 1840-1860: A Contemporary Account by Antun Dahir al 'Aqiqi and Other Documents.* American University of Beirut: Faculty of Arts and Sciences Publications, Oriental Series, No. 33. Beirut: Catholic Press, 1959.

Al Khalidy, al Shaykh Ahmad bin Muhammad. *'Ahd al Amir Fakhr al Din al Ma'ni.* Eds. Fu'ad Afram al Bustani and Asad Rustum. Beirut: Lebanese Government Publication, al Matba'ah al Kathulikiyyah, 1936.

Khatir, Lahad. *Kitab al Shaykh Bisharah al Khury al Faqih.* Beirut: Matabiʿ Nassar, 1956.

Khayrallah, Irinimus. *Tarikh Mujaz li al Rahbaniyyah al Antuniyyah al Maruniyyah.* Juniyah: n.p., 1940.

Khazen, Phillipe. *Perpétuelle Indépendance Législative et Judiciaire du Liban depuis la Conquête Ottomane en 1516.* Beirut: n.p., 1910.

Al Khazin, Shayban. *Tarikh Shayban,* in *UT,* III (1958).

Al Khazin, Simʿan. *Al Harb fi Sabil al Istqlal: aw Yusuf Bayk Karam wa Dawud Basha.* Juniyah: Matbaʿat al Kraym, 1957.

———. *Yusuf Bayk Karam fi al Manfa.* Tripoli: n.p., 1950.

———. *Yusuf Bayk Karam: Qa'immaqam Lubnan.* Juniyah: n.p., 1954.

Al Khury, Ighnatius. *Mustafa Agha Barbar Hakim Iyalat Tarablus wa Jablah wa Ladhiqiyyat al ʿArab: 1767-1843.* Beirut: Matbaʿat al Rahbaniyyah al Lubnaniyyah, 1957.

Kurd—ʿAli, Muhammad. *Kitab Khitat al Sham.* Vols. III-V. Damascus: Matbaʿat al Taraqqi, 1927.

Lamartine, Alphonse de. *Voyage en Orient.* 2 vols. Paris: Hachette et Cie-Furne, Jouvet et Cie-Pagnerre, 1875.

Lammens, Henri. *La Syrie: Précis Historique.* Vol. 1. Beirut: Imprimerie Catholique, 1921.

———. *Tasrih al Absar fi ma Yahtawi Lubnan min al Athar.* Vol. 1. Beirut: al Matbaʿah al Kathulikiyyah, 1913.

Laurent, Achille. *Relation Historique des Affaires de Syrie depuis 1840 Jusqu'en 1842: Statistique Générale du Mont Liban.* 2 vols. Paris: Gaume Frères, 1846.

Lenormant, François. *Histoire des Massacres de Syrie en 1860.* Paris: L. Hachette et Cie, 1861.

Lewis, Bernard, and P. M. Holt (eds.). *Historians of the Middle East.* London: Oxford University Press, 1962.

Lockroy, Edouard. *Ahmed le Boucher: La Syrie et l'Égypte au XVIIIᵉ Siècle.* Paris: L. P. Ollendorf, 1888.

Al Majma' al Lubnani. Ed. and trans. from the Latin by Bishop Yusuf Najm. Juniyah: Matba'at al Arz, 1900.

Al Ma'luf, 'Isa Iskandar. *Tarikh al Amir Fakhr al Din al Ma'ni al Thani min Sanat 1590-1635.* Juniyah: Matba'at al Risalah al Lubnaniyyah, 1934.

―――. *Dawani al Qutuf fi Tarikh Bani al Ma'luf.* B'abda, Lebanon: al Matba'ah al 'Uthmaniyyah, 1907-1908.

―――. *Tarikh al Amir Bashir al Shihabi al Kabir al Ma'ruf bi al Malti.* Zahlah, Lebanon: Matba'at Zahlah al Fatat, 1914.

―――. *Tarikh Madinat Zahlah.* Zahlah: Matba'at Zahlah al Fatat, 1911.

Mas'ad Bulus (patriarch). *Kitab al Durr al Manzum Radan 'ala al As'ilah wa al Ajwibah al Mumdat bi Ism al Sayyid al Batriyark Maksimus Mazlum.* Kisrwan, Lebanon: Matba'at al Ruhban fi Dayr Sayidat Tamish, 1863.

Mas'ad, Bulus. *Lubnan wa al Dustur al 'Uthmani.* Egypt: Matba'at al Ma'arif, 1909.

―――. *Al Dhikra fi Hayat al Mutran Jirmanus Farhat.* Juniyah: Matba'at al Mursalin al Lubnaniyyin, 1934.

――― (ed.). *Al Dhikra al Qarniyyah al Thaniyyah li al Majma' al Iqlimi al Lubnani.* Juniyah: Matba'at al Mursalin al Lubnaniyyin, 1936.

――― (ed.). *Al Majma' al Baladi.* Beirut: al Matba'ah al Kathulikiyyah, 1959.

―――. *Al Rad 'ala Mikha'il al Rajji.* Aleppo: al Matba'ah al Maruniyyah, 1937.

Mas'ad, Bulus, and Nasib Whaybah al Khazin (eds.). *Al Usul al Tarikhiyyah: Majmu'at Watha'iq.* 3 vols. Beirut: Matabi' Samya, 1956-1958.

Mashaqah, Mikha'il. *Muntakhabat min al Jawab 'ala Iqtirah al Ahbab.* Eds. Subhi Abu Shaqra and Asad Rustum. Lebanese Government Publication: Nusus wa Watha'iq. Beirut: al Matba'ah al Kathulikiyyah, 1955.

Al Munayyar, Hananiyya. *Kitab al Durr al Marsuf fi Tarikh*

al Shuf. Ed. and pub. by Ighnatius Sarkis in *MQ*, XLVIII-LI (1954-1957).

————. *Théogonie des Druses: ou Abrégé de leur Système Religieux.* Ed. and trans. from Arabic by Henri Guys. Paris: Imprimerie Impériale, 1863.

Murad, Niqula. *Notice Historique sur l'Origine de la Nation Maronite et sur ses Rapports avec la France, sur la Nation Druze et sur les Diverses Populations du Mont Liban.* Paris: le Clère, 1844.

Muzhir, Yusuf. *Tarikh Lubnan al 'Am.* 2 vols. [Beirut, 1952].

Nahoum, Haim (ed.). *Recueil des Firmans Impériaux Ottomans Addressés aux Valis et aux Khédives d'Égypte: 1006-1322 H. (1597-1904).* Cairo: Impr. de l'Institut Français d'Archéologie Orientale du Caire, 1934.

Nawfal, Nasim. *Batal Lubnan al Shahir al Ta'ir al Sit: Yusuf Karam.* Alexandria: al Matba'ah al Wataniyyah, 1896.

Perrier, Ferdinand. *La Syrie sous le Gouvernement de Mehemet-Ali Jusqu'en 1840.* Paris: Arthus, Bertrand, Librairie, 1842.

Poliak, A. N. *Feudalism in Egypt, Syria, Palestine and the Lebanon, 1250-1900.* London: The Royal Asiatic Society, 1939.

Polk, William R. *The Opening of South Lebanon, 1788-1840: A Study of the Impact of the West on the Middle East.* Cambridge, Mass.: Harvard University Press, 1963.

Poujade, Eugène. *Le Liban et la Syrie 1845-1860.* Paris: Librairie Nouvelle, 1860.

Poujoulat, Baptistin. *La Vérité sur la Syrie et sur l'Expédition Française.* Paris: Gaume Frères et Duprey, 1861.

Poujoulat, Jean Joseph, and Joseph Michaud. *Correspondance d'Orient: 1830-1831.* Vol. VII. Paris: Ducollet, 1835.

Qar'ali, 'Abdallah. *Al Misbah al Rahbani fi al Qanun al Lubnani.* Ed. by Jirjus Murani. Beirut: n.p., 1956.

Qar'ali, Bulus. *Al Amir Bashir.* Bayt Shabab, Lebanon: n.p., 1933.

Qar'ali, Bulus (ed.). *Aham Hawadith Halab.* Egypt: al Matba'ah al Suriyyah, n.d.

———. *Fakhr al Din al Ma'ni al Thani: Hakim Lubnan, wa Dawlat Tuscana.* 2 vols. Rome: Realte Accademia d'Italia, 1938.

——— (ed.). *Hurub Ibrahim Basha al Misri fi Suriyyah wa al Anadul.* 2 vols. Egypt: al Matba'ah al Suriyyah, 1927.

———. *Hurub al Muqaddamin: 1075-1450.* Bayt Shabab, Lebanon: n.p., 1937.

———. *Al La'ali fi Hayat al Mutran 'Abdallah Qar'ali.* Vols. I-III. Bayt Shabab: Matba'at la Patrie, 1932-1950.

———. *Al Mawarinah: Aqdamiyatuhum fi Lubnan wa Usaruhum.* Juniyah: n.p., 1949.

——— (ed.). *Tarikh 'Awd al Nasara ila Jurud Kisrwan.* Egypt: Matba'at al Muqtataf wa al Muqattam, n.d.

Rabbath, Antoine (comp.). *Documents Inédits pour Servir à l'Histoire du Christianisme en Orient, XVI-XIX Siècles.* 2 vols. Leipzig: Otto Harrassowitz, 1905-1910.

Raphael, Pierre. *Le Rôle du Collège Maronite Romain dans l'Orientalisme aux XVIIe et XVIIIe Siècles.* Beirut: Université de Saint Joseph de Beyrouth, 1950.

Ristelhueber, René. *Traditions Françaises au Liban.* Paris: Félix Alcan, 1918.

Rochemonteix, Camille de. *Le Liban et l'Expédition Française en Syrie (1860-1861).* Paris: Librairie Auguste Picard, 1921.

Rufa'il, Butrus. *Al Yad al Maruniyyah fi Irtidad al Kana'is al Sharqiyyah.* Trans. by Ighnatius al Khury. Aleppo: n.p., 1936.

Rustum, Asad. *Bashir Bayn al Sultan wa al 'Aziz: 1804-1841.* 2 vols. Beirut: Manshurat al Jami'ah al Lubnaniyyah, 1956-1957.

———. *Kanisat Madinat al Lah: Intakiyyah al 'Uzma.* 3 vols. Matba'at Dar al Funun, n.d.

——— (ed.). *Al Usul al 'Arabiyyah li Tarikh Suriyyah fi*

'Ahd Muhammad 'Ali Basha. 5 vols. Beirut: American University of Beirut, American Press, 1930-1934.

al Sabbagh, Mikha'il Niqula. *Tarikh al Shaykh Zahir al 'Umar al Zaydani: Hakim 'Akka wa Bilad Safad.* Ed. by Qustantin al Basha. Harisa: Matba'at al Qiddis Bulus, n.d.

Safa, Muhammad Jabir. *Tarikh Jabal 'Amil.* Beirut: Dar Matn al Lughah, n.d.

Salibi, Kamal S. *Maronite Historians of Mediaeval Lebanon.* American University of Beirut, Faculty of Arts and Sciences Publication: Oriental Series, No. 34. Beirut: Catholic Press, 1959.

———. *The Modern History of Lebanon.* New York: Praeger, 1965.

Scheltema, J. F. *The Lebanon in Turmoil.* Yale Oriental Series, No. 7. New Haven: n.p., 1920.

Sfayr, Butrus F. *Al Amir Bashir al Shihabi: Tara'if 'an Hayatihi wa Akhbarihi wa Akhlaqihi.* Beirut: Dar al Tiba'ah wa al Nashr, n.d.

al Shartuni, Rashid al Khury (ed.). *Al Majami' al Maruniyyah.* Beirut: al Matba'ah al Kathulikiyyah, 1904.

Shaykho, Lewis. *Al Adab al 'Arabiyyah fi al Qarn al Tasi' 'Ashar: 1800-1870.* 2 vols. Beirut: Matba'at al Aba' al Yasu'yyin, 1910.

al Shidiaq, Faris Yusuf. *Kitab al Saq 'ala al Saq fi ma Huwa al Fariaq.* Paris: Benjamin Dupart, 1855.

al Shidiaq, Tannus bin Yusuf. *Akhbar al A'yan fi Jabal Lubnan.* Ed. Munir al Khazin. 2 vols. Beirut: Matabi' Samya, 1954.

Shihab, Haydar Ahmad. *Kitab al Ghurar al Hisan fi Tawarikh Hawadith al Zaman.* Ed. Na'um Mughabghab. Egypt: Matba'at al Salam, 1900.

———. *Lubnan fi 'Ahd al Umara' al Shihabiyyin.* Eds. Asad Rustum and Fu'ad Afram al Bustani. Beirut: Lebanese Government Publication, n.p., 1933.

Shihab, Haydar Ahmad. *Tarikh Ahmad Basha al Jazzar*. Eds. Antonius Shibli and Ighnatius Khalifah. Beirut: Maktabat Antwan, 1955.

Temperley, Harold. *England and the Near East: The Crimea*. London: Longmans, Green and Co., 1936.

Testa, Baron I. de. *Recueil de Traités de la Porte Ottomane avec les Puissances Étrangères depuis le Premier Traité Conclu en 1536 entre Suleyman I et François Jusqu'à nos Jours*. Vols. III and V. Paris: Amyot, Bibliothèque Diplomatique, 1868.

Al Turk, Niqula. *Diwan al Mu'allim Niqula al Turk*. Ed. Fu'ad Afram al Bustani. Lebanese Government Publication: Nusus wa Watha'iq. Beirut, 1949.

Urquhart, David. *The Lebanon (Mount Souria): A History and a Diary*. 2 vols. London: T. C. Newby, 1860.

Volney, C.-F. *Travels Through Syria and Egypt in the Years 1783, 1784, and 1785*. Vol. II. London: G.G.J. and J. Robinson, 1788.

Al Waqi' al Durzi wa Hatmiyyat al Tatawwur: Majmu'at Muhadarat. Beirut: Lebanese Government, Ministry of Social Affairs, Rabitat al 'Amal al Ijtima'i, 1962.

Yahya, Salih bin. *Kitab Tarikh Bayrut wa Akhbar al Umara' al Buhturiyun min Bani al Gharb*. Ed. Lewis Shaykho. Beirut: al Matba'ah al Kathulikiyyah, 1898.

Al Yaziji, Kamal. *Ruwwad al Nahdah al Adabiyyah fi Lubnan al Hadith, 1800-1900*. Beirut: Maktabat Ras Beirut, 1962.

Al Yaziji, Nasif. *Risalah Tarikhiyyah fi Ahwal Lubnan fi 'Ahdihi al Iqta'i*. Ed. Qustantin al Basha. Harisa: Matba'at al Qiddis Bulus [1936].

Yazbak, Yusuf (ed.). *Awraq Lubnaniyyah*. 3 vols. Beirut: n.p., 1955-1957.

Ziadah, Yusuf. *Al Qada' al Maruni wa 'Alaqatuhu bi al Shar' al Rumani*. Juniyah: Matba'at al Mursalin al Lubnaniyyin, 1929.

———. *La Hiérarchie Maronite*. Edited by C.A.L. Beirut: Qirtbawi Press, 1959.

ARTICLES AND PERIODICALS

Abilla, Charles. "Risalatan li al Sayyid Jirmanus Farhat," *MQ*, xvi (1913).

Alaux, Gustave d'. "Le Liban et Davoud Pacha: L'Installation du Nouveau Gouvernement," *Revue des Deux-Mondes*, lviii (Juillet-Août, 1865).

Asaf, Yusuf. "Dukhul al Shar' al Islamy ila Lubnan," *al Manarah*, viii (1937).

'Ashur, 'Isam. "Nizam al Muraba'ah fi Suriyyah wa Lubnan wa Falastin," *Al Abhath*, i (September, 1948; December, 1948) and ii (March, 1949).

'Awwad, Mansur 'Awwad. "Al Batriyark al Lubnani, Ilias Butrus al Hwayyik, 1842-1931," *MQ*, xxx (1932).

Al Bash'alani, Istfan. "Al Amir Haydar al Lama'i wa 'Asruhu," *al Manarah*, i (1930) and ii (1931).

Al Bash'alani, Istfan. "Tanassur al Amir 'Abdallah al Lama'i," *MQ*, xiv (1921).

———. "Tarikh al 'Usar al Maruniyyah," *MQ*, xlv (1951).

———. "Wasiyyat al Amir Bashir al Kabir," *al Manarah*, i (1930).

Al Basha, Qustantin (ed.). "Jaridat Tawzi' Mal Kharaj Lubnan al Amiri fi 'Ahd al Amir Bashir al Shihabi," *MQ*, xxxiii (1935).

"Bashir Shihab," *The Encyclopedia of Islam* (1913).

Belin, M. "Du Régime des Fiefs Militaires dans l'Islamisme et Principalement en Turquie," *Journal Asiatique*, xv (1870).

Bulaybil, Lewis. "Nabdhah Tarikhiyyah 'an al Rahbaniyyah al Lubnaniyyah," ed. Antonius Shibli, *MQ*, li (1957).

——— (ed.). "Tahrir al Nasara mima Nusiba ilayhim fi Hawadith sanat 1860," *MQ*, xxvi (1928).

Bulaybil, Lewis (ed.). "Yawmiat al Sayyid Yusuf Sim'an al Sim'ani Sanat 1736," *MQ* (no volume number), 1927.

Al Bustani, Fu'ad Afram. "Al Hayat al 'Aqliyyah Qabl Mi'at Sanah," *MQ*, xxvii (1929).

———. "Al Mu'alim Niqula al Turk," *MQ*, xliii (1949).

Al Bustani, Ughustin. "Tarjamat al Batriyark Bulus Mas'ad," *MQ*, xxviii (1930).

Cahen, Claude. "L'Évolution de l'Iqta' du IXe au XIIIe Siècle: Contribution à une Histoire Comparée des Sociétés Médiévales," *Annales: Économies, Sociétés, Civilisations*, VIIIe Année (January-March 1953).

Chevallier, Dominique. "Aux Origines des Troubles Agraires Libanais en 1858," *Annales: Économies, Sociétés, Civilisations*, xiv, No. 1 (January-March 1959).

———. "Que Possédait un Cheikh Maronite en 1859?: Un Document de la Famille al Khazen," *Arabica*, vii (1960).

Charmes, Michel Gabriel. "La France et le Protectorat Catholique en Orient," *Revue des Deux-Mondes*, lv (15 February 1883).

Al Dahdah, Salim Khattar. "Al Abrashiyyat al Maruniyyah wa Silsilatu Asaqifatuha," *MQ*, vii (1904) and viii (1905).

———. "Al Amir Bashir al Shihabi al Kabir al Ma'ruf bi al Malti," *MQ*, xxii (1924).

———. "Intikhab Batarikat al Mawarinah," *MQ*, xxx (1932).

Al Dahdah, Salim Khattar. "Intikhab Batriyark Maruni fi al Qarn al Tasi' 'Ashar," *MQ*, xxx (1932).

———. "Al Kunt Rashid al Dahdah wa 'Usratuhu," *MQ*, iv (1901).

Al Dahdah, Sallum. "Rihlat al Amir Bashir al 'Ula ila Misr," ed. Salim al Dahdah, *MQ*, xviii (1920).

Dib, Butrus. "Al Huquq al Maruniyyah," *al Manarah*, vi (1935).

Dib, Pierre. "Maronite (église)," *Dictionnaire de Théologie Catholique*, ed. E. Amman, x, Part 1. Paris, 1928.

Duwayhi, Patriarch Istfan. "Silsilat Batarikat al Ta'ifah al Maruniyyah," ed. R. Shartuni, *MQ*, I (1898).

Faucher, Leon. "La Question d'Orient d'après les Documents Anglais," *Revue des Deux-Mondes*, IV (1841).

Fighali, Bakhus. "Watha'iq Tarikhiyyah 'an al Majma' al Lubnani," *MQ*, XLV-XLVI (1951-1952).

Ghalib, Butrus. "Al Ahwal al Shakhsiyyah," *MQ*, XXVIII-XXIX (1930-1931).

———. "Nawabigh al Madrasah al Maruniyyah al Ula," *MQ*, XXII (1924).

——— (ed.). "Taqrir al Sayyid Ghranji 'an Biladina fi al Qarn al Thamin 'Ashar," *MQ*, XXVIII (1930).

Ghanim, Ibrahim Abu Samra. "Al Misriyyun fi Lubnan wa Suriyyah Qabl Mi'at Sanah," *MQ*, XXX (1932).

Giradin, Saint-Marc. "Les Voyageurs en Orient: de la Condition des Chrétiens en Turquie," *Revue des Deux-Mondes*, XXXI (15 February 1861).

Gokbilgin, M. Tayyip. "1840 'tan 1861'e Cebel-i Lubnan Meselesi ve Durziler," *Belleten*, X (1946).

Harfush, Ibrahim. "Al Adyar al Qadimah fi Kisrwan," *MQ*, V-VIII (1902-1905).

———. "Al Baba Biyyus al Tasi' al Malik wa al Sultan 'Abd al Majid," *al Manarah*, II (1931).

——— (ed.). "Majma' Dayr Hrash wa al Majami' al Maruniyyah," *MQ*, VI (1903).

———. "Min Athar al Amir Bashir," *al Manarah*, II (1931).

———. "Mufawwad ibn Sallum al Tiyyan min Bayrut," *al Manarah*, VIII (1937).

———. "Nabdhah Tarikhiyyah fi al Usra al Shihabiyyah," *al Manarah*, I (1930).

———. "Talamidhat al Madrasah al Rumaniyyah al Maruniyyah al Qadimah," *al Manarah*, VI-VIII (1935-1937).

Harik, Iliya F. "The Iqta' System in Lebanon: A Comparative Political View," *Middle East Journal*, XIX (Autumn 1965).

Hodgson, Marshall G. S. "Al-Darazi and Hamza in the Origin

of the Druze Religion," *Journal of the American Oriental Society*, LXXXII, No. 1 (January-March 1962).

Hourani, Albert. "The Changing Face of the Fertile Crescent in the XVIIIth Century," *Studia Islamica*, VIII (1957).

Hubayqah, Butrus. "Tanassur al Umara' al Lama'iyyin al Matniyyin," *MQ*, XVIII (1920).

Hurewitz, J. C. "Lebanese Democracy in its International Setting," *Middle East Journal*, XVII, No. 5 (Autumn, 1963).

Al Khazin, Shahin. "Awqaf al 'A'ilah al Khaziniyyah 'ala al Tawa'if al Laji'ah ila Lubnan," *MQ*, IV (1901).

———. "Awqaf al 'A'ilah al Khaziniyyah 'ala Dhatiha," *MQ*, V (1902).

Khury, 'Abdallah. "Al Batriyark al Maruni wa Jamal Basha Ibban al Harb," *MQ*, XXII (1924).

Khury, Wajih. "Hawl al Qawanin al Fardiyyah 'ind al Ta'ifah al Maruniyyah fi Zaman al Umara' al Shihabiyyin," *MQ*, XXXII (1934).

———. "Al Qada' fi Lubnan 'ala 'Ahd al Hukm al Iqta'i," *MQ*, XXXI (1933).

Krader, Lawrence. "Feudalism and the Tatar Policy in the Middle Ages," *Comparative Studies in Society and History*, I, No. 1 (October 1958).

Al Labudi, Tuma. "Sirat al Mutran 'Abdallah Qar'ali," ed. A. Rabbat, *MQ*, X (1907).

Lammens, Henry. "Frère Gryphon et le Liban au XVᵉ Siècle," *Revue de l'Orient Chrétien*, IV (1899).

———. "Mardaites," *Encyclopaedia of Islam*, eds. M. Th. Houtswa and A. J. Wensink, III (1913).

———. "Tasrih al Absar fi ma Yahtawi Lubnan min al Athar," *MQ*, V (1902).

Lewis, Bernard. "The Quest for Freedom: A Sad Story of the Middle East," *Encounter*, XXII, No. 3 (March 1964).

Lewis, Norman N. "The Frontier of Settlement in Syria, 1800-1950," *International Affairs*, XXXI (1955).

Al Ma'luf, 'Isa Iskandar. "Al Amir Bashir min Akhbarihi al lati lam Tunshar Qablan," *al Manarah*, II (1931).

———. "Al Azjal fi al Amir Bashir al Shihabi al Kabir," *al Manarah*, VIII (1937).

———. "Lubnan fi 'Ahd al Amir Fakhr al Din," *MQ*, XXX (1932).

———. "Nukhbah min Amthal Hananiyyah al Munayyar," *MQ*, XII (1909).

———. "Al Qada' fi Lubnan bi Zaman al Umara' al Shihabiyyin," *MQ*, XXXI (1933).

Al Ma'luf, 'Isa Iskandar, and Salim al Dahdah. "Tanassur al Umara' al Shihabiyyin wa al Lama'iyyin fi Lubnan," *MQ*, XVIII (1920).

Mas'ad, Bulus. "Dhikra al Majma' al Lubnani," *al Manarah*, VII (1936).

Nau, F. "Opuscules Maronites," *Revue de l'Orient Chrétien*, IV (1899).

Poliak, A. N. "La Féodalite Islamique," *Revue des Études Islamiques*, X (1936).

Polk, William R. (ed.). "The British Connections with the Druzes," *Middle East Journal*, XVII, Nos. 1 and 2 (Winter-Spring 1963).

———. "Rural Syria in 1845," *Middle East Journal*, XVI, No. 4 (Autumn 1962).

Qar'ali, Bulus. "Al Batriyark Yusuf Hubaysh: Kalimah fi Siyasatihi al Ta'ifiyyah wa al Dawliyyah," *Al Bayraq* (Beirut), 3-4, 24-25, 29-30 October 1949.

———. "Al Mutran Jirmanus Farhat wa Saytaratu al Mashayikh 'ala Intikhab al Batarika wa al Matarinah," *Al Majallah al Batriyarkiyyah*, V (1930) and VII (1932).

Rajji, Mikha'il. "Nas Qadim bi al 'Arabiyyah li Majma'ay Qannubin 1596," *MQ*, XLVI (1952).

Al Rami, Yusuf. "Sahl al Biqa' fi Ayyam al Amir Bashir: Wakiluhu wa al Mal al Matlub Minhu," *al Manarah*, II (1931).

Ramya, Dimiyan. "Al 'Aqurah fi al Tarikh," *MQ*, xxx (1932).

"Rihlat al Mutran Ishaq al Shadrawi ila Faransa Sanat 1660," *MQ*, ii (1899).

Ristelhueber, René. "Les Maronites," *Revue des Deux-Mondes*, xxv (January 1915).

Rizqallah, Milad. "Min Tarikh Lubnan al Mu'asir: Sim'an al Labaki wa Ibnuhu Ghattas," *MQ*, xxxv (1937).

Rufa'il, Butrus. "Dawr al Mawarinah fi Irtidad al Kana'is al Sharqiyyah," *MQ*, xxxv (1937). ·

———. "Dlibta: Nabdhah Tarikhiyyah," *MQ*, xxiv (1931).

———. "Al Istiqlal al Madani fi al Kana'is al Sharqiyyah al Kathulikiyyah," *MQ*, xxvii (1929) and xxviii (1930).

Rustum, Asad. "Safhah Jadidah fi Tarikh al Thawrah al Durziyyah: 1834-1838," *MQ*, xxxv (1937).

———. "Al Shaykh Ahmad al Ghurr wa al Qada' fi Bayrut Qabl Mi'at 'Am," *MQ*, xxxi (1933).

Salibi, Kamal. "The Buhturids of al Gharb," *Arabica*, viii (January 1961).

———. "The Maronite Church in the Middle Ages and Its Union with Rome," *Oriens Chritianus*, xlii (1958).

Sarah, Butrus. "Dayr Kfayfan," *MQ*, xxvi (1928).

———. "Al Rahbaniyyah wa al 'Ilm," *MQ*, xxx (1932).

Al Shartuni, Rashid al Khury. "Majma' Day'at Musa," *MQ*, vii (1904).

———. "Al Majma' al Lubnani," *MQ*, iv (1901).

Shaw, Stanford J. "Archival Sources for Ottoman History: The Archives of Turkey," *Journal of the American Oriental Society*, lxxx, No. 1 (January-March 1960).

Shaykho, Lewis. "Bayrut: Akhbaruha wa Atharuha," *MQ*, xxiv (1926).

———. "Al Khury al Sha'ir Arsanius al Fakhury," *MQ*, iii (1900).

———. "Al Mu'alim Ilias Iddi al Sha'ir," *MQ*, ii (1899).

———. "Al Rahbaniyyah al Yasu'iyyah wa Risalatuha al Ajnabiyyah fi al Qarn al Akhir," *MQ*, xvii (1914-1919).

———. "Al Ta'ifah al Maruniyyah wa al Rahbaniyyah al Yasu'iyyah fi al Qarnayn al Sadis 'Ashar wa al Sabi' 'Ashar," *MQ*, xvii-xxi (1914-1923).

———. "Tarikh Fan al Tiba'ah fi al Mashriq," *MQ*, iv (1901).

———. "Thalath Bara'at li al Baba Banidiktus al Rabi' 'Ashar bi Khusus al Majma' al Lubnani," *MQ* (no volume number), 1927.

———. "Usul Fan al Tiba'ah," *MQ*, iii (1900).

Shibli, Antonius (ed.). "Al Athar al Matwiyyah," *MQ*, xlviii-lvi (1959-1962).

———. "Mulhaq: Nabdhah fi Tarikh Dayr Qizhayya wa Matba'atihi," *MQ*, xlvi (1952).

———. "Nabdhah Tarikhiyya fi Tanassur ba'd al Umara' al Lama'iyyin," *MQ*, xxviii (1930).

———. "Al Rahbaniyyah al Lubnaniyyah al Maruniyyah: Safaha Tarikhiyyah," ed. Butrus Sarah, *MQ*, xxx (1932).

———. "Rihlah ila Qannubin fi Jabal Lubnan Sanat 1721," *MQ*, xxix (1931).

———. "Al Ruhban wa A'mal al Risalah," *MQ*, xxxi (1933).

———. "Al Zira'ah wa al Sina'ah bayn al Ruhban," *MQ*, xxxi (1933).

Shibli, Michel. "Nuzuh al Amir Bashir ila Misr," *MQ*, xlv (1951).

———. "Al Tashri' wa al Qada' fi 'Ahd al Umara'," *MQ*, xlvi (1952).

Shihab, Maurice. "Al Ta'ifiyyah fi al 'Ahd al Iqta'i," *al Manarah*, xxi (1950).

Shihwan, Matta. "Hayat Matta Shihwan wa ma Jara fi Ayyamihi min al Hawadith fi Lubnan," ed. Basilius Qattan, *Kawkab al Bariyyah* (B'abda, Lebanon, 1911).

"Situation du Liban," *Revue des Deux-Mondes*, iv (1842).

Stavrou, Theofanis George. "Russian Interest in the Levant, 1843-1848," *Middle East Journal*, xvii, Nos. 1 and 2 (Winter-Spring 1963).

"Taqlid Ahmad Basha al Jazzar li al Amir Yusuf al Shihabi al Hukm 'ala al Shuf," *MQ*, XIII (1910).

Tawtal, (Ferdinan). "Jirmanus Farhat al 'Amil fi Khidmat al Nufus," *MQ*, XXXII (1934).

———. "Watha'iq Tarikhiyyah 'an Halab," *MQ*, XLII (1948) and L-LVI (1956-1962).

Yazbak, Yusuf (ed.). "Wulliya 'ala Lubnan," *MQ*, LIII (1959).

Ziadah, Yusuf. "Al Batriyark Mikha'il Fadil wa Nasabuhu," *MQ*, LIV (1960).

———. "Al Batriyark Yuhanna al Hilu," *al Manarah*, I, Nos. 4-10 and 12 (1930).

———. "Sijil al Ahkam," *al Manarah*, II (1931).

UNPUBLISHED MATERIAL

Works and Studies

Abi Dibs, Jirjus. "Tarikh Jirjus Abi Dibs." Jafeth Library, American University of Beirut, n.d.

Abkarius, Iskandar. "Nawadir al Zaman fi Malahim Jabal Lubnan." Jafeth Library, American University of Beirut, n.d.

Al Fakhury, Arsanius. "Tarikh ma Tawaqqa'a fi Jabal Lubnan min Shahr Ayyar Sanat 1840 wa Sa'idan." Jafeth Library, American University of Beirut, n.d.

Farah, Caesar E. "The Problem of the Ottoman Administration in the Lebanon: 1840-1861." Unpublished Ph.D. dissertation, Department of Oriental Studies, Princeton University, 1957.

"Hasr al Litham 'an Nakabat al Sham." Jafeth Library, American University of Beirut.

Ibn Sbat. "Tarikh ibn Sbat al 'Alihi." Jafeth Library, American University of Beirut, n.d. Photographed copy.

[Kharma, Jorj]. "Sirat al Amir Bashir al Kabir." MAA, no. 6469 (1914).

[Anonymous Shihabi amir]. "Makhtutat fi Tarikh al Umara' al Shihabiyyin." MAA, no. 6468 (n.d.).

Mas'ad, al Batriyark Bulus. "Tarikh Suriyyah wa Lubnan fi 'Ahd al Dawlah al Misriyyah." Jafeth Library, American University of Beirut, n.d.[1] Incomplete.

Mashaqah, Mikha'il. "Al Jawab 'ala Iqtirah al Ahbab." Jafeth Library, American University of Beirut, n.d. The complete text.

Nakad, Nasib bin Sa'id. "Tarikh al Nakadiyyin." Jafeth Library, American University of Beirut, n.d.

Nawfal, ibn Ni'mtallah bin Jirjus Nawfal. "Kitab Kashf al Litham 'an Muhayya al Hukumah wa al Ahkam fi Iqlimay Misr wa Barr al Sham." Jafeth Library, American University of Beirut, n.d.

Al Rajji, Mikha'il. "Hawl al Majma' al Lubnani." A paper read to the Conference on the Second Centennial of the Lebanese Council, Beirut. Personal copy of the author.

Rustum, Asad. "Syria under Mehemet Ali." Unpublished Ph.D. dissertation, Department of Oriental Languages and Literatures, University of Chicago, 1923.

Shihab, Haydar. "Kitab Nuzhat al Zaman fi Hawadithy, 'Arabistan wa fi Akhirihi, Mulhaq Tarikh Lubnan wa Sukkanuhu li al Yaziji." Jafeth Library, American University of Beirut, n.d.

Al Yaziji, Nasif. "Fi Taqsim Jabal Lubnan." Jafeth Library, American University of Beirut, n.d. The published edition of Yaziji's treatise on the iqta' system in Lebanon shows some variations from this manuscript.

Archives

Maronite Diocese of Sayda, Bayt al Din, Lebanon.

Ministère des Affaires Étrangères: Correspondance Consulaire (microfilm). National Department of Antiquities, Ministry of Education, Republic of Lebanon.

[1] Patriarch Mas'ad's incomplete manuscript was published by Bulus Qar'ali in *Al Majallah al Batriyarkiyyah*, January 1930. However, this document is listed under unpublished materials because my citations happen to be from the manuscript rather than the published edition, which was not convenient to use.

Monastery of the Lebanese-Aleppine Monks in Rome.

Mudiriyyat al Athar 'Ammah (National Department of Antiquities), Ministry of Education, Republic of Lebanon.

Patriarchal Archives of Bkirki. Bkirki, Lebanon.

The papers of each patriarch are placed under his name in separate drawers of a large cupboard. The serial numbers are in an imperfect condition. Sometimes the same number appears twice on different manuscripts, or it may be marked so faintly as to make it impossible to read. The series are also sometimes discontinuous either because a paper is missing or because of imperfect cataloguing. It is therefore suggested that the reader who wishes to check the Bkirki sources should make use of dates where possible in addition to serial numbers. It would also be advisable to search a whole drawer rather than just where the number belongs.

Sacra Congregazione de Propaganda Fide, Congressi Maroniti, Rome.

Index

Melkite Orthodox Church, 85
mercenaries, 41, 42, 175
miri, 38, 48, 64, 117, 209, 292, 294
Misk, Francis, 259
monasteries, al Luwayzah, 88; Tamish, 88, 159; Mar Musa al Habashi, 159; Mar Hanna, 160
monks, orders of, 105, 111-17, 156;
Antonines, 81; land ownership,
112-14; educational and ideological role, 113, 156-58. *See also* Lebanese Order of Monks
Mount Lebanon, inhabitants, 12ff, 16,
18; geographic definition, 13-17,
129; relations with Ottoman valis,
30; unification, 31-34; political division, 35, 36; concept of nationhood, 146; division plan, 268, 271
mudabbir, office of, 51, 167-69, 196,
197, 250, 283, 284, 290; recruitment, 170-73, 177; education of,
172; effects of office, 197-99; relations with the Church, 199-205
Muhammed 'Ali of Egypt, 34, 224,
225, 235, 236, 247
Muhasib, Bishop Ilias, 99, 119
Mukhtarah, 70, 223, 225, 226; school,
27; the Mukhtarah affair, 222-28,
229, 243
al Munayyar, Hananiyyah, 179, 185
muqaddam, title, 49
muqata'ah, 65, 66
muqati'jis, office of, 27, 38, 49, 68; relations with subjects, 42-46; relations with Hakims, 48-51; autonomy, 61; military service, 61, 62;
functions of office, 62-64; relations
with monks, 114-17
Murad, Bishop Niqula, 139-43, 149,
150, 151, 163, 164, 239, 271
Mutasarrif, 36
Mutasarrifiyyah, 149, 276
Muzhir, Yusuf, 30n; house, 50

Na'imah, custom house, 294
Napoleon Bonaparte, 97, 180, 202-203
nationalism, 286; Lebanese, 128, 140-
42, 146; Maronite, 140, 141, 149,
151, 152, 165, 166, 199, 254, 277,
284
nobility, 49, 50, 51

Ottoman Empire, Christians in, 173
Ottoman government, 239, 247, 254,
255, 256, 259, 265, 277, 285; sultan, 19, 28, 255, 256, 267; role in
Lebanese civil war, 34-36, 252, 266-
77; as a higher civil order, 38, 39;
relations with Hakims, 39, 40; relations with Maronites, 244
Ottoman reforms, 251, 266-69; effects
on Lebanese crisis, 267-73

political actors, 10, 71, 72; concept of,
5, 6, 278, 286; differentiation, 49
political allegiance in the iqta' system,
42-48
political institutions, *see* institutions
political change, 8, 278; principles of,
4; in the iqta' system, 9, 10
political system, 5; transformation of,
10
Pope, *see* Gregory XIII, Leo X
Poujade, Eugène, 120, 248
primogeniture, principle of, 54
printing press, 159, 160
property, private, 21, 27, 69
Protestant missionaries, 158, 235

qadi, office, 51, 169
al Qadi, Shaykh 'Abdallah, 179
Qa'immaqamiyyah, 35, 147, 150, 271;
council of, 272-73
Qannubin, 87, 91, 119, 120, 206, 238
Qar'ali, Bishop 'Abdallah, 99, 110,
121, 157
al Qati', 159, 296
Qaysi faction, 30, 31, 52

Rashid Pasha, 267
religious, allegiance, 42, 43; freedom
in the Imarah, 94, 156; societies,
157, 158-59, 166
Roman Catholic Church, *see* Church
of Rome
Rome, 128, 131, 159, 161, 202

Salibi, Kamal, 128
Sayda, 16; Vali of, 15, 30, 34, 38, 40,
273; Vilayet of, 30; diocese of, 239,
296
schools, 160-66
secularism, 47